IMPLIED TERMS IN ENGLISH CONTRACT LAW

Second Edition

ELGAR COMMERCIAL LAW AND PRACTICE

The *Elgar Commercial Law and Practice* series is a library of works by leading practitioners and scholars covering discrete areas of law in the field of Commercial Law. Each title will be analytical in approach, highlighting and unpicking the legal issues that are most critical and relevant to practice. Designed to be detailed, focused reference works, the books in this series aim to offer an authoritative statement on the law and practice in key topics within the field, from corporate contracts and dispute resolution to insurance and the sale of goods and services. Presented in a format that allows for ease of navigation to a particular point of law, each title in the series is written by specialists in their respective fields, often with insight either from private practice or from an academic perspective.

IMPLIED TERMS IN ENGLISH CONTRACT LAW

Second Edition

RICHARD AUSTEN-BAKER

of Gray's Inn, Barrister
Senior Lecturer in Law, University of Lancaster, UK

ELGAR COMMERCIAL LAW AND PRACTICE

Edward Elgar
PUBLISHING

Cheltenham, UK • Northampton, MA, USA

Published by
Edward Elgar Publishing Limited
The Lypiatts
15 Lansdown Road
Cheltenham
Glos GL50 2JA
UK

Edward Elgar Publishing, Inc.
William Pratt House
9 Dewey Court
Northampton
Massachusetts 01060
USA

A catalogue record for this book
is available from the British Library

Library of Congress Control Number: 2016953956

This book is available electronically in the Elgaronline
Law subject collection
DOI 10.4337/9781785365287

ISBN 978 1 78536 527 0 (cased)
ISBN 978 1 78536 528 7 (eBook)

Typeset by Columns Design XML Ltd, Reading

Printed on FSC approved paper

Printed and bound in Great Britain by Marston Book Services Ltd, Oxfordshire

To the Late Professor Jill Poole
to whom I am indebted for much

CONTENTS

EXTENDED TABLE OF CONTENTS

PREFACE TO FIRST EDITION

The idea for this book grew out of writing an article on terms implied in fact, the inspiration for which grew from a remark made to me by a very distinguished law professor. I had referred to the case of *The Moorcock* as one example of the flexibility of contract law. He dismissed this, airily saying that a Law Lord had told him that he (the Law Lord) knew that counsel were scraping the barrel as soon as they cited *The Moorcock*. I was not terribly pleased to have my argument dismissed on the basis of what one judge, however distinguished, had remarked to a professor, however distinguished, perhaps over a glass of port or a gin and tonic in the pension room of an Inn of Court (as I imagine the conversation taking place). This irritation led to an article about terms implied in fact, and the interest that stirred in me ultimately resulted in this book. That article was published as 'Implied Terms in English Contract Law: The Long Voyage of *The Moorcock*' (2009) 38 *Common Law World Review* 56, and the substance of it is reproduced in Chapter 7 of this book.

Implication of terms is, to my mind, one of the most important weapons in the armoury of lawyerly and judicial technique. A thorough knowledge by the practitioner of what terms are and are not likely to be implied will permit him or her to advise a client what is likely to happen if anything goes wrong in the absence of an express clause providing for that event, and perhaps guide the client away from unnecessary negotiations, conflict, concessions payment of price for terms that are unlikely ever to be needed (since relatively few contracts ever result in breakdown and the causes of breakdowns are so multifarious that nearly all contractual terms are in fact completely redundant) and where the client would be perfectly content with the effect of the likely implied term. As a judicial technique, it permits the court to 'discover' an interpretation of a contract more clearly aligned to its view on any particular occasion of what is common sense or fair, without ever having to admit to doing such a heinous thing. For parties who are entirely conscious of the terms usually implied in their trade, it saves time and ink. Yet, in spite of all this, the textbooks, student and practitioner ones alike, skip rather briefly over this subject and there is no current specialist volume on the subject of implied terms in English law. It is this deficiency which this volume is intended to supply. I hope that it will be of assistance to the practitioner as well as being of interest to the academic and student. To this end, I have emphasized the task of stating the law as best I can, with detailed and critical discussion of the leading cases, focussing rather less on the purely theoretical aspects, though I hope it will not be felt that I have unduly neglected these.

I would like to acknowledge with gratitude the considerable assistance furnished to me by Donna Neill, a former student of mine, now a research student at Bristol University. Donna provided many, many hours of painstaking research assistance which tremendously speeded the process of researching and writing this book. Another former student, Emma Smith, also deserves my gratitude for her work in gathering cases related to *The Moorcock* in preparation for the work on terms implied in fact. I have also benefitted from research leave in Lent Term 2009 from Lancaster University, which helped enormously.

I have endeavoured to state the law as at 1st May 2010.

PREFACE TO SECOND EDITION

To what I have said in the Preface to the first edition, above, I should like to add the following thanks. First, to Andrew Phang, Justice of the Singapore Court of Appeal, who kindly suggested in a review in the *Journal of Contract Law* that a new edition of this work would be timely and welcome. Secondly, I wish to thank my doctoral student Miss Kate Hunter who provided research assistance for this edition with startling efficiency and despatch. And thirdly, Lancaster University Law School for providing funds to pay for that assistance.

I have endeavoured to state the law as at 1st March 2016.

TABLE OF CASES

[Paragraph numbers in **bold** indicate a mention in the text]

TABLE OF STATUTES AND STATUTORY INSTRUMENTS

[Paragraph numbers in **bold** indicate a mention in the text]

Statutory Instruments

1

INTRODUCTION

A. GENERAL

The content of an agreement consists in its terms, express and implied. Even a **1.01** contract made in writing, purporting to contain all its terms within the four corners of the document is likely, on careful examination, to be found to contain implied as well as express terms. Any contract of sale, for example, will contain such terms as are implied by the Sale of Goods Act 1979, unless expressly excluded (and even then, the exclusion may be held invalid). In an oral contract, whether or not subsequently evidenced in writing, or a part-oral, part-written contract, many of the terms are likely to be implied terms. In *British Crane Hire Corp Ltd v. Ipswich Plant Hire Ltd*,[1] the whole contents of a written standard hire contract were implied into the oral contract for hire of a piece of machinery. It is obvious, then, that an understanding of implied terms is essential to an understanding of the contents of a contract and, therefore of what amounts to breach and how damages should be calculated.

This book aims to set out in some detail the law of England and Wales on **1.02** implication of terms in contracts. An attempt is made later in this chapter to trace the origins of implied terms in English law, while in Chapter 2 we discuss the theoretical context of implication of terms, before turning to the detail of the various aspects of the doctrine in Chapters 3 to 7, with a detailed consideration of the leading authorities. Since England & Wales remains a significant jurisdiction of choice for parties to international contract-related litigation, including many cases where neither party has any link to the jurisdiction, and decisions of the English courts continue to be influential in

---

1 [1975] Q.B. 303; [1974] 2 W.L.R. 856 (C.A.).

many other common law jurisdictions, it is hoped that this book will be of value to practitioners, academics and students far beyond these shores.

1.03 Implication of terms presents a difficulty for the law in common law jurisdictions. It conflicts with fundamental ideas about contract that have had, and still enjoy, significant influence on the common lawyer's mind. First, it offends against the idea of sanctity of contract. Neither Parliament nor the court is a party to a contract and it is therefore not for the court to intermeddle in the terms the parties have agreed. Arguably, this should be the case even if the lack of a particular term makes the contract unworkable, since the unworkable contract is the only deal made between the parties and they should not be taken to have agreed to a quite different, albeit workable contract. Secondly, it offends against the idea of freedom of contract, for precisely the same reasons. Indeed parties sometimes insert clauses known to one party to be wholly unenforceable but put there for tactical reasons (e.g., penalty clauses and not a few exemption clauses), or make whole 'contracts' that are not enforceable as such, as with agreements 'binding in honour only'. In these cases the courts strike down the offending clause, leaving the contract to be interpreted in its absence, or decline to enforce the agreement as a contract: they do not rewrite the clause to make it legitimate (or, say, strike down a penalty and then imply a liquidated damages clause), or conclude that an honour clause makes for such a failure of consideration that the parties as reasonable business-people cannot have intended.

1.04 With regard to terms implied by statute, there is no question that implication cuts across the parties' freedom of contract where the term cannot be excluded by an express term, as is the case with the implied terms in sections 12 to 15 of the Sale of Goods Act 1979 in contracts involving a consumer buyer.[2] Whether or not the parties are at liberty to exclude such a term and whether or not they have done so in fact, such terms still cut across the sanctity of contract, since if the parties do not in fact refer to them so as to exclude them (if they may) this may be through ignorance rather than deliberation and in that case it is not possible to say that they meant such terms to form a part of their contract. And the necessity of excluding such a term expressly dictates part of the contract where this is done. It is submitted that the same applies to terms implied by law as an automatic incident of any given species of contract.[3]

---

2   Unfair Contract Terms Act 1977, ss. 6(1)(a) and 6(2)(a). The implied term in s. 12 SGA 1979 cannot be excluded against any buyer, consumer or otherwise: s. 6(1)(a) UCTA 1977 while the terms in ss. 13 to 15 cannot be excluded as against a consumer, and can only be excluded against a buyer in the course of business if exclusion is reasonable: s. 6(3).
3   See below, Chapter 3.

Where terms are implied from custom,[4] however, or are implied 'in fact',[5] the **1.05** law's explanation is one of interpretation of the contract made between the parties, of ascertaining actual intention, which might only imperfectly have been expressed in words, oral or written. So far as this explanation is justified, then there is no interference with either freedom or sanctity of contract. On the contrary: the parties' intentions are being more completely recognized and upheld by the implication of a term in these cases. That, at any rate, is the justification, and it draws strength from commercial convenience, in that parties engaged in a particular trade, for example, would generally expect that they are operating within the customary matrix of that trade so that opting out of a custom is easier than having to opt in every time, while parties generally cannot actually anticipate every possibility and provide for it, so that implication in fact is a useful part of the litigation content of contract, provision of which is the function of contract law and upon which parties can rely.

Civil law jurisdictions typically do not require any general doctrines of implied **1.06** terms. The approach, typified in French law, is to prescribe quite closely the terms on which different kinds of contracts are made. Coupled with a 'good faith' approach, this dispenses with the requirement for implied terms.[6] Since the civilian approach does not place such an emphasis on freedom of contract as common law jurisdictions do, an implied term approach, though unnecessary, would not present the conceptual difficulties it poses for the common law, and good faith takes care of lacunae left by the codes, with no problem presented by belief in contractual freedom and party autonomy.

It may be argued, as the Australians Carter and Peden have, that implied terms **1.07** are one of the common law's inbuilt mechanisms for achieving the same ends as good faith in the civil law.[7] The lack of a general requirement of good faith in contracting is a notable characteristic of the common law approach, though the extent of the rejection of good faith varies between different common law jurisdictions. Good faith is almost entirely absent as a doctrinal concept in the law of England and Wales,[8] while in U.S. law the Uniform Commercial Code

---

4   See below, Chapter 5.
5   See below, Chapter 7.
6   However, implied terms may still live in otherwise civilian-style legal environments. Japanese law, for example, has a Civil Code and a Commercial Code, yet also uses terms implied from course of performance and from trade usage: seeZ. Kitigawa, 'Use and Non-Use of Contracts in Japanese Business Relations' in H. Baum (ed), *Japan, Economic Success and Legal System* (deGruyter: Berlin and New York, 1997).
7   J. Carter and E. Peden, 'Good Faith in Australian Contract Law' (2003) 19 *Journal of Contract Law* 155, E. Peden, 'Policy Concerns in Terms Implied in Law' (2001) 117 L.Q.R. 459.
8   Insurance contracts are contracts *uberrimae fidei*, and the Unfair Terms in Consumer Contract Regulations 1999 (originally 1994), implementing an E.U. directive, makes reference to good faith in the terms of consumer contracts.

enjoins good faith in performance and enforcement, but not negotiation.[9] The extent to which good faith is a requirement at the negotiation stage in any jurisdiction is questionable, whatever might be claimed. The idea of negotiating with all cards on the table is not only alien to the common law but is only very partially applicable in any jurisdiction. It is unlikely in the extreme, for example, that a customer in a French car showroom in France, on enquiring about the suitability to his requirements of its flagship vehicle would be told that it is very stylish and comfortable but that if reliability is important to him then a Japanese car would be more suitable as the French manufacturer in question has had many complaints on this score. Moreover, no French court would be likely to uphold a contention that the failure of the showroom staff to point out the shortcomings of their goods is a breach of good faith. Good faith at this stage requires mainly specific information and an avoidance of what in common law jurisdictions would be called 'misrepresentation'.

1.08 Lord Denning's attempt in *Liverpool City Council v. Irwin*[10] to make reasonableness not merely necessary in defining an implied obligation but also sufficient to justify making an implication in the first place, could be regarded as an attempt to introduce a good faith requirement as to terms, that is to say a requirement that the terms of the contract meet with broad notions of fairness. This attempt failed, of course, when this approach was firmly rejected by the House of Lords in the same case.[11]

1.09 It can further be argued that civil law does have implied terms, if not quite to the same extent as common law. The compulsory terms in a civil code provided as incidences of different types of contract are surely no different from terms implied by statute, save that terms implied by statute may in some, but not all, instances be excluded by express agreement (see Chapter 6). Indeed, these also fulfil the role of terms implied by law and by custom and usage, though again without the option of contracting out and, necessarily, by a different mechanism. The 'implied terms' of the civilians are what are called 'mandatory terms' rather than 'default terms'. That is to say that the court applying the code does one of two things: either imposes a term on the parties different from one to which they had agreed, or supplies a term to fill some gap in the

---

9   UCC §1–203: 'Every contract or duty within this Act imposes an obligation of good faith in its performance or enforcement.' This provision should be read together with § 1–102(3):

> The effect of provisions of this Act may be varied by agreement, except as otherwise provided in this Act and except that the obligations of good faith, diligence, reasonableness and care prescribed by this Act may not be disclaimed by agreement but the parties may by agreement determine the standards by which the performance of such obligations is to be measured if such standards are not manifestly unreasonable.

10 [1976] 1 Q.B. 319 (C.A.).

11 [1977] A.C. 239. See especially at 258 per Lord Cross and at 254 per Lord Wilberforce.

contract's provision which the parties did not want the court to fill.[12] Where the common law differs is primarily in the fact that in the common law most implied terms supply default rather than mandatory rules and in the possibility of implying terms in fact into individual contracts when disputes reach judgment.[13]

B. CATEGORIZATION

There are a number of ways one can categorize implied terms. Textbooks tend **1.10** to split them into the categories of terms implied by statute, terms implied in law, terms implied in fact, and terms implied by trade usage or custom. Alternatively, 'terms implied by common law' is sometimes adopted to cover both implications in fact and implications into all contracts of a particular type as a matter of law. There is no reason why usage and custom should not also fall under this heading. Lord Steyn in *Equitable Life Assurance Society v. Hyman* divided implied terms into 'general default rules' and 'ad hoc gap fillers'.[14] This has the limitation, however, of neither distinguishing sufficiently between the sources nor indicating the degree of mandatoriness that might be expected. Terms implied by statute, for instance, may well prove mandatory and unavoidable, as discussed below. In this sense, Lord Steyn's division also lacks clarity as it does not acknowledge that some implied terms are not default rules at all, but mandatory.[15]

A law-and-economics approach might be to divide implied terms into manda- **1.11** tory and default rules. Mandatory terms are those which cannot be avoided by the parties expressly agreeing to inconsistent terms. Such rules would include UCC 1–203, section 12 of the Sale of Goods Act 1979, and sections 13 to 15 of the same Act in sales from business sellers to consumer buyers. Default terms are ones which apply if the parties do not agree otherwise.

It would also be possible to categorize implied terms into fixed litigation **1.12** content, comprising statute-implied terms, terms implied by usage or custom and terms implied as a matter of law, and *eo instante* litigation content, covering terms implied in fact.

---

12   See G.M. Cohen, 'Implied Terms and Interpretation in Contract Law' in B. Bouckaert and G. deGeest (eds), *Encyclopedia of Law and Economics* (Edward Elgar: Cheltenham, UK and Northampton, Mass, 2000) 78 at p. 84.

13   Discussed below in Chapter 7.

14   [2002] 1 A.C. 408, 458 and 459.

15   McMeel points out that the origin of Lord Steyn's terminology is in fact North American: see G. McMeel, *The Construction of Contracts* (OUP: Oxford, 2007) at 10.04 n. 7.

1.13 It is the first manner of categorization, however, which has most often commended itself to the textbook writers, that seems to fit most closely with the language of the judiciary when one looks across the cases as a body, and that makes readiest sense of the subject from the point of view of the practitioner. This is the approach adopted in this book, therefore, in which terms implied by statute, terms implied as a matter of law, terms implied from usage or custom and terms implied in fact are dealt with in separate chapters. This should not, however, be taken as a theoretical preference on the part of the author; a number of ways are equally satisfactory for different purposes.

C. PURPOSES OF IMPLIED TERMS

1.14 From a practical perspective, implied terms might be viewed as a technique of construction or interpretation of contracts. That does not say very much, however, as it says nothing about why implied terms should be adopted for use in interpretation, and nothing about whether they should be so used or to what end.

1.15 As an interpretative technique, implied terms leave something to be desired. To what extent, for instance, does any implied term represent a 'reading' of a contract? The answers to such questions, though, are both a matter of degree and a matter of individual preference. We might draw an analogy with interpretation in the arts, distant as this world may seem from the world of contract law. If a Shakespeare play is performed in a reconstructed Elizabethan theatre, with boys playing women, costumes and sets as close as we can manage to what would likely have been experienced in Elizabethan times, and actors sticking faithfully to the words of the First Folio, then that is as faithful an interpretation as we can probably manage. But do we really want boys playing women? Is that part of the intention of the playwright or just a result of operative limitations in Shakespeare's time? And would Shakespeare want 'authentic' dress if he could return today? Or would he be surprised that actors were not dressed in more normal garb? If, in order to evoke similar feelings of familiarity as might have been enjoyed by the Elizabethan audience we transpose Romeo and Juliet to modern-day street gangs, are we interpreting more accurately or just taking an astounding liberty?

1.16 Moving to music, should performances of Mozart require an orchestral pitch of A 5 421 instead of A 5 440, so that everything is played a semitone lower than it appears to be written, and should the modern concert grand piano be eschewed for something that sounds like a battered upright in a bar, so that the performance will sound more like it would have done in Mozart's day? How can we know he would have wanted it to sound like that if he had had the choice of having it played on modern instruments? And does the realm of legitimate 'interpretation' of history, or 'artistic licence' run out before or after making a film showing the Enigma machine captured by Americans from U571 (actually sunk by the Royal Australian Airforce) rather than by the Royal Navy from U110 before the U.S. even joined the war, as actually happened?

What these examples demonstrate is that one's purpose and 'taste' (which in law translates to 'policy') must determine one's answers. The final example above, moreover, demonstrates that we are likely to have divergent views about the difference between interpretation and invention. And though we probably all will be able to draw, at least to our own satisfaction, a reasonably clear dividing line between interpretation and invention, we will also have differing views about the legitimacy of pure invention in different contexts. **1.17**

It is submitted that it is easier to see terms implied by law as default but not generally mandatory terms, as interpretative techniques aimed at the better understanding of parties' intentions as imperfectly expressed in their words, since parties might be taken, if they are in a particular trade, or if they have engaged lawyers to draft the contract document, to be aware of the implications that will be made if they do not express an intention to the contrary. But there are still important 'ifs' here: they may not be in the trade, or might not have familiarized themselves with trade usage (particularly if they have not had a dispute of this nature before), and lawyers may not be fully competent or expert in the relevant trade, or the courts may not have determined yet that such and such is in fact a usage of that trade. Moreover, if we exclude mandatory implied terms and terms implied in fact from our consideration, then we have hardly achieved a legitimate categorization of implication as an interpretative technique. **1.18**

So, can mandatory implied terms be seen as interpretative? It is submitted that they clearly are not. Rules of interpretation, of which there is a considerable number, have as their function the eliciting of the joint intention of the parties at the time the contract was made, consistent so far as possible with the policy of maximizing certainty. Certainty is achieved, so far as it can be, by consistent application of rules of what might be called legal grammar. But this is an exercise that is necessarily bounded by what the parties have actually said or, preferably, written. The parties may or may not have had in mind the existence and content of any relevant mandatory terms. One implication of the findings of Beale and Dugdale's classic survey is that parties might well not have them **1.19** in mind, owing to an ignorance (deliberate or otherwise) of contract law which may well go as far as not actually achieving legally-binding agreements at all.[16]

1.20   On the other hand, parties may well develop some knowledge of mandatory terms relevant to their business from experience of disputes and from simply being in the trade; the tacit knowledge of nearly every retailer, for instance, as to the general thrust of section 14 of the Sale of Goods Act 1979. Such knowledge might be taken to have been part of the backdrop against which the express agreement was made. Although the parties might have preferred to contract without such mandatory terms, that does not mean that they did not *intend* the mandatory terms to have effect; they intended to contract and that in itself imports a good deal into the bargain.

1.21   That said, this is still not an interpretative action on the part of the court, any more than the calculation of damages or the application of the requirement to mitigate loss or the rule against penalties. These are positive rules of law affecting every contract, not a device of interpretation, unless all of contract law is merely interpretative, and that is an extreme position indeed.

1.22   If mandatory terms are not devices of interpretation or construction, what about default terms drawn from legislation, the common law, or trade usage and custom? These seem to have a better claim, in that the parties can contract out of them and therefore might be taken to have accepted them if they fail to contract out. Thus, the contract, properly construed, includes such default terms as are not inconsistent with the express terms. Again, however, it is submitted that this places too great a strain on the idea of interpretation, certainly of construction. To return to our theatrical analogy, to call such an act interpretation, let alone construction, is very like assuming that any characters left alive at the end of the play as written must be assumed to have the fate similar characters have in other plays of the type and period, so a new act can be written in detailing these fates and called 'interpretation'. Would we generally consider, in ordinary language, that this was 'interpretation'? It is submitted that some would and others would not, so categorizing such behaviour as interpretation would be at least suspect and by no means necessarily a consensus position.

1.23   The difficulties with seeing the use of such terms as an interpretative device become even greater when the law of agency is taken into account. In this case a principal is taken to agree to any practices or customs of the market

---

16   H. Beale and T. Dugdale, 'Contracts Between Businessmen' (1975) 2 *Brit. Jo. Law & Society* 45.

concerned unless directly contrary to the express terms of the agency agreement.[17] It must often be the case that principals are not aware of what such terms might be, and the trouble of ascertaining them (even the chances against knowing what questions to ask to ascertain them) will generally be too great. Which of us, in instructing our stockbroker to buy or sell shares on our behalf is fully aware of the customs of the stock exchange in question?

Which leaves us with terms implied in fact. This category of implied term is **1.24** perhaps the most debated, indeed contested. Here there is no resource of established terms; instead a term is devised from the ground up by the court, which deems it to have been a term the parties really intended to apply but didn't actually discuss. This is not the place for a detailed consideration of the debates around terms implied in fact, the law on which has its own chapter in this book, where these matters can be discussed more fully. Nevertheless, some observations seem to be called for here.

The first leading case on terms implied in fact is *The Moorcock*.[18] It is the **1.25** judgment of Bowen LJ that is best known, and it is known particularly for his test of necessity to give business efficacy to a contract. In *Reigate v. Union Manufacturing (Ramsbottom) Ltd*,[19] Scrutton LJ also adopted this business efficacy test, though in the slightly different phrase 'necessary in a business sense to give efficacy to the contract' and went on to explain that this meant

> if it is such a term that it can confidently be said that if at the time the contract was being negotiated some one had said to the parties, 'What will happen in such a case,' they would both have replied, 'Of course, so and so will happen; we did not trouble to say that; it is too clear'.[20]

And in *Shirlaw v. Southern Foundries (1926) Ltd*,[21] Mackinnon LJ adopted the same formula with 'some one' replaced by an 'officious bystander'.[22] Whether the business efficacy test and the 'officious bystander' test are two tests or one, and how best the test(s) can be described is discussed in detail in Chapter 7. But the thrust is clearly that terms implied in fact are implied from some sort of 'necessity' and must be 'reasonable' (again, this requirement is discussed in Chapter 7).

---

17 See, for example, *Cunliffe-Owen v. Teather & Greenwood* [1967] 3 All E.R. 561; [1967] 1 W.L.R. 1421 (Ch.D.).
18 (1889) 14 P.D. 64.
19 [1918] 1 K.B. 592.
20 At 605.
21 [1939] 2 K.B. 206.
22 At 227.

1.26   Bowen LJ asked himself this question in *The Moorcock*:

> how much of the peril of the safety of this berth is it necessary to assume that the shipowner and the jetty owner intended respectively to bear – in order that such a minimum of efficacy should be secured for the transaction, as both parties must have intended it to bear?[23]

1.27   Three inferences are being made. First, that the parties intended the contract to have business efficacy. Secondly, what that business efficacy amounted to in fact: that is to say, what was the purpose of the contract. Thirdly, what term is then to be implied as the least which must have been intended by the parties to give effect to that purpose.

1.28   The first is natural enough and does not require discussion. The second is not always quite so clear. In *Couturier v. Hastie*,[24] for example, the purpose of the contract for sale of a quantity of corn in transit was disputed. One party argued that the purpose was the acquisition of corn; the other party argued that in fact it was simply a venture, and what was contracted for was the chance of corn or of receiving money under insurance covering the corn. The court concluded that the former was the true purpose of the contract and held that the contract was void, as we would say for mistake, on the basis that it was a contract for *res extincta*. But the argument might just as well have gone the other way, and surely the idea of a contract for an adventure is far the more realistic in the context of many modern day sales of goods in transit, an example being oil, which is often sold a hundred or more times while at sea.

1.   Implied terms and positive rules of law

1.29   The distinction between implied terms and positive rules of law is not, it is submitted, a clear one at all. It has, for instance, been suggested on occasion that a term implied in law is in actuality a positive rule of law. As mentioned above (para **1.10**), Lord Steyn in *Equitable Life Assurance Society v. Hyman*,[25] for example, described terms implied by law as 'general default rules'.[26]

1.30   The default rules created by terms implied in law can usually be excluded by express terms inconsistent with the implied terms. Terms implied by statute

---

23   (1889) 14 P.D. 64, 69.

24   (1856) 5 H.L.C. 673.

25   [2002] 1 A.C. 408; [2000] 3 All E.R. 961.

26   [2002] 1 A.C. 408, 459. McMeel suggests, no doubt correctly, that the terminology of 'default rules' (terms implied in law, by statute, or custom, etc.) and 'ad hoc gap-fillers' (terms implied in fact) is North American in origin, citing T.D. Rakoff 'Implied Terms: Of "Default Rules" and "Situation Sense"' in J. Beatson and D. Friedmann (eds.), *Good Faith and Fault in Contract Law* (OUP: Oxford, 1995): McMeel, 10.02 n. 7.

can sometimes be displaced or excluded by express terms, and sometimes not. Default rules such as those in sections 17 and 18 of the Sale of Goods Act 1979 only take effect in the absence of express provision in the contract. A full discussion of this question would be a lengthy one, and beyond what is possible within the scope of a book of this length. A couple of observations will therefore have to suffice.

First, a term implied by law, custom or statute might (but not in all cases) be **1.31** ousted by an express term inconsistent with the implied term. Similarly, default rules such as those in sections 17 and 18 of the Sale of Goods Act 1979, only apply where the contract is silent on the relevant point. To this extent, such implied terms operate in the same way as default rules. They are arguably, however, different from positive rules of law, in that we tend to think of such rules as being non-optional, as with the rule that a contract for immoral or illegal purposes is void. On the other hand, if the positive rule is expressed as 'unless … then', such a rule takes effect in precisely the same way as either implied terms or default provisions. Thus, implied terms could be expressed as positive rules of the 'unless … then' type.

Secondly, bearing the first point in mind, the distinction between a positive or **1.32** default rule and an implied term is one without a difference at a practical level. This is only untrue where we say that one cannot resile from a positive rule. But this is also the case with some undoubted implied terms, for example the implied term in section 12 of the Sale of Goods Act 1979. It is fair to conclude, then, that discussion of whether a particular rule or term is an implied term or a positive rule of law is not only doomed to inconclusiveness in the case of at least some such terms or rules, but ultimately sterile in any case.

D. HISTORY OF IMPLIED TERMS

It is by no means easy to attempt to fix the date or method of entry into **1.33** English contract law of the implied term. Part of the problem is conceptual: the first treatise on contract, as such, was that of Powell in 1790, followed first by Chitty in 1826 and then by a series of treatises starting with Addison in 1847 and culminating in Anson in 1879. Before the 19th century, what we should today call 'the law of contract' was not readily grasped as a discrete system at all.

Actions for what we would call a breach of contract took various forms, not **1.34** just over time, but at any one time. Often the action was really tortious in nature: damages claimed for, say, injuring a horse while shoeing it. Wherein lay the duty not to injure it? In the promise of the farrier, or more precisely in the fact that the farrier had 'taken it in hand' ('assumpsit') to shoe the horse. Why should the farrier be held to that? The plaintiff had provided him a consideration.

1.35   So we cannot easily look for 'contract' cases, and it is hard to trace the ancestry of those we do identify, as the reported judgments frequently make no reference to the cases relied on in reaching the decision.

1.36   Nonetheless, there do appear to be some promising lines of inquiry. First, implied contracts, properly so called; these were often a device of lawyers to bring another kind of case under the umbrella of assumpsit. For instance, a case of debt might be brought within the ambit of assumpsit by alleging an implied promise to pay the debt. A debt could not be recovered in assumpsit; it must be recovered through an action in debt, but the breach of the promise to pay the debt was a breach of undertaking and was therefore actionable in indebitatus assumpsit. The idea of the implied contract also permitted recovery in what became known as quasi-contract, or more commonly today, restitution. And though restitutionary claims no longer need to hide behind a fiction of implied contract, implied contracts remain of significance in shipping law, as with the implied contracts between the shipowner and the buyer in a c.i.f. sale, the shipowner and the seller in an f.o.b. sale, the shipowner and shipper where the ship is let on a time charter, and so on. Sales law offers another promising line of enquiry. One could also consider landlord and tenant cases, but only at the risk of clouding the issue of contractual terms with property law issues, manorial rights and so on.

1.   Sales

1.37   Simpson states that 'in sale of goods the original position was caveat emptor' and that 'on an *express* warranty if one had been given, it was possible to sue in tort for deceit'.[27] The *caveat emptor* rule applied as much to title as to quality or conformity with description. Simpson records that the earliest reported case where an action was brought on the contract for breach of an express warranty was *Stuart v. Wilkinson*,[28] as late as 1778, but that the practice began around 1750. However, he also notes that the insistence on express terms began to be

---

27   A.W.B. Simpson, 'Historical Introduction' in M. Furmston, *Cheshire, Fifoot & Furmston's Law of Contract*, 15th edn (OUP: Oxford, 2007), p. 17.

28   (1778) 6 Doug. K.B. 18.

eroded from the case of *Medina v. Stoughton* as early as 1700,[29] and that 'by the time of the decision in *Eichholz v. Bannister* (1864)[30] the exception had for all practical purposes eaten up the rule'.[31]

The implied term as to title (so called) has its origin in the common law. As **1.38** already noted, the original position appears to have been caveat emptor,[32] but as early as 1688 it was held that a warranty of title was to be inferred from mere affirmation and circumstance. In *Crosse v. Gardner*,[33] a case concerning a sale of oxen, it was held that mere affirmation amounted to a warranty (though the plaintiff had failed to allege a warranty) that the defendant was entitled to sell, since the oxen were in his possession and the plaintiff had no way of knowing of the rights of another (the true owner having recovered the oxen from the plaintiff). Shortly after, in *Medina v. Stoughton* the defendant sold a lottery ticket to the plaintiff, affirming it to be his own. In fact it belonged to a third party. It did not avail the defendant to say that he bought it bona fide then sold it to the plaintiff. Holt C.J. held that 'where one having the possession of any personal chattel sells it, the bare affirming it to be his amounts to a warranty, and an action lies on the affirmation, for his having the possession is a colour of title, and perhaps no other title can be made out'.[34] This is not quite what we mean by an implied term, since there is an affirmation involved, but it required a sort of implication in the law at the time, and the case represented an inroad into the caveat emptor principle in respect of entitlement to sell a chattel.

The rule was still being stated as caveat emptor in 1849, but with extensive **1.39** exceptions which had clearly developed over time and in part amounted to an extension of *Crosse v. Gardner* and *Medina v. Stoughton*, and had to a large extent nullified the rule itself in the ordinary commercial context at least. In the case of *Morley v. Attenborough*,[35] which concerned the sale of a harp, the headnote explains:

> There is no implied warranty in the contract of sale of a personal chattel; and in the absence of fraud, a vendor is not liable for a defect of title, unless there be an express warranty or an equivalent to it, by declaration or conduct. A warranty may be inferred from usage of trade, or from the nature of the trade being such as to lead to the conclusion that the person carrying it on must be understood to engage that the

---

29 (1770) Holt 208; 1 Salk. 210; 1 Ld Raym. 593; 90 E.R. 1014.
30 17 C.B.N.S. 708; 144 E.R. 284.
31 Simpson, n.27, above, p. 17.
32 See, for example, *Deering v. Farrington* (1675) 3 Keble 303; 84 E.R. 734.
33 (1688) Carthew 90; 90 E.R. 656.
34 (1770) 1 Salk. 210, 210; 91 E.R. 188.
35 (1849) 3 Exch. 500; 154 E.R. 943.

purchaser should enjoy that which he buys, as against all persons; as where goods are bought in a shop professedly carried on for the sale of goods …

1.40   By 1864, the implied term was clearly established. *Eichholz v. Bannister*[36] involved a sale of cloth by the defendant warehouseman in Manchester for £18/4s.[37] The plaintiff purchaser then resold them a few days later for £19/15s. The goods, however, were recognized as stolen goods and returned to the plaintiff from whom they were in turn taken by the police. The defendant argued that there was no warranty of title in a sale of goods and a plaintiff in such cases would be confined to an action in deceit, if deceit there had been. The old authorities were said to support this strongly, though it was noted that Blackstone J. (presumably in his *Commentaries*) had said that 'in contracts for sale it is constantly understood that the seller undertakes that the commodity he sells is his own',[38] indicating an early view as to implied warranty of title. The court, Erle C.J., Byles J. and Keating JJ., held that there was a warranty of title. The judgment of Byles J. is short and pithy and representative of the views of his brother judges, and it warrants reproduction here almost in full.

> […] It has been said over and over again that there is no implied warranty of title on the mere sale of a chattel. But it is certainly as [Erle C.J.] has observed, barren ground; not a single judgment has been given upon it. In every case, there has been, subject to one single exception, either declaration or conduct. Chancellor Kent, 2 Com. 478, says: "In every sale of a chattel, if the possession be at the time in another, and there be no covenant or warranty of title, the rule of caveat emptor applies, and the party buys at his peril;" for which he cites the dicta of Lord Holt in *Medina v. Stoughton* … and of Buller, J., in *Pasley v. Freeman* [[39]]
>
> … "But," he goes on, "if the seller has possession of the article, and he sells it as his own, and not as agent for another, and for a fair price, he is understood to warrant the *title*." Thus the law stands that, if there be declaration or conduct or warranty whereby the buyer is induced to believe that the seller has title to the goods he professes to sell, an action lies for a breach. There can seldom be a sale of goods where one of these circumstances is not present. I think Lord Campbell was right when he observed that the exceptions had well nigh eaten up the rule.

1.41   Simpson traces an implied term that goods sold by description be merchantable, even where the seller was not proven to have known of the defect, to the case of *Laing v. Fidgeon*.[40] This case involved the sale and purchase of, among

---

36   (1864) 17 C.B.N.S. 708; 144 E.R. 284.
37   Apparently, at least. The invoice shows a price of £19/0/0d, less a 1.5 per cent cash reduction rounded to 6 shillings, but a total of £18/4/0d, which should, of course, have been £18/14s.
38   (1864) 17 C.B.N.S. 708, 713.
39   (1789) 3 T.R. 51; 100 E.R. 450.
40   (1815) 6 Taunt. 108; 128 E.R. 974.

other goods, 48 saddles from a manufacturer in Birmingham, for reasonable prices between 24 s. and 26 s. each.[41] The goods were shipped to North America and on inspection there were found to be unmerchantable without being restuffed and relined. Although it was contended by counsel for the defendant that the price was one at which merchantable goods of that description could not have been supplied, that the plaintiff must have known this and that, therefore, there could be no warranty of merchantable quality, the court (Gibbs C.J.) held that this was no argument: the defendant could have declined the order if he thought the price inadequate; accepting the order meant undertaking to supply goods of merchantable quality. Neither Taunton's report nor Campbell's report, however, mentions any prior authority at all.

The case of *Jones v. Bright*[42] concerned the sale of copper for sheathing a ship. **1.42** The defendants knew the purpose for which the copper was required. A mutual acquaintance of the parties, one Fisher, told the defendants 'Mr Jones is in want of copper for sheathing a vessel and I have pleasure in recommending him to you, knowing that you will sell him a good article,' to which one of the defendants replied 'Your friend may depend on it, we will supply him well.' The actual copper sheets were selected by the plaintiff's shipwright and the price paid was that commanded by top quality sheet copper. The copper, however, lasted only about four months, rather than the four or five years normally expected. The evidence differed as to whether the problem was extrinsic ('the inveteracy of the barnacles in the river at Sierra Leone'[43]) or intrinsic (perhaps too much oxygen during the process of manufacturing the sheets[44]). This question was left to the jury, which found that the defect was intrinsic. Judgment was then directed in favour of the plaintiff.

On appeal, counsel for the plaintiffs argued that 'when an article is sold for a **1.43** particular purpose, a warranty is implied that it is fit for that purpose'.[45] The case of *Fisher v. Samuda*[46] was alluded to as a case where the quality of the goods had not been allowed to be raised, but it was distinguished on the grounds that the problem there had been procedural, because the defendant (being sued for the price of beer) had not raised the quality in his defence to the original action. In fact, in that case Lord Ellenborough clearly indicated that poor quality was a legitimate defence which should have been raised in

---

41 Though according to Campbell's report, the contract was for '50 saddles, to be charged about 28 s. each': 4 Camp. 169; 171 E.R. 55. Campbell was counsel for the plaintiff in this case.
42 (1829) 5 Bing. 533; 130 E.R. 1167.
43 At 534.
44 At 534.
45 At 535.
46 (1808) 1 Camp. 190; 170 E.R. 925.

the first place.[47] While in *Gardiner v. Gray*,[48] a case concerned with waste silk that was not saleable under that denomination, the same judge held that:

> The purchaser has a right to expect a saleable article answering the description in the contract. Without any particular warranty, there is an implied term in every such contract. Where there is no opportunity to inspect the commodity, the maxim of caveat emptor does not apply. He cannot, without a warranty, insist that it shall be of any particular quality or fitness; but the intention of both parties must be taken to be, that it shall be saleable in the market under the denomination mentioned in the contract between them.[49]

The same principle appears to have been adopted by Lord Ellenborough in *Bluett v. Osborne*.[50]

1.44 In *Parkinson v. Lee*,[51] however, it was held that there was no implied warranty of merchantable quality in sales by sample, presumably on the application of the other side of the same principle: where there is no inspection there is a warranty, where there is an inspection, as with a sale by sample, then there is no warranty as to merchantable quality since the buyer is able to make up his own mind on this point. Though in *Okell v. Smith*,[52] a case concerning the sale of 16 copper pans, Bayley J. held that a buyer was entitled in appropriate circumstances to make a reasonable trial use of goods and if they were not fit for the purpose for which they were sold the seller would be obliged to take them back.

2. Implication of assumpsit

1.45 Of course, the implied terms discussed above are nothing like the first implications. Mediaeval sales were enforced through the actions of debt and detinue. The first allowed the seller to recover the price as a debt; the second allowed a buyer to oblige the seller to deliver up the goods. Both were problematic as the mode of trial was wager of law. This meant that a defendant could escape liability by swearing and getting 11 others (compurgators) to swear likewise, that he did not owe the money or was not obliged to deliver the goods. Assumpsit, on the other hand, came with trial by jury. The problem was that there was no outstanding promise to sue on in assumpsit. The lawyers got

---

47   At 191.
48   (1815) 4 Camp. 144; 171 E.R. 46.
49   At 145.
50   (1816) 1 Stark. 384; 171 E.R. 504.
51   (1802) 2 East 314; 102 E.R. 389. There was in this case, incidentally, an express warranty that the bulk (of hops) would correspond with the sample.
52   (1815) 1 Stark. 107; 171 E.R. 416.

around this by claiming an implied promise to pay the debt. So, the sale contract raised the debt, but the assumpsit was the promise to pay the debt.

Whether this should properly be seen as an implied term, however, seems **1.46** doubtful: it is clearly more in the nature of an implied contract: the whole assumpsit, that is to say the 'taking in hand' or what we would today call the contract, is implied from the debt. That said, what is clear is that there was no room for implied terms in debt or detinue, or in covenant (an action on a sealed document which seems, for reasons unknown, never to have been popular) either, as requirements in covenant were formal in the extreme.[53] The development of implied terms was, at any rate, a development belonging to the actions of special and indebitatus assumpsit.

3. Summary

We can conclude, it is submitted, that while sales seem to have given rise to **1.47** implied contracts at a very early date, the technique of implication as such may well have first arisen in the implication of the assumpsit arising from a debt. Sales, however, may well have provided the main arena for the development of implication of terms, since implication of terms is, in its character, oil for the wheels of commerce. However, the difficulties in tracing clear genealogies through judgments, particularly because so many older judgments cite no prior authority for what is being held to be the law, mean that it is unlikely that it will ever be possible to say with any certainty or even with reasonable confidence.

---

53   See, generally, A.W.B. Simpson, *A History of the Common Law of Contract*, (OUP: Oxford, 1975), pp. 281ff.

2

SOME THEORETICAL CONSIDERATIONS

A. INTRODUCTION

2.01 The existence of the technique of implication of terms necessarily raises questions about the nature of the exercise and its relation to fundamental principles such as freedom of contract and sanctity of contract. In this short chapter the author purposes to explore these issues to some extent, though the degree to which definite conclusions can be reached about such vexed questions is necessarily indeterminate.

2.02 Two approaches are possible: either to consider the, surprisingly limited but diffuse, literature on the question, or to take, as it were, a clean slate and discuss these matters from first principles with just the occasional nod to work already done. It is this author's intention to adopt a *tabula rasa* approach, since space is limited and at least some readers will already be familiar with the existing literature. Some of the issues canvassed below have also been touched upon in Chapter 1, which should be read together with this chapter.

B. THE NATURE OF THE TECHNIQUE

2.03 Hitherto, the most thorough current treatment of implication of terms in a book by an English author is probably that of Gerard McMeel. But it is not a book on implication of terms; rather it is entitled *The Construction of Contracts* and subtitled *Interpretation, Implication and Rectification*.[1] The implication of the title and subtitle read together is that implication of terms is a technique of

---

1 G. McMeel, *The Construction of Contracts* (OUP: Oxford, 2007).

18

construction, but not of interpretation. Two words are really necessary to describe the different activities: 'interpretation' must mean the process of gleaning the actual meaning of the wording of a contract; and 'construction' can be taken to refer to the process of ascertaining the effect of the contract as a whole. Interpretation does not apply to implied terms, but to express terms. Implication of terms, on the other hand, can be seen as part of the toolkit available to the lawyer or jurist in construing a contract.

In plain English, however, 'construction' has more than one meaning. On the one hand, it may be defined as the activity or result of construing something; on the other, the making or building of something. The difference between these two meanings is fundamental to the question of the nature of the process of implication and for what implication of terms says about freedom and sanctity of contract. Is implication of terms merely an exercise in discerning the true intentions of the parties as to the contents of contractual obligations freely entered into, respecting both freedom and sanctity at once? Or is a court which implies a term into a contract engaged in making a contract for the parties? It has often been said that implication of terms is rooted in the intention of the parties. Bowen L.J. said as much in *The Moorcock*: 'Now, an implied warranty, or, as it is called, a covenant in law, as distinguished from an express contract or express warranty, really is in all cases founded on the presumed intention of the parties, and upon reason.'[2]   **2.04**

However, this is not an unchallenged position. Elizabeth Peden, writing about terms implied in law states that they are so 'because of the nature of the contract, rather than the supposed intentions of the parties'.[3] But Bowen L.J. does not seem to have been speaking only of terms implied in fact. His words do not bear that construction and although *The Moorcock* is today seen primarily as a case about implication in fact (and lies at the heart of our chapter on such terms), it was also relied upon as importing a term implied in law into contracts of the wharfage and mooring types.[4] The difference is important but may arise from an examination of the issue at two quite different levels and even from using words in different senses. If one says 'this implied term is designed to give effect to the parties' intentions' when speaking of a term implied in law, that is true and untrue in a number of different ways. It is untrue if by it we mean 'the court has concluded that in order to give effect to the subjective intentions of these two parties before it, as judged by objective evidence, an implied term must be inserted to this particular effect'.   **2.05**

---

2   (1889) 14 P.D. 64, 68.
3   E. Peden, 'Policy Concerns Behind Implication of Terms in Law' (2001) 117 L.Q.R. 459, 459.
4   See further, Chapter 7.

This would be a direct misrepresentation of the process by which the term has been arrived at, for one thing. If, however, we say 'these parties intended to enter into a perfectly normal contract for employing a legal secretary', for instance, then go on to say 'surely, therefore, they must have intended all the usual unspoken terms that you get in such contracts, particularly ones which courts in the past have held to be a necessary incident of contracts of this particular type', then this is quite likely true to some extent at least. The employer, who might well know of such terms, would be expected, in what is normally a contract of adhesion, to have sought to exclude any such normally implied terms that were not wanted. The employee probably would not know of such terms, but equally is likely to want to have all the usual incidents of such contracts and expect the usual burdens as well as benefits. We could also say, with some truth, that 'this term is one which parties *in general* intend to operate within their contractual relation', as opposed to the particular parties involved in the particular contract before the court.

2.06 Peden's view when taken, as this author takes it to be intended, as a reflection on the actual process of implication in the case of terms implied in law,[5] is entirely legitimate in respect of already identified instances. That is to say when it is argued that a particular implied term exists in all such contracts of the relevant type and there is prior authority to support this contention. The view seems to this author to be less legitimate, however, when a court is invited for the first time, so far as the court is aware, to conclude that a suggested implied term is one which the law implies into all contracts of that kind as a necessary incident of the species of contract. And there has to be a first time for every such implied term. The process is discussed in Chapter 3.

2.07 What one sees from an examination of the judgments in such cases is that the judiciary certainly appear to place the strongest emphasis on the intentions of the parties. In *Miller v. Hancock*, for instance, Bowen L.J. says:

> It appears to me obvious, when one considers what a flat of this kind is, and the only way in which it can be enjoyed, that the parties to the demise of it must have intended [the proposed term] by necessary implication, as a basis without which the whole transaction would be futile …[6]

He said much the same thing in *Lamb v. Evans*:

---

5   Her argument is far wider than this, in fact, and her main point, that the implied term is a means for ensuring a degree of fairness in contracting, will be considered further, below.
6   [1893] 2 Q.B. 177 at 181.

> What is an implied contract or an implied promise in law? It is that promise which the law implies and authorizes us to infer in order to give the transaction that effect which the parties must have intended it to have, and without which it would be futile.[7]

Again, the emphasis is on the supposed intentions of the parties.

2.08 But judicial rationales are, of course, not always the same as actual reasons. With a theory of contracts which emphasizes party autonomy it is natural to rationalize rules relating to implication of terms in the language of ascertaining the true intentions of the parties. Whether this rationalization is an accurate reflection of the reasons is not a matter that can be solved with the greatest facility. The first question might well be: what do we mean by the intentions of the parties? This is, it is submitted, essentially a technical question, in the sense that it goes to the matter of whether the technique is interpretive in nature or creative.

2.09 The underlying viewpoint of English contract law is objectivism. Giving effect to the intention of the parties does not involve an exercise in ascertaining the subjective intentions. The endeavour is always to ascertain objectively what the intentions of the parties were. That is to say, that it is outward appearances that matter. This objectivity might be promisee objectivity: what would the promisor's words and actions convey to someone in the position of the promisee? It could be promisor objectivity: what would someone in the position of the promisor typically think he was promising if using those words or performing those actions? Or it might be third party objectivity: what would a third party observer think it was to which the parties had agreed? Whichever approach is being adopted, however, it must necessarily be assumed that this someone is a reasonable person, since it would clearly be perverse to assume an unreasonable or irrational observer. This is an assumption which necessarily excludes much that individual parties might say they intended or might actually have intended, since people can be and frequently are unreasonable. Moreover, subjectively we may intend something to which we know the other party would not assent, hoping to 'get away with it'.

2.10 For instance, this author, by sheer disorganization in failing to cancel it at the end of the 'free' period, found himself with mobile telephone insurance. When the instrument was lost or stolen he claimed on the insurance and the claim was declined on the basis of a contract, which had never before been sent or shown to him, and which contained some quite astonishing terms. Indeed, reading all the clauses together, practically the only circumstance in which a

---

7 [1893] 1 Ch. 218 at 229.

valid claim could be made in respect of loss or theft would be as a result of a burglary of the policyholder's own home by means of forced entry (a distraction burglary would not do); a circumstance which surely accounts for only a fraction of a per cent of all thefts and losses of telephones. Moreover, the policy purported to allow the insurer to pay not for a replacement instrument of comparable cost, features and quality but any one they pleased, which could include the cheapest on the market, at a cost of a fraction of the annual premium. To put it into a familiar context, the policy was the equivalent of insuring a £40 000 motor car fully-comprehensive, paying a premium of £20 000 per annum and finding that one is only covered for theft if it is stolen during a forcible entry to one's own garage.

2.11 The issue of County Court proceedings coupled with the allegation that the terms were not incorporated as they had not been brought to the attention of the claimant, brought speedy settlement of the claim. But how many other policyholders are not lawyers and do not sue? The calculation must be that if customers are unaware of the terms and do not know that claims need only be met in the most unlikely circumstances then they will pay the outrageous premiums which the insurer can then pocket in the knowledge that if a claim is made it will reject it relying on terms to which no reasonable customer would have been prepared to accede. A tiny number will in fact sue and these suits can then be settled at once when proceedings are actually issued. Now, if the terms in the policy are not incorporated then some terms must be implied. Should a court give effect to the actual intentions of the insurer in such a case? Surely not.

2.12 Of course, whatever terms were implied into such a contract as this, where there is a failure effectively to incorporate one party's adhesion terms (assuming a court accepted the argument that they were not incorporated), would be construction of a wholly different type. Not a construing of the parties' words but the creative process of building a contract from the ground up; our other meaning of 'construction'. This is an extreme case but not without precedent. For instance, the leading case of *Liverpool City Council v. Irwin*,[8] which is discussed in some detail in Chapter 3, involved a tenancy in writing wherein the only terms concerned the tenant's obligations. The court was not obliged to construct the entirety of the landlord's obligations, only to decide whether one of these involved keeping lifts in operation and stairways lit, since this was the substance of the principal complaint. But the process is nonetheless a creative one. Not construction of the words of the parties since there were none to construe in respect of the landlord's obligations, but a process of

---

8 [1977] A.C. 239.

ground-up construction. What the court did was to discover a term implied by law into all tenancies of multiple-occupancy, multiple-storey local authority-owned apartment blocks that the landlord had to take reasonable care to ensure the operation of the means of access falling within the common parts of the building. The Law Lords all agreed that this was not a case for a *Moorcock* term, that is, a term implied in fact (see Chapter 7) and this seems to have been because the council might have rejected any such term had it been suggested, since it had all the bargaining power and prospective tenants had, in effect, none at all. This certainly gives some weight to Peden's argument, mentioned above, that terms implied in fact are the result of an attempt to give effect to what the intention of the parties must be supposed to have been, while terms implied at common law are the law's attempt to supply a degree of fairness to the content of contracts.

That of course does not really answer the question in relation to terms implied **2.13** from custom or trade usage. Where, however, such customs are, as they must be to result in an implied term (see Chapter 5), notorious, it may be taken that if the parties have not excluded the operation of the term, the implication simply reflects the intention of the parties: there is no need to state expressly what is regarded as automatically part of the deal. Similarly, where a term is implied from a prior course of dealing between the parties, if they have not taken the trouble specifically to indicate that such a term is no longer to be considered part of their deal, it seems probable that they intended to carry on with the same terms. In these cases, then, they are part of the armoury of construction of contracts in the sense of construing the proper meaning of the parties' words and actions.

On the other hand, terms implied by statute are evidently an attempt at **2.14** imposing either a mandatory or a default solution on the parties to particular types of contracts, but these are a parliamentary rather than a judicial construction of a contract for the parties.

It seems reasonable to conclude, then, that the technique of implication of **2.15** terms into contracts is both a technique of construction in the sense of construing a contract and a technique of construction in the sense of making a contract for the parties. Which of these it is in a particular case would seem to depend on the type (mode) of implication.

C. CONTEXTUALIZING WITHIN A THEORETICAL PARADIGM

2.16 The present author has argued elsewhere that implication of terms is one means by which contract law gives effect to various of the relational norms proposed by Macneil[9] and certainly accepted by this author. Placing ourselves within the theoretical paradigm of relational contract seems reasonable, as even the formalist Robert Scott has noted:

> The debate that divides the academics who thinks about these questions is not over the nature of *contract* as an institution. We are all relationalists now. In that sense Macneil and Macaulay have swept the field. Contract, we now know, is complex and subjective and synthetic in every sense of those terms. The debate, rather, is over the proper nature of *contract law*. All contracts are relational, complex and subjective. But contract law, whether we like it or not, is none of those things. Contract law is formal, simple, and (returning to Macneil's terminology) classical.[10]

The present author respectfully disagrees with the last sentence of this passage, for the reasons he set out in the article referred to above, but this does not concern us here insofar as we justify adopting the relational paradigm to provide a theoretical context for our discussion. It is, however, relevant for considering the position of implied terms within our chosen context, as will be seen presently.

2.17 For the reader who is unfamiliar with relational contract theory, it would be as well to set out here the briefest of outlines of the theory. In essence, the theory rejects viewing contracts as sharp-in-sharp-out deals, each discrete from everything outside itself. Instead, contracts are seen as more or less complex relations. The simple transaction of buying, say, a vacuum cleaner is not in fact a wholly discrete transaction. The buyer obtains rights against the seller for the quality of the goods by virtue of the sale, but much wider considerations are at play than these rights or this seller. The decision of the customer to buy a particular product is likely influenced considerably by the reputation not of the seller but of the manufacturer. There are different expectations relating to each manufacturer and the buyer may well rely on these, if they are disappointed, in dealing with the seller, who made no specific promises in relation to the goods. Often such goods will be accompanied by a manufacturer's warranty, and the manufacturer will often be concerned to maintain its reputation and go far beyond any contractual obligations it may have entered into with the buyer, if any, in order to protect that reputation. The seller may have a reputation to

---

9 R. Austen-Baker, 'A Relational Law of Contract?' (2004) 20 *Journal of Contract Law* 125.

10 R.E. Scott, 'The Case for Formalism in Relational Contract' (2000) 94 *Northwestern University Law Rev.* 847 at 852.

protect which leads it to treat customers as though they had rights far beyond their actual contractual rights, so that they gain and retain a degree of goodwill amongst the public by being known to treat customers particularly well. In both cases, the further up the expense tree the supplier is, the more they are likely to treat customers as if they had far wider rights than are actually contained within the four corners of the contract.

An employer may give effect to far wider views of employee rights than the **2.18** employees actually have in law or are granted in their actual contract of employment, because the employer seeks to retain talent, avoid recruitment costs, maintain morale and so on, and because typically such decisions are being made not by the employer as such, which will usually be a corporate body rather than a physical person, but by managers, who will themselves bring their own values and conceptions of fairness and right dealing into play (though obviously not always).

The longer the period for which the contract is anticipated to last, the greater **2.19** the personal involvement of the parties, and so on, the more complex and fuzzy the relationship is likely to be, and the stronger the non-legal glue holding the relationship together is likely to be. The stronger that non-legal glue, the more important it is compared with actual legal rules.

The late Professor Ian Macneil developed the most sophisticated version of **2.20** relational contract theory, positing a number of norms of contract. These are not norms in the sense of prescriptions for how contracting parties ought to behave, but rather descriptions of how contracting parties do in fact normally behave and how contracts do in fact normally work out, including the overwhelming majority of contracts that actually work quite successfully and never end up in a court of law. A discussion of these norms, with references to the work of Macneil, together with a simplified, four-norm version of the theory can be found in the present author's article 'Comprehensive Contract Theory: A Four-Norm Model of Contract Relations'[11] and the reader is referred to that article for a more detailed exposition.

Viewed through the useful lens of relational contract theory, then, what is the **2.21** role or position of implication of terms? It is submitted that implied terms are supportive of the norm of implementation of planning, in the sense of enabling effective planning. It is impossible for any party to imagine every possible permutation of circumstances which may arise in the course of the performance of a contract, particularly where the contractual relationship is

---

11   (2009) 25 *Journal of Contract Law* 216.

likely to be complex, involve whole-person relations, or of extended duration. Implication of terms as a gap-filling device enables the implementation of plans according to their broad intention without burdening the planners with the need for omniscience and perfect precognition. The technique can thereby also be said to effectuate the parties' consent.

2.22   Implied terms, whether default or mandatory also serve the norm of mutuality or reciprocity by ensuring certain minimum standards (or, if the term is sought to be excluded by an express term, highlighting the want of an acceptable level of reciprocity). The implied terms in the Sale of Goods Act 1979 certainly perform this function to a large extent, and particularly in relation to consumers, since they cannot be excluded (see Chapter 6). By insisting that as good a title as claimed is passed, that the goods conform to description or the bulk corresponds with the sample and that goods are of satisfactory quality, a minimum level of reciprocity is exacted from the seller willy-nilly. Even when there is scope for exclusion of the term by express provision, the attempt to do this clearly puts the buyer on notice to take particular care in proceeding and to demand a lower price, thus normalizing the reciprocation.

2.23   In terms of the present author's own version[12] of Macneil's norm-based theory of contractual relations,[13] implied terms serve to support the norms of 'substantial fairness' and 'satisfying performance expectations'.[14] To the extent that there is a norm of substantial fairness (that is to say, rough and approximate fairness, or reasonable reciprocity) in contract, a measure which will always vary according to the bargaining position of the parties, and insofar as the technique of implication in one or more of its forms, this chimes in with Peden's argument, alluded to above, that implied terms serve in England to supply the need met in other jurisdictions by generalized doctrines of good faith in contract.

D. CONCLUSIONS

2.24   The argument for the technique of implication of terms is rooted in the need to serve norms of contractual relations. In essence, that something needs to be supplied by the law if there are to be as few broken contractual relations as reasonably feasible, be it a doctrine of good faith or implication of terms, only

---

12   Which he calls 'comprehensive contract theory'; see above, note to paragraph 2.20.

13   Which Macneil called 'essential contract theory', see I.R. Macneil, 'Contracting Worlds and Essential Contract Theory' (2000) 9 *Social & Legal Studies* 431.

14   For further explanation see R. Austen-Baker, 'Comprehensive Contract Theory: A Four-Norm Model of Contract Relations' (2009) 25 *Journal of Contract Law* 216.

explains them to an extent. The way in which they achieve the ends of helping to ensure substantial fairness and the fulfilment of contractual expectations, thus helping to hold contracts together, are obvious enough to pass without further explanation, but why are the aims desirable (or, why are such norms norms at all?) and why is this a desirable way of achieving them? And can various theories sit together at the same table?

A number of arguments might be posited. One is that really what is being **2.25** achieved by many implied terms, particularly those implied at common law and by statute, is a species of good faith, but one which sits more easily with the common law's assumption of adversarial bargaining than civilian-type good faith doctrines. This does not answer why good faith needs to be supplied in some way. It is submitted that it is equally sufficient to say that good faith (using the term in a general way) is a good in itself, morally right and therefore ought to be enforced against bad people, or to say that insisting on some degree of good faith results in a more efficient distribution of resources because parties know better what the subject matter of the contract is in fact and can value it more accurately, or else that if parties are encouraged to act broadly in good faith fewer contracts will break down, particularly litigiously, saving transaction costs. None of these can be proven to be the one true explanation.

Alternatively, one might argue that implied terms are nothing to do with good **2.26** faith. They give effect to the will theory of contract by allowing the court to use objective methods of ascertaining the joint will of the parties to the extent that implied terms typically identify what would likely have been agreed had the matter been discussed.

Can these sit at the same table? The present author thinks they can. First, such **2.27** theories are enduring features of the landscape of contract theory. If someone or other were demonstrably at fault in being unable to explain some significant aspect of contract law, then it would fall away. All these explanations are capable of being right and all might be right in their different ways. What is surely beyond doubt is that parties enter into contractual relations with the intention that they should not break down in acrimony and litigation but rather should be seen through in the manner anticipated. This is the will of the parties to every contract. That being the case, a technique which ascribes some detail to the intentions of the parties, even though they had not addressed their minds to it so far as objective evidence can tell us, implements the will of the parties to have a workable contract. (Of course, one party might want a demonstrably unfair contract, but if he is not prepared to be open about this and suggest positive unfair terms then his will cannot be judged objectively.)

Contracting itself is a more or less universal phenomenon, presumably because it has been found efficient. It would be the task of a moral philosopher to ask whether good faith for good faith's sake is the result of innate human morality, divine will or an instinctive tendency to economically efficient solutions. All the present author can say is that insofar as such requirements exist in our law, contracting parties can be considered to have willed them as part of their contract and implied terms can all, therefore, be imputed to the will of the parties.

3

TERMS IMPLIED AT COMMON LAW I: GENERAL PRINCIPLES

A. INTRODUCTION

This chapter concerns terms which are implied into all contracts of a particular **3.01** type (unless the express words of the contract contradict the proposed implied term), where the implication is made by the courts as a necessary incident of the type of contract concerned, rather than being implied either by statute or else from custom or usage of the trade. As Lord Cross of Chelsea put it in *Liverpool City Council v. Irwin*:

> When it implies a term in a contract the court is sometimes laying down a general rule that in all contracts of a certain type – sale of goods, master and servant, landlord and tenant and so on – some provision is to be implied unless the parties have expressly excluded it.[1]

Probably the leading cases on this are now the House of Lords decisions in **3.02** *Lister v. Romford Ice and Cold Storage Co. Ltd,*[2] and *Liverpool City Council v. Irwin*.[3] However, it would be useful to consider the development of case law on this subject before proceeding to consider these cases in detail.

---

1 [1977] A.C. 239 at 257.
2 [1957] A.C. 555; [1957] 2 W.L.R. 158.
3 [1977] A.C. 239; [1976] 2 All E.R. 39; [1976] 2 W.L.R. 562. Applied in *Ferguson v. John Dawson & Partners (Contractors) Ltd* [1976] 3 All E.R. 817; [1976] 1 W.L.R. 1213; [1976] 2 Lloyd's Rep. 669 (C.A.), *Wettern Electric Ltd v. Welsh Development Agency* [1983] Q.B. 796; [1983] 2 All E.R. 629; [1983] 2 W.L.R. 897 (Q.B.D.), *Southern Water Authority v. Carey* [1985] 2 All E.R. 1077 (Q.B.D.), *Tadd v. Eastwood* [1985] I.C.R. 132; [1985] I.R.L.R. 119 (C.A.), *Hughes v. London Borough of Greenwich* (1992) 65 P.&C.R. 12 (C.A.), *O'Connor v. Old Etonians Housing Assoc.* (2001) 82 P.&C.R. 378 (Ch.D.), *Stroude v. Beazer Homes Ltd* [2005] E.W.H.C. 2686; [2006] 2 P.&C.R. 75, *Aymard v. SISU Capital Ltd* [2009] E.W.H.C. 3214 (Q.B.), *Rutherford v. Seymour Pierce Ltd* [2010] E.W.H.C. 375 (Q.B.); [2010] I.R.L.R. 606, *Dhamija v. Sunningdale Joineries Ltd*

3.03 A good place to start might be with the late 19th century case of *Miller v. Hancock*.[4] This was an action for personal injuries, brought by a collector for the Midland Railway Company. He had been visiting the offices of a customer, Messrs Gwynne & Co., engineers, who were tenants of the defendant, in order to collect sums owing to the railway company, but fell on (or rather, through) the stairs due to a defectively maintained step. The building was let in chambers (what would today be called office suites), with the stairs, which were the only means of access to the upper floors (Gwynne & Co's office was on the second floor), being retained in the control of the landlord. The tenants, naturally, had an easement over the stairs. It was accepted law that the owner of the dominant tenement must maintain the easement if he wished to use it, unless it was agreed otherwise with the owner of the servient tenement. The case turned on whether there was such an agreement between tenants of the building and the landlords. There was no such term in writing, so the plaintiff depended upon the existence of an implied term in the agreement between the landlords and Gwynne & Co., who had invited him onto the premises, in order to place upon the defendant landlord a duty to maintain, breach of which would give rise to a right of action for the plaintiff in respect of his injuries (a broken leg, for which the jury at first instance had awarded the sum of £200).

3.04 We see in this case the Court of Appeal going to some trouble to ensure that the plaintiff (who certainly had a good case to be compensated) did not fail, have to pay the defendant's costs and then sue Gwynne & Co. The crucial question was whose duty it was to keep the staircase in repair. If it was Gwynne & Co., then the plaintiff's action must fail. If, to the contrary, it was the landlord's duty, then the plaintiff must succeed. The defendant's argument, therefore, was dedicated to showing that Gwynne & Co. were responsible. The argument ran thus: the staircase was not demised to the tenant but retained by the landlord; however, the tenants had an easement over the staircase, and it

---

[2010] E.W.H.C. 2396 9T.C.C.); [2011] P.N.L.R. 9 and *Cometson v. Merthyr Tydfil C.B.C.* [2010] E.W.H.C. 23446 (Ch.); [2012] 50 E.G. 101 (C.S.) among others. Individual dicta have been applied in *Mears v. Safecar Security Ltd* [1983] Q.B. 54; [1982] 2 All E.R. 865; [1982] 3 W.L.R. 366; [1982] I.C.R. 626; [1982] I.R.L.R. 183 (C.A.), *Sim v. Rotherham M.B.C.* [1987] Ch. 216; [1986] 3 All E.R. 387; [1986] 3 W.L.R. 851; [1986] I.C.R. 897; [1986] I.R.L.R. 391 (Ch.D.), *Bank of Nova Scotia v. Hellenic Mutual War Risks Assoc. (Bermuda) Ltd (The 'Good Luck')* [1990] 1 Q.B. 818; [1989] 3 All E.R. 628; [1990] 2 W.L.R. 547; [1989] 2 Lloyd's Rep. 238 (C.A.), *National Bank of Greece S.A. v. Pinios Shipping Co. (The 'Maira')* [1990] 1 A.C. 637; [1989] 1 All E.R. 213; [1989] 3 W.L.R. 185; [1988] 2 Lloyd's Rep. 126 and in the Court of Appeal in *Spring v. Guardian Assurance plc* [1993] 2 All E.R. 273; [1993] I.C.R. 412; [1993] I.R.L.R. 122 (C.A.). It was distinguished in *Harvela Investments Ltd v. Royal Trust Co. of Canada (C.I.) Ltd* [1985] Ch. 103; [1985] 1 All E.R. 261; [1984] 3 W.L.R. 1280 (C.A.).

4   [1893] 2 Q.B. 177; [1891–4] All E.R. Rep. 736 (C.A.). Applied in *Liverpool C.C. v. Irwin*, n.3, above. Overruled as to landlord's liability to visitors in *Fairman v. Perpetual Investment B.S.* [1923] A.C. 74. See now, on this point, Occupier's Liability Act 1957 and associated case law.

was well-established law that the keeping in repair of an easement was the responsibility of the owner of the dominant tenement, in this case the tenants of the chambers, that is to say Gwynne & Co. The case of *Pomfret v. Ricroft* was cited in support,[5] along with *Gale on Easements*.

Lord Esher's judgment focussed on the relationship between the parties, and **3.05** revolved around the case of *Smith v. London & St Katharine Docks Co.*[6] Thus, the question for him seemed to be whether the landlord necessarily held a responsibility for the safety of visitors using the staircase, rather than on the, for us, more pertinent question of responsibility as between landlord and tenant. Bowen L.J., however, focussed his attention on the relationship between the defendant landlord and Gwynne & Co., and he found as follows:

> It appears to me obvious, when one considers what a flat of this kind is, and the only way in which it can be enjoyed, that the parties to the demise of it must have intended by necessary implication, as a basis without which the whole transaction would be futile, that the landlord should maintain the staircase, which is essential to the enjoyment of the premises demised, and should keep it reasonably safe for the use of the tenants, and also of those persons who would necessarily go up and down the stairs in the ordinary course of business with the tenants; because, of course, a landlord must know when he lets a flat that tradesmen and other persons having business with the tenant must have access to it. It seems to me that it would render the whole transaction inefficacious and absurd if an implied undertaking were not assumed on the part of the landlord to maintain the staircase so far as might be necessary for the reasonable enjoyment of the demised premises.[7]

We can see from this judgment that the test for implication in law is couched **3.06** in a way not far detached from the principle for implication in fact, that is to say that without the implied term the transaction would be rendered 'inefficacious', an echo of 'business efficacy' from Bowen L.J.'s judgment in *The Moorcock* four years before.[8] *Miller v. Hancock* was overruled by the House of Lords in *Fairman v. Perpetual Investment Building Society*,[9] but it was overruled on the question of the extent of a landlord's liability to visitors, not on the basis for the implication of the term between landlord and tenant.

---

5 (1666) 1 Wm Saund. 321; 85 E.R. 454.
6 (1868) L.R. 3 C.P. 236; [1861–73] All E.R. Rep. 580 (C.P.). Applied in *Miller v. Hancock* [1893] 2 Q.B. 177; [1891–4] All E.R. Rep. 736 (C.A.).
7 [1893] 2 Q.B. 177 at 181.
8 (1889) 14 P.D. 64 (C.A.). See further, Chapter 7.
9 [1923] A.C. 74. Applied in *Anderson v. Guinness Trust* [1949] 1 All E.R. 530.

3.07 Two of the same court (Lord Esher M.R. and Kay L.J., sitting with A.L. Smith L.J.) also heard the appeal in *Robb v. Green*.[10] This concerned an employee's duty of fidelity. The employee made a list of customers of his employer, copied from the order book, with a view to using it subsequently to solicit orders once he had left the employer's service. It was held that it was an implied term of the contract of service that the defendant would act in good faith towards the employer during the existence of the relationship of confidence between them. The decision was based in part on the authority of Bowen L.J. in *Lamb v. Evans*,[11] to the effect that there is such an implication in a contract of service.[12] Lord Esher M.R. said:

> I think that in a contract of service the Court must imply such a stipulation as I have mentioned, because it is a thing which must necessarily have been in view of both parties when they entered into the contract. It is impossible to suppose that a master would have put a servant into a confidential position of this kind, unless he thought that the servant would be bound to use good faith towards him; or that the servant would not know, when entered into that position, that the master would rely on his observance of good faith in the confidential relation between them.[13]

3.08 The reasoning adopted from *Lamb v. Evans* was expressed by Bowen L.J. in that case in the following terms:

> The common law, it is true, treats the matter from the point of view of an implied contract, and assumes that there is a promise to do that which is part of the bargain, or which can be fairly implied as part of the good faith which is necessary to make the bargain effectual. What is an implied contract or an implied promise in law? It is that promise which the law implies and authorizes us to infer in order to give the transaction that effect which the parties must have intended it to have, and without which it would be futile.[14]

3.09 This is nearly identical with the wording used by Bowen L.J. in *The Moorcock*.[15] What Bowen L.J. said there was that in all the cases on

---

10 [1895] 2 Q.B. 315; [1895–99] All E.R. Rep. 1053 (C.A.). Applied in *Kirchner & Co. v. Gruban* [1909] 1 Ch. 413; [1908–10] All E.R. Rep. 242 (Ch.D.), *Measures Bros Ltd v. Measures* [1910] 1 Ch. 336 (Ch.D.), *Amber Size & Chemical Co. Ltd v. Menzel* [1913] 2 Ch. 239 (Ch.D.), *Bents Brewery Co. Ltd v. Hogan* [1945] 2 All E.R. 570 (Assizes), and *Essarelle Ltd v. Bodycombe* [2001] All E.R. (D) 196 (Nov.)(Ch.D.). See also *R. v. Fuller ex. p. Earles & McKee* (1968) 70 D.L.R. (2d) 108, *Balston Ltd v. Headline Filters (No.2)* [1990] F.S.R. 385 (Ch.D.), and *Item Software (U.K.) Ltd v. Fassihi* [2003] E.W.H.C. 3116; [2003] I.R.L.R. 769 (Ch.D.).

11 [1893] 1 Ch. 218; (1893) 62 L.J. Ch. 404 (C.A.). Applied in *Robb v. Green* [1895] 2 Q.B. 315 (C.A.), *Louis v. Smellie* [1895–9] All E.R. Rep. 875 (C.A.), *Walter v. Lane* [1900] A.C. 539, *Lawrence & Bullen Ltd v. Aflalo* [1904] A.C. 17, *Measures Bros Ltd v. Measures* [1910] 1 Ch. 336 (Ch.D.), and *Alperton Rubber Co. v. Manning* (1917) 86 L.J. Ch. 377 (Ch.D.).

12 [1895] 2 Q.B. 315, 317, per Lord Esher M.R.

13 At 317.

14 [1893] 1 Ch. 218 at 229.

15 (1889) 14 P.D. 64 (C.A.).

implication of terms 'it will be found that … the law is raising an implication from the presumed intention of the parties with the object of giving to the transaction such efficacy as both parties must have intended … it should have'.[16] What seems open to criticism is the suggestion that the transaction without the term would be 'futile' and the natural inference from that that the degree of necessity required is such that the implication can only be made when without it the transaction would be futile. It is understandable that such a test might be set in relation to a term to be implied in fact, but the test, if such it is, seems inappropriate in the context. If one considers the employment relationship in question, there is not even the suggestion that the employee is competing with the employer's business. The information is being acquired for later use. In the meantime, the employer has the benefit of the work of the employee in his day-to-day functions. What is 'futile' about that? Employment contracts are not generally made primarily to prevent the employee subsequently competing with the employer. Professional firms, for example, will generally expect that employees will leave at some point and use the knowledge, skill and very often the contacts they have made while in their employment to compete, *inter alia*, against themselves.

In *Wessex Dairies Ltd v. Smith*,[17] in which the Court of Appeal had to consider **3.10** the situation of a milkman who left the plaintiff's service to go into business on his own account, and solicited the customers of the plaintiff, the court considered *Robb v. Green* and Maugham L.J. had this to say:

> First, after the employment terminates, the servant may, in the absence of special stipulation, canvass the customers of the late employer, and further he may send a circular to every customer. On the other hand, it has been held that while the servant is in the employment of the master he is not justified in making a list of the master's customers, and he can be restrained, as he was in *Robb v. Green*, from making such a list, or if he has made one, he will be ordered to give it up. But it is to be noted that in *Robb v. Green* the defendant was not restrained from sending out circulars to customers whose names he could remember. Another thing to be borne in mind is that although the servant is not entitled to make use of information which he has obtained in confidence in his master's service he is entitled to make use of the knowledge and skill which he acquired while in that service, including knowledge and skill directly obtained from the master in teaching him his business. It follows, in my opinion, that the servant may, while in the employment of the master, be as agreeable, attentive and

---

16 At 68.
17 [1935] 2 K.B. 80; [1935] All E.R. Rep. 75 (C.A.). Applied in *Diamond Stylus Co. Ltd v. Bauden Precision Diamonds Ltd* [1973] R.P.C. 675 (Ch.D.), *Marshall (Thomas) Exports Ltd v. Guinle* [1979] Ch. 227; [1978] 3 All E.R. 193; [1978] 3 W.L.R. 116; [1979] F.S.R. 208, [1978] I.C.R. 905; [1978] I.R.L.R. 174 (Ch.D.), and *Faccenda Chicken Ltd v. Fowler* [1985] 1 All E.R. 724; [1985] F.S.R. 105; [1984] I.C.R. 589; [1984] I.R.L.R. 61 (Ch.D.) (affirmed, [1987] Ch. 117; [1986] 1 All E.R. 617; [1986] 3 W.L.R. 288; [1986] I.C.R. 297; [1986] I.R.L.R. 69 (C.A.).

skilful as it is in his power to be to others with the ultimate view of obtaining the benefit of the customers' friendly feelings when he calls upon them if and when he sets up business for himself. That is, of course, where there is no valid restrictive clause preventing him doing so.[18]

In the instant case, however, the employee had circulated customers during the final days of his employment, which was not permissible.

3.11 The same line was subsequently taken in *Faccenda Chicken Ltd v. Fowler*.[19] So, it clearly is not futile to have an employment contract wherein an employee with a good memory may acquire detailed knowledge of the employer's business and customers and then use that later to compete against the former employer. That being the case, how can it be futile to employ a person with a less good memory on the understanding that he should not make notes to use in the same way? It is submitted that 'futility', or anything like it, cannot be the test for implication in law. The extent to which it is necessary to have such a degree of failure of consideration without the term where implication in fact is sought is considered in the relevant chapter.

B. LEADING AUTHORITIES ON THE TEST FOR IMPLICATION IN LAW

3.12 In any individual case, the question of whether a term alleged to be implied in common law is in fact implied is one that will generally be settled by reference to prior authority on the point. For example, for the term that an employee will serve his employer with good faith and fidelity, it is enough to cite *Robb v. Green*[20] and, for added force, *Wessex Dairies Ltd v. Smith*.[21] Nothing more is really needed. In some cases it might be argued that such a term supported by prior authority should no longer have force because expectations and society generally have changed so much in the meanwhile; but that argument must be pressed against the authorities. However, clearly it is otherwise if the argument is that a term ought to be implied in law into all contracts falling within the same category as the contract in question, but there is no prior authority to that effect. What principles must then be observed in considering such a plea?

---

18   At 89.
19   [1987] Ch. 117; [1986] 1 All E.R. 617; [1986] 3 W.L.R. 288; [1986] I.C.R. 297; [1986] I.R.L.R. 69 (C.A.). Applied in *Berkeley Administration Inc. v. McClelland* [1990] F.S.R. 505 (Q.B.D.), *A.T. Poeton (Gloucester Plating) Ltd v. Horton* [2001] F.S.R. 169 (C.A.), *Montis Surgical Ltd v. Tregenza* [2007] E.W.H.C. 1545 (Q.B.), *Crowson Fabrics Ltd v. Rider* [2007] E.W.H.C. 2942 (Ch.); [2008] I.R.L.R. 288, *Goldenfry Foods Ltd v. Austin* [2011] E.W.H.C. 137 (Q.B.) and *Clear Edge U.K. Ltd v. Elliot* [2011] E.W.H.C. 3376 (Q.B.).
20   [1895] 2 Q.B. 315, n.10, above.
21   [1935] 2 K.B. 80, n.17, above.

The leading cases on this question are generally regarded as being *Lister v.* **3.13**
Romford Ice & Cold Storage Ltd,[22] and *Liverpool City Council v. Irwin*.[23] The
former concerning whether an employee is entitled to be indemnified by his
employer against civil liability for his own negligent acts carried out during the
course of his duties, and the latter concerning the duties of a landlord of blocks
of multi-storeyed flats.

1. *Lister v. Romford*

In *Lister* a young man was employed by the respondent (the plaintiff in the **3.14**
action) as a lorry driver. He had originally been engaged as an unskilled
labourer, but from 17 years of age was employed driving the company's lorries,
which duties he had performed for some 10 years. The company had liability
insurance pursuant to the Road Traffic Act 1930 and this insurance extended
beyond the minimum requirements of the Act in that it covered accidents off
public roads as well as on them. It was usual at the time for lorry drivers to be
accompanied by a 'driver's mate'. On the relevant occasion the driver's mate
was Mr Lister's father. On a visit to a yard in Romford to collect waste, Lister
Junior had to reverse the lorry. At the time Lister Senior was out of the lorry.
Lister Junior carried out the reversing manoeuvre negligently, injuring Lister
Senior, who then sued the company on the basis of its vicarious liability. He
received some £1600 in damages, and £200 costs.

The company (in reality its insurers under a right of subrogation – the **3.15**
company would not have contemplated such a move) began proceedings
against Lister Junior to recover a contribution of 100 per cent. This claim
could be made out in any of three alternative ways. First, that they were
entitled to a contribution from him as a joint tortfeasor under the Law Reform
(Married Women and Tortfeasors) Act 1935. Secondly, that Lister's negligence had caused a loss to his employer.[24] Thirdly, that he was in breach of an
implied term of employment contracts that employees should carry out their
duties with due skill and care. It made no practical difference on what basis the
company should succeed.

---

22 [1957] A.C. 555; [1957] 1 All E.R. 125; [1957] 2 W.L.R. 158; [1956] 2 Lloyd's Rep. 505. Applied in
    Matthews v. Kuwait Bechtel Corp. [1959] 2 Q.B. 57; [1959] 2 All E.R. 345; [1959] 2 W.L.R. 702 (C.A.),
    Liverpool C.C. v. Irwin, [1977] A.C. 239; [1976] 2 All E.R. 39; [1976] 2 W.L.R. 562, *Keegan v. Young* [1963]
    N.Z.L.R. 720 (Sup. Ct of N.Z.), and *Janata Bank v. Ahmed* [1981] I.C.R. 791; [1981] I.R.L.R. 457 (C.A.).
23 [1977] A.C. 239.
24 Though this cause of action was not pleaded against Lister and had not been considered in the courts below,
    and therefore had not to be decided by the House.

3.16 The defence was complex and was amended twice. We need not go into the question of whether the 1935 Act could properly be relied upon, as it is not germane to our discussion here. Nor need we go into the question of whether there is indeed an implied term that employees should act with due skill and care in the execution of their duties, as this was found to be well-established. What is relevant to our purposes was an allegation by the defendant that one or more implied terms prevented the company suing him to recover its loss, a sum that would doubtless be ruinous to someone in his position in life.

3.17 The House of Lords held unanimously that Lister was under a contractual obligation to his employers to exercise care in the performance of his duties as a driver. It also held by a majority (Lord Somervell of Harrow dissenting) that the company could recover damages for breach of that obligation and that there was no implied obligation that Lister should be indemnified by the company, whether or not it in fact had insurance or needed to have insurance.

3.18 The implied term as originally pleaded was very wide in its scope. The indemnity was to be absolute and did not depend on the degree of carelessness, recklessness or indeed criminality of the employee's conduct. Their Lordships, however, considered whether a much narrower term, restricted to civil liability might be implied. A number of problems were identified in making such an implication. If it was an implied term of any sort, can it be defined with sufficient precision? If it was implied in law, when did such a term first come into the law? Viscount Simonds put the latter problem like this:

> When, then, did it first arise? Not, surely, when the first country squire exchanged his carriage and horses for a motor-car or the first haulage contractor bought a motor-lorry. Was it when the practice of insurance against third party risk became so common that it was to be expected of the reasonable man or was it only when the Act of 1930 made compulsory and therefore universal what had previously been reasonable and usual?[25]

3.19 The process of implication was also problematic. Viscount Simonds asked:

> [I]s it certain that if the imaginary driver had said to his employer: 'Of course you will indemnify me against any damage that I may do however gross my negligence may be,' the employer would have said: 'Yes, of course!'? For myself I cannot answer confidently that he would have said so or ought to have said so.[26]

---

25   At 578.
26   At 578.

Extent was problematic, so also was policy. Drivers were not the only **3.20** employees who were placed in charge of dangerous machinery. The example of a crane driver was given. Should crane drivers be held indemnified if they injured another, however gross their negligence? If not, was that because there are fewer cranes than lorries? And if staff in charge of dangerous machines were to be held indemnified would that not induce in them a feeling of irresponsibility? A final problem was that such a term would have the effect of depriving an insurer of its right of subrogation, through a contract to which the insurer was not a party. This last seems somewhat suspect as an objection, since if such a term were implied in law then insurers would know about it (as Viscount Simonds pointed out[27]) and could adjust their premiums accordingly.

There appear from *Lister* to be a number of factors to be taken into account in **3.21** deciding whether a term should be implied in law, including, most particularly, the inherent nature of the relationship between the parties, and the demands of public policy. What seems to be clear, however, is that the business efficacy test of *The Moorcock* was not a solution in cases where the term was to apply to all contracts of a given type. Viscount Simonds pointed out, if he were to apply the doctrine to cases of the latter type '… I should lose myself in the attempt to formulate it with the necessary precision.'[28]

It is submitted, however, that the approach in *Lister v. Romford* is problematic. **3.22** As is argued in Chapter 7 on implication in fact, the officious bystander test, to which Viscount Simonds appealed,[29] can be viewed as a restatement, or explanation, or operationalization of the business efficacy test, rather than a distinct test (in the sense of requirement) in its own right. Therefore, if one cannot apply the business efficacy test, then it would hardly be appropriate to apply the officious bystander test. The only conclusion capable of resolving that difficulty, is to suppose that while the officious bystander test began as a restatement in simpler and more concrete language of the business efficacy test, it has a meaning in implication-in-law cases distinct from its meaning in implication-in-fact cases. This is not a very happy solution, but Viscount Simonds' problem with applying the business efficacy test to cases of implication-in-law goes against prior authority (admittedly only of the Court of Appeal). *Miller v. Hancock*, as we have already seen, involved a question of whether a term could be implied in law into contracts for the letting of multi-storey buildings let out in flats, as to the maintenance of staircases. The

---

27 At 579.
28 At 579.
29 See above, paragraph **3.19**.

business efficacy test was certainly applied in *Miller v. Hancock*, so neither the principle nor its application appears to have presented a fundamental difficulty in implication in law at that time. This is, however, a matter to which we shall have to return, and can best return to after we have considered *Liverpool City Council v. Irwin*.

2. Liverpool City Council v. Irwin

3.23 Moving on now to consider *Liverpool City Council v. Irwin*,[30] we can see much the same factors in play. This case was brought by Liverpool City Council as landlord of a tenement block called 'Haigh Heights', in the Everton area of the city, consisting of some 70 'maisonettes' arranged over 15 storeys. The block had been constructed in the 1960s to replace houses demolished in a slum-clearance programme, and formed part of the council's stock of housing with which it performed its legal obligation to house those in need of accommodation.

3.24 By the time the events occurred which gave rise to the action, Haigh Heights, in spite of its newness, had itself become a scene of squalor. The communal parts had been extensively vandalized; the lifts worked only intermittently; the lighting on the communal stairs was also intermittent; and the chutes through which rubbish was intended to pass from all floors down to large waste bins at ground level were frequently blocked (supposedly the result of misuse by some tenants of the block). It had become a horrid place to live, particularly since the maisonettes were intended for occupation by families with young children. We may well imagine that many of the occupants probably found conditions little if at all improved compared with the old slums from which they had been rescued by their beneficent council.

3.25 Just such occupants were Leslie and Maureen Irwin, whose maisonette was located on the ninth and tenth floors of the block. No doubt having despaired of the council keeping the block in acceptable condition, they joined with others in a 'rent strike'. This in turn led to the council instituting possession proceedings in the County Court. The Irwins counterclaimed for nominal damages in respect of breaches of implied covenants, in respect of the common parts, to repair and maintain lifts, staircases, rubbish chutes and passages and, in relation to the demised premises (i.e., their maisonette) breach of an implied covenant of quiet enjoyment and of the implied covenant under section 32(1) of the Housing Act 1961, which has the effect of imposing on the landlord an obligation to keep the structure and specific installations in repair and proper

---

30   [1977] A.C. 239. Above, n. 3.

working order. The Irwins complained, in this respect, that the lavatory cistern was not kept in repair: Housing Act 1961, s.32(1)(b)(i) applies to sanitation including 'sanitary conveniences' and imposes an obligation to keep these 'in repair and proper working order'.

The maisonettes were let unfurnished and the only documentation in relation **3.26** to the tenancy was a list of obligations and restrictions on the tenants, described as 'conditions of tenancy'. There were no words of demise or lease, nor any obligations on the part of the landlord specified in this document.

It was common ground that there is no implied term of fitness for human **3.27** habitation in a lease of unfurnished dwellings: *Hart v. Windsor.*[31] So, the Irwins would have to establish the existence of more specific terms. At trial in the Liverpool County Court, His Honour Judge T.A. Cunliffe granted possession to the council but also £10 nominal damages on the counterclaim on the basis that there was a breach of an implied covenant under which the council was to keep the common parts in repair and properly lit, that the council was in breach of this covenant and also of the implied covenant for quiet enjoyment and the repairing covenant implied by the 1961 Act.

The council appealed against the judgment on the counterclaim, an appeal **3.28** which the Court of Appeal (Lord Denning M.R., Roskill and Ormrod L.JJ.) unanimously allowed. The reasoning of the judges, however, differed. Roskill and Ormrod L.J.J. held that there was no implied covenant to keep the common parts in repair. They arrived at this view after considering whether a term could be implied on *Moorcock* lines, that is to say that the term should be one necessary to give business efficacy to the contract and no more. They could conceive of five possible terms to meet the minimum of business efficacy and therefore rejected the argument that any one of them could be necessary. Lord Denning, on the other hand, took the view that there was an implied covenant to take reasonable care to keep the common parts in reasonable working order, but that the council had not breached this covenant. He implied the covenant on the basis that the courts are empowered to imply into contracts such terms as are reasonable. All three judges agreed there was no breach of the implied covenant under the 1961 Act and the Irwins did not pursue the point on the alleged breach of the covenant of quiet enjoyment. The Irwins appealed to the House of Lords where it was heard by Lords Wilberforce, Cross of Chelsea, Salmon, Edmund-Davies and Fraser of Tullybelton.

---

31   (1843) 12 M. & W. 68; 13 L.J. Ex. 129; 152 E.R. 114 (Exch.). Applied in *Sleafer v. Lambeth B.C.* [1960] 1
      Q.B. 43; [1959] 3 All E.R. 378; [1959] 3 W.L.R. 485 (C.A.).

3.29 The House of Lords upheld the appeal in part, agreeing that there was a breach of the implied covenant in the 1961 Act, and also that there was an implied duty on the lines proposed by Lord Denning, but dismissed the rest of the Irwins' arguments. Their Lordships took occasion to disapprove unanimously of Lord Denning's approach. However, they also disagreed with the majority of the Court of Appeal. Lord Wilberforce was at pains to explain that a clear distinction should be drawn between implication into a particular contract and only that contract, on the one hand, which should be on *Moorcock* principles, and implication at common law of a term as a legal incident of all contracts of a given type, unless excluded by express terms, where the principles were somewhat different. The majority in the Court of Appeal, having found the *Moorcock* test inapplicable, took the view that there could therefore be no implied term. Lord Wilberforce agreed that *Moorcock* was not applicable in this sort of case. *Moorcock* terms were terms imported into an otherwise complete agreement in order to give it business efficacy. Here there was barely anything in the contract: it had an entirely one-sided character, so the court had to decide not what term was necessary to give business efficacy to the contract, but what terms must be supposed to be in the contract from the very nature of the transaction.

3.30 Lord Wilberforce thought that 'to leave the landlord free of contractual obligation … is, in my opinion, inconsistent totally with the nature of this relationship. The subject matter of the lease (high rise blocks) and the relationship created by the tenancy demand, of their nature, some contractual obligation on the landlord.'[32] He went on to say that the need to 'have regard to the inherent nature of a contract and of the relationship thereby established' was stated by the House of Lords in *Lister v. Romford*.[33] Further, Viscount Simonds had rejected the idea of searching in such a case for a *Moorcock* term on the basis that if he attempted this he would 'lose [himself] in the attempt to formulate it with the necessary precision'.[34] Essentially the same problem, in fact, experienced by the majority of the Court of Appeal in the *Irwin* case.

3.31 He found assistance in the judgment of Bowen L.J. in *Miller v. Hancock*, already discussed above,[35] and observed that although that case had been overruled in *Fairman*, he cited the passage in question 'for its common sense as between landlord and tenant, and you cannot overrule common sense'.[36] He then went on to consider two cases of specifically landlord and tenant where

---

32 At 254.
33 At 254–5, citing the judgment of Viscount Simonds in *Lister v. Romford* [1957] A.C. 555, 579.
34 [1957] A.C. 555, 576.
35 At paragraphs **3.03** and following.
36 *Liverpool C.C. v. Irwin*, [1977] A.C. 239, 255.

the use of some equipment was included in the letting (a lift in the case of *De Meza v. Ve-Ri-Best Manufacturing Co. Ltd*,[37] and a refrigerator in *Penn v. Gatenex Co. Ltd*[38]) before observing that these 'are all reflections of what necessarily arises whenever a landlord lets portions of a building for multiple occupation, retaining essential means of access'.[39] Having considered the matter of what arises naturally in multiple occupation tenancy cases, Lord Wilberforce continued:

> It remains to define the standard. My Lords, if, as I think, the test of the existence of the term is necessity the standard must surely not exceed what is necessary having regard to the circumstances. To imply an absolute obligation to repair would go beyond what is a necessary legal incident and would indeed be unreasonable. An obligation to take reasonable care to keep in reasonable repair and usability is what fits the requirements of the case.[40]

This echoes his earlier statement that in his opinion implied terms could only be those which 'should be read into the contract as the nature of the contract itself implicitly requires, no more no less: a test in other words, of necessity'.[41]

Lord Cross of Chelsea, in his speech, referred to the distinction between implication in fact and implication in law, and clearly viewed the 'officious bystander' test as being applicable only to implication in fact: **3.32**

> When it implies a term in a contract the court is sometimes laying down a general rule that in all contracts of a certain type ... some provision is to be implied unless the parties have expressly excluded it. In deciding whether or not to lay down such a prima facie rule the court will naturally ask itself whether in the general run of such cases the term in question would be one which it would be reasonable to insert. Sometimes, however ... what the court is being in effect asked to do is to rectify a particular ... contract by inserting in it a term which the parties have not expressed. Here it is not enough for the court to say that the suggested term is a reasonable one ... it must be able to say that the insertion of the term is necessary to give ... 'business efficacy' to the contract and that if its absence had been pointed out at the time both parties − assuming them to have been reasonable men − would have agreed without hesitation to its insertion. The distinction between the two types of case was pointed out by Viscount Simonds and Lord Tucker in their speeches in *Lister v. Romford Ice and Cold Storage Co. Ltd* [1957] AC 555, 579, 594, but I think that Lord Denning M.R. in

---

37 (1952) 160 E.G. 369 (C.A.).
38 [1958] 2 Q.B. 210; [1958] 1 All E.R. 712; [1958] 2 W.L.R. 606 (C.A.).
39 *Liverpool City Council v. Irwin* [1977] A.C. 239, 256.
40 At 256.
41 At 254.

proceeding – albeit with some trepidation – to 'kill off' MacKinnon L.J.'s 'officious bystander' … must have overlooked it.[42]

3.33   What is not so clear from Lord Cross's speech is in what way, precisely, he was disagreeing with Lord Denning M.R. in the Court of Appeal. So far as Lord Denning had confused the two categories and felt the need to 'kill off' the officious bystander, the basis for disagreement is clear. But Lord Denning's proposed basis for implication that the court can imply such a term as it deems reasonable, seems no different from Lord Cross's statement in the second sentence of the passage quoted above, save that Lord Cross would confine this to implication in law or 'legal incident' cases. This is not consonant with the approach taken by the rest of the House, who thought that something much more was required than that a term be reasonable, though doubtless reasonableness is a vital ingredient, and it must be reasonable to imply such a term in 'the general run of such cases'.[43]

3.34   It can only be presumed that Lord Cross did not mean to say that any term that happened to be reasonable should therefore be implied. As Lord Salmon pointed out:

> To say, as Lord Reid said in *Young & Marten Ltd v. McManus Childs Ltd* [1969] 1 A.C. 454, 465, that '… no warranty ought to be implied in a contract unless it is in all the circumstances reasonable' is, in my view, quite different from saying that any warranty or term which is, in all the circumstances reasonable, ought to be implied into a contract. I am confident that Lord Reid meant no more than that unless a warranty or term is in all the circumstances reasonable there can be no question of implying it into a contract, but before it is implied much else besides is necessary, for example that without it the contract would be inefficacious, futile and absurd.[44]

3.35   Lord Edmund-Davies also took the view, in common particularly with Lord Wilberforce, that the test is one of 'necessity', though he thought it did not matter very much whether necessity or reasonableness be the touchstone, as

---

42   At 257–8.

43   Lord Cross also considered whether there ought to be a different situation as regards implied obligations of the landlord between cases where the landlord is a local authority and cases of private landlords. He rejected this idea on the basis that there was not enough distinction between the two cases. However, the reasoning here may no longer be applicable. Clearly the most significant difference between 'social' housing and the private rental sector is that rents in the former are artificially low, often to a very considerable degree. Lord Cross, however, pointed to the fact that at the time he was speaking 'most tenants pay less than the full economic rent for their accommodation, though in the case of privately owned properties the subsidy is at the expense of the landlord and not of the local community'. This, of course, was at a time when most rented property in England was subject to rent controls – 'fair rents' or 'reasonable rents' determined by Rent Officers. This is no longer the case.

44   *Liverpool C.C. v. Irwin* [1977] A.C. 239, 262.

the exercise was really 'ascertaining the presumed intention of the parties'.[45] He went on to consider the authorities on landlord and tenant cases where buildings were in multiple occupation with means of access retained in the control of the landlord, and concluded that in such cases the rule is that the landlord take reasonable care to keep such access in reasonable repair (and lit, in the case of stairs and passages).[46] His Lordship cited[47] *Miller v. Hancock*,[48] *De Meza v. Ve-Ri-Best Manufacturing Co. Ltd*[49] and *Penn v. Gatenex Co. Ltd*[50] as the foundation of the basic obligation and *Dunster v. Hollis*[51] and *Cockburn v. Smith*[52] as limiting the duty to one of taking reasonable care.

3.36 Lord Fraser of Tullybelton agreed with Lord Wilberforce that an obligation on the landlord to take reasonable care to maintain common areas and means of access is an implied term as a legal incident of 'the kind of contract between these landlords and these tenants', without making clear whether he would distinguish between contracts for social housing and private or commercial lettings, or indeed explain what he thought was the basis of term or the basis for making such implications if invited to do so in a novel instance.[53] All of their Lordships agreed that Liverpool City Council was not in breach of that term, though all also agreed that the council was in breach of the implied duty under the Housing Act 1961 in respect of the lavatory cistern.

C. A TEST FOR TERMS TO BE IMPLIED IN LAW

3.37 It is submitted that while the *Romford* case offers significant clues to the approach to be taken where a novel term is alleged to be a legal incident of contracts of a given type, neither that case nor *Liverpool C.C. v. Irwin* offer any clear 'test'. In spite of which, both cases (and especially *Irwin*) have been extensively cited in the courts, the textbooks and the classroom, and by judges themselves.[54] What can be drawn from these two cases, taken together?

3.38 First, it may be said that for a term to be implied as a necessary legal incident of a type of contract, that is to say, to be implied in law as opposed to being

---

45   At 266.
46   At 267–9.
47   At 269.
48   [1893] 2 Q.B. 177. See n. 4, above.
49   (1952) 160 E.G. 364 (C.A.).
50   [1958] 2 Q.B. 210 (C.A.). See n. 38, above.
51   [1918] 2 K.B. 795; [1918–19] All E.R. Rep. 949.
52   [1924] 2 K.B. 119; [1924] All E.R. Rep. 59 (C.A.).
53   *Liverpool C.C. v. Irwin* [1977] A.C. 239, 270.
54   See, especially, n. 3, above.

implied in fact in an individual case, it must be established that such a term is 'necessary'. But what is meant by this, we really cannot say. It seems that it is not so strict a test of necessity as that in the case of '*Moorcock* terms'. If that is so, then it can only be that such a term must be *reasonably necessary*. The courts have used language such as 'inefficacious, futile and absurd' to describe the necessary condition of a contract without the proposed term.[55] However, as has been shown, the language and the actuality have tended to differ, since terms have been implied on the basis that without them the contract would be 'futile' when plainly the contract would not be futile in the ordinary sense of the word.[56] It might be better, then, to say that a term will be implied when without it the contract, viewed as a whole, would be unreasonable. This is not the same as saying that any reasonable term may be implied. A great many terms may be entirely reasonable because they are fair and decent, but that does not justify the implication of all of them. If that were the case, then the tradition of adversarial, arm's-length bargaining would be a thing of the past in the common law of contract. It is a foundation of our system of contract that the parties might seek to obtain a bigger share of the pie for themselves, to the disadvantage of the other party, so long as the means used are not actually illegitimate (fraud, misrepresentation, economic duress, and so on).

3.39 The term must only be implied that is necessary to prevent the contract being *unreasonable* to the point of being an affront to common sense. A contract may be very one-sided indeed, without being an affront to common sense. 'Unreasonable' is not the same as 'unfair'. *Irwin* gives us a good example of this in action, whatever the language of the judges, in that if we propose the opposite of the proposed term (that is, if we propose that the landlord is not under any duty at all in relation to the lifts and stairs to a 15-storey apartment building) we are clearly suggesting something absurd, in common-sense terms. That opposite position is what will be left if *some* term is not implied, and we can then consider what reasonable term might be implied, but only such term as is necessary to avoid the absurdity.

3.40 Secondly, the 'officious bystander' test is not to be applied in these cases, but is confined to cases where it is sought to imply a term in fact into a particular contract rather than all contracts of a particular type.

3.41 Thirdly, the touchstones are arguably 'common sense' and reasonableness, but the mere fact that a term would be reasonable is not enough to justify its implication. Fourthly, reasonableness of a term must be judged not simply

---

55 *Liverpool C.C. v. Irwin* [1977] A.C. 239, 262 per Lord Salmon.
56 See above, paragraphs **3.09–3.11**.

between the parties before the court, but bearing in mind the generality of parties entering into contracts of the type in question, with due consideration being given to the possible effects of implication of such a term in other instances and what message the general implication of such a term would send out to contracting parties generally. That is to say, that any implied term proposed as a necessary legal incident must accord with the policy of the law and general public policy considerations.

So much for what can be drawn from those two cases. We are still left to some **3.42** extent trudging stickily about in a semantic mire. Some assistance may be had from the case of *Scally v. Southern Health and Social Services Board*.[57] In considering whether a term ought to be implied into the contract between doctors and the Health Board that employed them, to the effect that the Board was under an obligation to draw the doctors' attention to the right to buy additional years in a pension scheme, under a complex, lengthy and collectively negotiated contract, Lord Bridge of Harwich observed that:

> The implication cannot, of course, be justified as necessary to give business efficacy to the contract of employment as a whole. I think there is force in the submission that, since the employee's entitlement to enhance his pension rights by the purchase of added years is of no effect unless he is aware of it and since he cannot be expected to become aware of it unless it is drawn to his attention, it is necessary to imply an obligation on the employer to bring it to his attention to render efficacious the very benefit which the contractual right to purchase added years was intended to confer. But this may be stretching the doctrine of implication for the sake of business efficacy beyond its proper reach. A clear distinction is drawn in the speeches of Viscount Simonds in *Lister v. Romford Ice and Cold Storage Co. Ltd.* [1957] A.C. 555 and Lord Wilberforce in *Liverpool City Council v. Irwin* [1977] A.C. 239 between the search for an implied term necessary to give business efficacy to a particular contract and the search, based on wider considerations, for a term which the law will imply as a necessary incident of a definable category of contractual relationship.[58]

This passage clearly indicates a separation between notions of necessity. And it is the meaning of 'necessary' which presents us with most difficulty.

An appeal to the dictionary supplies us with a variety of subtly but signifi- **3.43** cantly different meanings. The *Shorter Oxford English Dictionary* defines the word thus (insofar as is relevant to us here):

---

57 [1992] 1 A.C. 294; [1991] 4 All E.R. 563; [1991] 3 W.L.R. 778; [1991] I.R.L.R. 522. The dictum of Lord Bridge was applied in *Spring v. Guardian Assurance plc* [1993] 2 All E.R. 273; [1993] I.C.R. 412; [1993] I.R.L.R. 122 (C.A.).

58 At 306–7.

I. 1. Indispensable, requisite, needful; that cannot be done without … **b.** Commodious, convenient (*rare*) … **II. 1.** Inevitably determined or fixed by predestination or natural laws' happening or existing by an inherent necessity …

b. Of mental concepts or processes: Inevitably resulting from the constitution of things or of the mind itself …[59]

Viewed in this light, it is submitted that what the judges have been attempting to clarify is that when a term is sought to be implied in fact into a particular contract, it must be 'necessary' in sense **I. 1.** above, whereas when a term is suggested as being implied in law as a 'necessary incident' of a particular type of contract, 'necessary' is meant in a sense closer to **II. 1.** and **II. 1. b.**, which is to say that it is an inevitable incident of the type of contract under consideration, deriving from the nature of the contractual relationship itself. The (rare) sense of **I. 1. b.** is also not without value here, if we take 'convenient' in a broad sense. The suggested term in *Lister v. Romford* was considered distinctly 'inconvenient' because of what were perceived to be its likely results in future instances.

3.44 Having established what we mean by 'necessary'[60] it is, however, another matter to define how we should determine whether a term is 'necessary', that is to say that 'necessity' is the attribute we seek, not the test: a test must be found to apply to a proposed term in order to discover the existence or non-existence of this attribute. In the case of terms implied in fact, we have the 'business efficacy' test. A term is 'necessary' if the want of it deprives the contract of such business sense as the parties to the contract, as reasonable businesspeople, must have intended it to have. To assist us in applying this we have the so-called 'officious bystander test' whereby the court should ask itself whether had an officious bystander been listening in on the parties' negotiations and butted in to suggest the term in issue, the parties would have testily dismissed him with a common 'Oh, of course!'[61]

3.45 In relation to terms implied in law, however, it is submitted that we lack an equivalent test, but it is surely not impossible to formulate one. It is submitted that the lacuna could be closed by a test requiring the court to ask 'would the generality of contracting parties, assuming they are reasonable people situated in the respective roles of the parties to such a contract as this, naturally expect

---

59 Onions, C.T. (ed.), *The Shorter Oxford English Dictionary*, 3rd edn., 3rd reprint (Clarendon Press: Oxford, 1988) p. 1390.

60 And it is an approach that appears to be supported by Treitel (Sir G.H. Treitel, *The Law of Contract*, 11th edn. Sweet & Maxwell, London, 2003, pp. 208–9) and to be implicitly supported by *Scally v. Southern Health & Social Services Board* [1992] 1 A.C. 294 at 307.

61 For a discussion of the business efficacy and officious bystander tests, see Chapter 7, on terms implied in fact.

such an obligation to be considered a part of the contractual obligations, whether or not explicitly stated'? It might be necessary then to apply a policy test: 'would the proposed term, if made general, be contrary to the public interest'? Whether a single-stage or a two-stage test is required depends on the view taken of reasonable people. If the most restrictively drawn version of the term proposed in *Lister v. Romford* was submitted to the first test, then quite likely one would have to conclude that it would pass. Most reasonable people, then as now, situated as employer on the one hand and employed professional driver on the other, would probably consider it natural to suppose that the employer would not only hold appropriate insurance to cover all activity in the course of duty, but would not seek to shift the burden of possibly enormous damages arising from a slight slip onto a modestly-paid employee. Nonetheless, the House felt that there were policy considerations that made such a term undesirable in that workers such as lorry and crane drivers might become blasé about safety if they were indemnified and held harmless for the results of such errors. If it continues to be felt that the generality of reasonable people cannot be trusted to take account of possible negative consequences (real or perceived), then the second, public policy, limb could be adopted.

Nevertheless, no such test has yet been established by the courts, and the author can do more than humbly suggest it. There has, however, been some movement in this direction. In *Crossley v. Faithful & Gould Holdings Ltd*, Dyson L.J. opined that: **3.46**

> It seems to me that, rather than focus on the elusive concept of necessity, it is better to recognise that, to some extent at least, the existence and scope of standardised implied terms raise questions of reasonableness, fairness and the balancing of competing policy considerations.[62]

Sir Andrew Morritt V-C and Thomas L.J. concurred with Dyson L.J.[63] However, this statement is worryingly close to that of Lord Denning M.R. in *Liverpool C.C. v. Irwin*.[64] It is to be hoped that cases in years to come will, without too much delay, come to agree on a reasonably well-defined, applicable but flexible test for implication of this sort.

---

62 [2004] EWCA Civ 293; [2004] 4 All E.R. 447; [2004] I.R.L.R. 377, at [36].

63 For a detailed discussion of the role of policy factors in implication of terms, the reader is commended to Elisabeth Peden, 'Policy Concerns Behind Implication of Terms in Law' (2001) 111 L.Q.R. 459 (also cited by Dyson L.J. in *Crossley*, n. 62, above, at [36]).

64 See above, paragraph **3.28**.

D. RELATIONSHIP OF TERMS IMPLIED IN LAW TO EXPRESS TERMS

3.47 Terms implied at common law are as a rule ousted by inconsistent express terms, but the application depends on a proper reading of the extent of the express term. So where a contract of employment stipulated a working week, but allowed the employer to require the employee to work in excess of his normal maximum working hours, this was subject to an overriding duty not to injure the health and wellbeing of the employee: *Johnstone v. Bloomsbury Area Health Authority.*[65]

---

65 [1992] 2 Q.B. 333; [1991] 2 All E.R. 293; [1991] 2 W.L.R. 1362 (C.A.). Considered in *Rayment v. Ministry of Defence* [2010] E.W.H.C. 218; [2010] All E.R. (D) 211 (Feb.) (Q.B.D.).

4

TERMS IMPLIED AT COMMON LAW II: SPECIFIC INSTANCES

A. INTRODUCTION

It is not possible, certainly not within the scope of a book of this length, to **4.01** enumerate all terms currently implied at common law. Such terms are numerous and also specialized, requiring for proper understanding an appreciation of specialist areas of legal practice. Moreover, such a list would doubtless soon be out of date as new terms are implied arising from the exigencies of litigation in many different fields of industrial and commercial endeavour. Therefore, the best repository of information on such terms is inevitably specialist practitioner works on such areas as construction law, charterparties, maritime law generally, employment law and so on. Nonetheless, it is possible to highlight some of the more commonly found terms of this type, illustrative and exemplary as they are, and we will attempt to do so here.

We shall consider in this chapter implied terms in employment contracts in **4.02** some detail, before touching in less detail on a small range of other instances of terms in common contracts. Some terms implied in law have now been put into statutory form, particularly in the fields of sale and supply of goods, supply of services, and hire purchase agreements. These instances will be discussed in their proper place in Chapter 6, on terms implied by statute.

B. EMPLOYMENT CONTRACTS: THE EMPLOYEE'S OBLIGATIONS[1]

4.03 The field of employment law has been particularly fecund in respect of terms implied in law, and especially so over the last 20 years or so. In the older cases, some of which have been discussed above, we see the courts placing particular duties of fidelity, competence, care and so forth on employees. The most distinctive feature of more recent cases is that greater obligations are being placed on employers than hitherto. This is well summarized in the comment of Lord Slynn of Hadley in *Spring v. Guardian Assurance* that he thought that it is now relevant to consider 'the changes which have taken place in the employer/employee relationship, with far greater duties imposed on the employer than in the past, whether by statute or by judicial decision, to care for the physical, financial and even psychological welfare of the employee'.[2]

1. Employee's duty of fidelity

4.04 In *Lamb v. Evans*[3] and *Robb v. Green*,[4] as we have seen,[5] a servant was held to owe a general duty of fidelity to the master and specifically not to make lists of clients for future solicitation or to solicit clients of the master while still in his employ. This was followed, though modified a little in *Wessex Dairies Ltd v. Smith*,[6] and the limits were made clearer still in *Faccenda Chicken Ltd v. Fowler*.[7] There is not only a duty not to compete, or take certain steps while in employment with a view to competing later, but also a duty not to work for a

---

1   On employment contracts generally, see R.W. Rideout (1996), 'Implied Terms in the Employment Relationship' in D.R. Halson (ed.), Exploring the Boundaries of Contract.

2   [1995] 2 A.C. 296 at 335; [1994] 3 All E.R. 129; [1994] I.R.L.R. 460. Applied in *Cox v. Sun Alliance Life Ltd* [2001] E.W.C.A. Civ. 649; [2001] I.R.L.R. 448, *Crossley v. Faithful & Gould Holdings Ltd* [2004] E.W.C.A. Civ. 293; [2004] 4 All E.R. 447, and *Lennon v. Metropolitan Police Commissioner* [2004] E.W.C.A. Civ. 130; [2004] 4 All E.R. 447. Distinguished in *Desmond v. Chief Constable of Nottinghamshire* [2011] E.W.C.A. Civ. 3; [2011] P.T.S.R. 1369.

3   [1893] 1 Ch. 218; (1893) 62 L.J. Ch. 404 (C.A.). See above, paragraph **3.07**.

4   [1895] 2 Q.B. 315; [1895–99] All E.R. Rep. 1053 (C.A.). See above, paragraph **3.07**.

5   Above, paragraphs **3.07–3.09**.

6   [1935] 2 K.B. 80; [1935] All E.R. Rep. 75 (C.A.). See above, paragraph **3.10**. See also *Sanders v. Parry* [1967] 2 All E.R. 803; [1967] 1 W.L.R. 753 (Q.B.D.) in which an assistant solicitor, who made arrangements with an important client to set up in an office of his own to handle the client's work, was in breach of the implied covenant of fidelity.

7   [1987] Ch. 117; [1986] 1 All E.R. 617 (C.A.). See above, paragraph **3.11**.

competitor during the employment, as in the case of *Hivac Ltd v. Park Royal Scientific Instruments Ltd and Others*.[8] In this case two of the defendants, Raymond and Gladys Davis had worked for some considerable time for the plaintiff company, which made midget valves for hearing aids, in which it thought it enjoyed a monopoly. Gladys, who had been a foreman for six years in charge of around 80 girls, had left on grounds of ill-health, but Raymond continued to work for the company in a highly-skilled and responsible position, with access to confidential design materials. Raymond and Gladys began working with Park Royal on producing a midget valve in competition with Hivac, and induced other Hivac employees to do likewise. None of this work was done in company time. The Court of Appeal held, however, notwithstanding the rightness of the principle that an employee sells his time to his employer for a fixed number of hours each week and should be free to use his spare time however he likes, including supplementing his income through other employment, there was a duty of fidelity owed by the employee. This duty would vary in extent according to the circumstances of individual cases, including factors such as the degree of skill and knowledge possessed by the employee, the degree of trust reposed in the employee by the employer and the effects or likely effects of any given behaviour. That is to say, that a duty of fidelity on the part of the employee is implied in any employment contract, but what will amount to a breach will depend on the particular circumstances.

These formulations of the employee's implied duty of fidelity are not, it is **4.05** submitted, entirely without an air of unreality or artificiality. It is not, perhaps, entirely unreasonable to object to a milk roundsman leafleting households on his round with a view to enticing those households to switch their business from his current employer to himself when he leaves that employment immediately afterwards, as in the *Wessex Dairies* case, since he could be expected to take his chances the day after his employment ends. It certainly does not seem unreasonable, also, to expect that trusted and skilled employees will not 'moonlight' for a competitor, especially when that work involves giving the competitor the very means of competition. But is it really to be expected that, for instance, even the most skilled barman should not work at other bars on other nights than those on which his principal employer requires his labour? And if he is popular with customers, is it not to be expected that they might go to those other bars when he is there? It is open, surely, to his employer to require an express term of his contract to be that he does not work elsewhere, and open to our putative barman to ask, in that case, that he should be given fuller employment and more money in exchange? Likewise, does a solicitor's firm, for example, really expect that an associate, if considering a

---

8   [1946] Ch. 169; [1946] 1 All E.R. 360 (C.A.).

move to another firm, or into the in-house legal department of a client of the firm, will first resign before entering into any discussions with his possible future employer? Statements of employees' duties of fidelity should be understood as having been made in the context of the case before the court at the time, and therefore a formulation cannot always be adopted and applied from one case to another without some difficulty. The duty can be stated in general terms, but it must be applied with care in specific contexts. Moreover, as employment patterns change, and social mores too, what amounts to a breach of such a term will also change in line with employers' and employees' usual expectations around the employment relation. What amounts to a breach of duty will also, plainly, differ not only over time, but also with the nature of the employer's business.

2. Employee's warranty of competence

4.06 An employee also impliedly warrants to his employer that he is reasonably skilled. In *Harmer v. Cornelius*[9] the Court of Common Pleas (Williams, Willes and Byles J.J.) considered the case of a painter, employed at £2/10s per week for 'more than a month'. The plaintiff painter was discharged, he alleged wrongfully, within the month. At first instance the jury found that the plaintiff was incompetent but, though the evidence showed he had represented himself as being possessed of the requisite skill, he had not fraudulently represented that he was competent. A verdict was given for the plaintiff, accordingly, but leave was given to the defendant to move for the verdict to be entered in his favour. The defendant obtained a rule nisi to this effect. Giving the judgment of the court, making the rule absolute, Willes J. held that:

> When a skilled labourer, artisan or artist is employed, there is on his part an implied warranty that he is of skill reasonably competent to the task he undertakes. *Spondes peritiam artis.*[10] Thus, if an apothecary, a watchmaker, or an attorney be employed for reward, they each impliedly undertake to possess and exercise reasonable skill in their several arts. The public profession of an art is a representation and undertaking to all the world that the professor possesses the requisite ability and skill ...[11]

---

9 [1843–60] All E.R. Rep 624; (1858) 5 C.B.N.S. 236 (C.P.). Applied in *Cuckson v. Stones* (1881) 1 E.&E. 248; 120 E.R. 902; [1843–60] All E.R. Rep. 390. Distinguished in *Andrews v. Garstin* (1861) 10 C.B.N.S. 444, *Re Elmslie & Co. ex p. Tower Subway Co.* (1873) L.R. 16 Eq. 326, and *Re Layton, Steele & Co.* [1890] W.N. 112.

10 'The art promises the skill.' (Note that this is the present author's own translation, but he does not promise particular skill in Latin translation.)

11 At 625.

Breach of this implied warranty can justify dismissal: **4.07**

> This is a question, upon which we have been furnished by the Bar with no authority, probably because labour, being seldom retained for a long time certain, the question has not often arisen. It seems, however, very unreasonable that an employer should be compelled to go on employing a man who, having represented himself as competent, turns out to be incompetent.[12]

Willes J. referred to a dictum of Lord Ellenborough in *Spain v. Arnott*,[13] speaking of a servant who had refused to perform his duty:

> 'The master is not bound to keep him on as a burdensome and useless servant to the end of the year', and went on to observe that '[i]t appears to us that there is no material difference between a servant who will not, and a servant who cannot, perform the duty for which he was hired'.[14]

This does not, however, mean that all workers warrant their own skill. It   **4.08** depends on the circumstances, as Willes J. went on to observe:

> It may be that if there is no general and no particular representation of ability and skill, the workman undertakes no responsibility. If a gentleman, for example, should employ a man who is known never to have done anything but sweep a crossing, to clean and mend a watch, the employer would probably be held to have undertaken all risk himself.[15]

And in *Jones v. Manchester Corporation*,[16] in which a hospital board sought indemnity from an inexperienced doctor for the damages it was liable to pay to a patient injured by the negligent administration of anaesthesia, it was held that there is no general implied term that a servant will indemnify his master for the consequences of his (the servant's) incompetence. In this instance the Court of Appeal held that the board had taken the benefit of employing junior and inexperienced doctors to do work that ought to have been done by more experienced practitioners and it would be unjust to allow it to escape the consequences by shifting liability onto the shoulders of the doctor (who was not, indeed, to blame for being inappropriately deployed on this occasion).

---

12 At 625–6, per Willes J.
13 (1817) 2 Stark. 256; 171 E.R. 638 (N.P.).
14 *Harmer v. Cornelius* at 626.
15 At 625.
16 [1952] Q.B. 852 (C.A.).

3. Duty of professional staff to co-operate

4.09 Employees who are considered a member of a profession may be under an additional duty to co-operate with colleagues and managers to ensure the proper discharge of the organization's professional functions. In *Sim v. Rotherham M.B.C.*[17] Scott J. held that teachers were members of a profession and were therefore obliged to co-operate in the proper running of the school, which included complying with the headmaster's reasonable arrangements to cover the lessons of absent colleagues. Deductions from their salaries for refusal to cover colleagues' lessons were therefore permissible.

4. Duty to indemnify employer in respect of employee's unlawful acts

4.10 This has already been alluded to in the foregoing paragraph. *Jones v. Manchester Corporation*[18] starts from the assumption of such a duty, but distinguishes the case where the employee's unlawful actions (in that case negligent treatment of a patient) are really the result of the employer's own default, in which case the employee ought not to have the burden cast upon him. *Lister v. Romford*, also discussed above, is an example of a case in which the employee's duty to carry out his duties skilfully and carefully or face indemnifying the employer was enforced by the courts insofar as the failure to do so constituted an unlawful act, which entitled another to claim against the employer. This duty is clearly bound up with the warranty of skill or competence (see paragraph **4.06**, above), but it equally clearly extends further, as an unlawful act by an employee might have nothing to do with the possession or otherwise of the proper level of skill. At the risk of appearing unduly pedantic, there is a difference between warranting that one possesses a skill, actually exercising that skill if one does have it, and not committing unlawful acts entitling another to claim against one's employer.

C. EMPLOYMENT CONTRACTS: THE EMPLOYER'S OBLIGATIONS

1. Employer's 'duty of trust and confidence'

4.11 In more recent times the courts have placed balancing obligations on employers. The servant's duty of fidelity, clearly established in the earlier cases, can now be said to be matched by a duty of fidelity on the part of the master.

---

17   [1987] Ch. 216; [1986] 3 All E.R. 387; [1986] 3 W.L.R. 851; [1986] I.C.R. 897; [1986] I.R.L.R. 391 (Ch.D.).

18   [1952] Q.B. 852; [1952] 2 All E.R. 125 (C.A.).

McMeel observes[19] that this duty, established in *Malik v. Bank of Credit and Commerce International S.A. (In Liquidation)*,[20] was derived from the principles adumbrated by Lord Bridge in *Scally v. Southern Health and Social Services Board*[21] (of which more, below), presumably referring to the remark in *Malik* of Lord Steyn:

> Lord Slynn of Hadley recently noted 'the changes which have taken place in the employer-employee relationship, with far greater duties imposed on the employer than in the past, whether by statute or by judicial decision, to care for the physical, financial and even psychological welfare of the employee': *Spring v. Guardian Assurance Plc.*[22] A striking illustration of this change is Scally's case … to which I have already referred, where the House of Lords implied a term that all employees in a certain category had to be notified by an employer of their entitlement to certain benefits. It was the change in legal culture which made possible the evolution of the implied term of trust and confidence.[23]

It seems tolerably clear, however, that what is here being said to pave the way for an implied term of trust and confidence placing a duty on the employer, is the change in employer-employee relations, not the decision or reasoning in *Scally*. Indeed the above is the only substantive mention of *Scally* to be found in the judgments in *Malik*.

The root in social change of wider obligations on employers is also emphasized **4.12** in the following statement of Lord Hoffmann in *Johnson v. Unisys Ltd*:

> [O]ver the last 30 years or so, the nature of the contract of employment has been transformed. It has been recognised that a person's employment is usually one of the most important things in his or her life. It gives not only a livelihood but an occupation, an identity and a sense of self-esteem. The law has changed to recognise this social reality.[24]

---

19 G. McMeel (2007), *The Construction of Contracts* (Oxford: Oxford University Press), at 10.20.
20 [1998] A.C. 20; [1997] 3 All E.R. 1; [1997] 3 W.L.R. 95. Applied in *Horkulak v. Cantor Fitzgerald International* [2003] E.W.H.C. 1918; [2004] I.C.R. 697; [2003] I.R.L.R. 756 (Q.B.D.), *Meikle v. Nottinghamshire C.C.* [2004] E.W.C.A. Civ. 859; [2004] 4 All E.R. 97, *Omilaju v. Waltham Forest L.B.C. (No. 2)* [2004] E.W.C.A Civ. 1493; [2005] 1 All E.R. 75, *McCabe v. Greenwich L.B.C.* [2005] E.W.C.A. Civ. 1364, *R.D.F. Media Group plc v. Clements* [2007] E.W.H.C. 2892 (Q.B.) [2008] I.R.L.R. 207, *Bournemouth University Higher Education Corp. v. Buckland* [2009] I.C.R. 1042; [2009] I.R.L.R. 606 (E.A.T.), *Tullett Prebon plc v. B.G.C. Brokers LP* [2010] E.W.H.C. 484 (Q.B.); [2010] I.R.L.R. 648, and in a number of unreported E.A.T. cases.
21 [1992] 1 A.C. 294; [1991] 4 All E.R. 563; [1991] 3 W.L.R. 778; [1991] I.R.L.R. 522.
22 [1995] 2 A.C. 296, 335.
23 [1998] A.C. 20, 46.
24 [2001] U.K.H.L. 13; [2003] 1 A.C. 519 at [35].

4.13   *Malik* concerned the after-effects of a notorious banking scandal. The bank concerned (B.C.C.I.) was a large privately-owned bank, founded in Pakistan in 1972 and incorporated in Luxembourg. It operated in nearly 80 countries and claimed assets of around $20 billion. The bank had many legitimate customers around the world including at its network of branches in major U.K. cities. It was, however, a front for criminality on a large scale, allegedly including money-laundering, organized crime, terrorism, arms-trafficking and fraud. It collapsed in 1991, with an estimated $13 billion unaccounted for. It may well be imagined, in the circumstances, that many entirely honest staff found themselves unemployed (at a time of recession) and with their personal reputations tarnished by association with their former employer.

4.14   The House heard consolidated appeals from Raihan Nasir Mahmud and Qaiser Mansoor Malik, who had both lost their jobs in the collapse of the bank and who sought to prove in the liquidation for damages for loss of notice money and statutory redundancy pay and for 'stigma' which they said attached to them from association with the bank and made it harder for them to find new jobs. The claims in respect of notice money and statutory redundancy pay were not in dispute, but the liquidators rejected the claim for damages in relation to stigma. The two men appealed to the court and the registrar directed a trial of a preliminary point of law as to whether their claims in this respect disclosed a reasonable cause of action or a sustainable claim for damages. At first instance, Evans-Lombe J. held that they did not, and this decision was upheld by the Court of Appeal (Glidewell, Morritt and Aldous L.JJ.). The House of Lords, unanimously, disagreed with the courts below.

4.15   Discussion centred on the exact scope of the employer's implied obligation. The parties agreed both in the Court of Appeal and in the House of Lords that employers owed a duty 'not, without reasonable and proper cause, [to] conduct itself in a manner likely to destroy or seriously damage the relationship of confidence and trust between employer and employee'.[25] However, the liquidators contended that a breach of this term had to be referable to conduct directed at particular employees or groups of employees, while the appellants argued that really this term was a portmanteau of implied obligations, including an obligation not to conduct a corrupt or dishonest business. There was also argument as to whether the employee needed to know of the trust-destroying conduct while still employed and whether the employee's trust must be shown actually to have been undermined. Lord Nicholls considered that breaches of some terms would entitle an employee to leave at once, and went on:

---

25   [1998] A.C. 20, 34, per Lord Nicholls of Birkenhead.

[a]s a matter of legal analysis, the innocent employee's entitlement to leave at once must derive from the bank being in breach of a term of the contract of employment which the employee is entitled to treat as a repudiation by the bank of its contractual obligations. That is the source of his right to step away from the contract forthwith.

In other words, and this is the necessary corollary of the employee's right to leave at once, the bank was under an implied obligation to its employees not to conduct a dishonest or corrupt business. This implied obligation is no more than one particular aspect of the portmanteau, general obligation not to engage in conduct likely to undermine the trust and confidence required if the employment relationship is to continue in the manner the employment contract implicitly envisages.[26]

The House also rejected the contention that the offending conduct must, to be actionable, be targeted at the particular employee either individually or as one of a group: **4.16**

I do not accept the liquidators' submission that the conduct of which complaint is made must be targeted in some way at the employee or a group of employees. No doubt that will often be the position, perhaps usually so. But there is no reason in principle why this must always be so. The trust and confidence required in the employment relationship can be undermined by an employer, or indeed an employee, in many different ways. I can see no justification for the law giving the employee a remedy if the unjustified trust-destroying conduct occurs in some ways but refusing a remedy if it occurs in others. The conduct must, of course, impinge on the relationship in the sense that, looked at objectively, it is likely to destroy or seriously damage the degree of trust and confidence the employee is reasonably entitled to have in his employer. That requires one to look at all the circumstances.[27]

In summary, then, an employer has a duty to refrain from conduct, unless justified, that tends to undermine its relationship of trust and confidence with its employee. This is a fairly general duty, and includes a duty not to conduct a dishonest business. *Malik* has since been applied or followed in a number of cases.[28] **4.17**

---

26 At 34–5.
27 At 35, per Lord Nicholls.
28 See, *Atlantic Air Ltd v. Hoff* [2008] All E.R. (D) 314 (Mar.) (E.A.T.), *Bank of Credit & Commerce International S.A. (in Liquidation) v. Ali* [1999] 4 All E.R. 83; [2000] I.C.R. 1354; [1999] I.R.L.R. 508, *Bates Wells & Braithwaite (a firm) v. MacFarlane* [2003] All E.R. (D) 484 (Oct.) (E.A.T.), *Bristol United Press Ltd v. Beckett* [2005] All E.R. (D.) 225 (Apr.) (E.A.T.), *Cape Industrial Services Ltd v. Ambler* [2002] E.W.C.A. Civ. 1264; [2002] All E.R. (D) 49 (Sep.), *Horkulak v. Cantor Fitzgerald International* [2003] E.W.H.C. 1918; [2004] I.C.R. 697; [2003] I.R.L.R. 756 (Q.B.D.), *Huggins v. Micrel Semiconductor (UK) Ltd* [2004] All E.R. (D) 07 (Sep.) (E.A.T. (Sc.)), *Diffang v. Lewisham Hospital N.H.S. Trust* [2005] All E.R. (D) 68 (Aug.) (E.A.T.), *M.P.I. Ltd v. Woodland* [2007] All E.R. (D) 100 (May) (E.A.T.), *McCabe v. Greenwich L.B.C.* [2005] E.W.C.A. Civ. 1364; [2005] All E.R. (D) 102 (Oct.), *Meikle v. Nottinghamshire C.C.* [2004] E.W.C.A. Civ. 859; [2004] 4 All E.R. 97; [2005] I.C.R. 1; [2004] I.R.L.R. 703, *Omilaju v. Waltham Forest L.B.C. (No.2)* [2004] E.W.C.A. Civ. 1493; [2004] 1 All E.R. 75; [2005] I.C.R. 481; [2005] I.R.L.R. 35, *R.D.F. Media Group plc v. Clements* [2007] E.W.H.C. 2892; [2008] I.R.L.R. 207 (Q.B.), *T. & N. Ltd (in*

4.18 The case of *Scally v. Southern Health and Social Services Board*[29] has already been mentioned.[30] This can be seen as an instance of the operation of the general obligation of trust and confidence or simply as an obligation in its own right, where there is a complex employment contract and a range of benefits, negotiated collectively perhaps, to which the employee simply signs up. In short, like most employment contracts, it is a complex contract of adhesion. In such cases the employer would seem to have a duty to draw valuable benefits to the attention of the employee, since the employee did not negotiate these and cannot be expected to know all of them, let alone the actions to be taken to secure the value of them, while the employer can certainly be imputed with such knowledge.

4.19 In *University of Nottingham v. Eyett*,[31] an employee of the university, John Eyett, took early retirement at the age of 60 and asked the university for information about his pension entitlement if he retired on 31 July 1994. While the university provided him with correct information, it did not go so far as to tell him that if he retired on the earliest possible date after 31 July 1994 to which the university would agree (that is, 31 August 1994) he would enjoy an increased pension entitlement, because his pensionable salary would have risen by that date and thus his benefits under the final salary scheme would have increased. On discovering this, Mr Eyett complained to the Pensions Ombudsman, who upheld his complaint. The university applied by originating motion to the Chancery Division to set aside this decision and the motion was heard by Hart J., who held for the university. The Ombudsman had considered the failure to warn Mr Eyett of the consequences of choosing a date before 1 August rather than after it was a breach of its obligation of trust and confidence. The university owed a:

> contractual duty which extended to providing him with sufficient information to enable him reasonably to realise that 1 August 1994 rather than 31 July 1994 would have been the most advantageous date on which he should retire and begin drawing his retirement benefits. If the information actually provided was not sufficient for this

---

Administration) v. Royal & Sun Alliance plc [2003] E.W.H.C. 1016; [2003] 2 All E.R. (Comm.) 939; [2004] Lloyd's Rep. I.R. 106, *Transco plc (formerly B.G. plc) v. O'Brien* [2001] I.R.L.R. 496, *Visa International Service Association v. Paul* [2004] I.R.L.R. 42 (E.A.T.), *Wright v. Weed Control Ltd* [2008] All E.R. (D) 235 (Feb.) (E.A.T.).

29 [1992] 1 A.C. 294; [1991] 4 All E.R. 563; [1991] 3 W.L.R. 778; [1991] I.R.L.R. 522. Dictum of Lord Bridge applied in *Spring v. Guardian Assurance plc* [1993] 2 All E.R. 273; [1993] I.C.R. 412; [1993] I.R.L.R. 122 (C.A.).

30 See above, paragraphs **3.42** and **4.11**.

31 [1999] 2 All E.R. 437; [1999] 1 W.L.R. 594; [1999] I.C.R. 721. Applied in *Transco plc (formerly BG plc) v. O'Brien* [2001] I.R.L.R. 496 (E.A.T.).

purpose, reasonable steps would not have been taken within the *Scally v. Southern Health and Social Services Board* principle.[32]

The Ombudsman held as a fact that the literature provided to Mr Eyett was insufficient. The *Scally* argument was conceded by counsel for the Ombudsman (Mr Eyett was not represented) and Hart J. in any event found that the literature was sufficient for Mr Eyett to realise for himself the financial disadvantage of retiring before 1 August. He further found that the university could not have been expected to suppose that Mr Eyett had not taken this into account, since he was also choosing to sacrifice a month's salary and a further month's pensionable service.

Hart J. doubted that the employer's duty of trust and confidence extended to positive duties. It was a negative duty not to act so as to destroy or seriously damage the relationship. *Scally*, in imposing a measure of positive duty, depended on definite conditions, set out by Lord Bridge in the following terms: **4.20**

> (1) the terms of the contract of employment have not been negotiated with the individual employee but result from negotiation with a representative body or are otherwise incorporated by reference; (2) a particular term of the contract makes available to the employee a valuable right contingent upon action being taken by him to avail himself of its benefit; (3) the employee cannot, in all the circumstances, reasonably be expected to be aware of the term unless it is drawn to his attention.[33]

Eyett was a decision at first instance, that is largely explicable on its facts, but the Court of Appeal in *Crossley v. Faithful & Gould Holdings Ltd*[34] also rejected a general positive duty to care for an employee's economic well-being, and in that case the employee making the damaging decision had suffered from a nervous breakdown, so might be expected to be less able to take care in his affairs (though, on the other hand, he was a managing director, and even with a nervous breakdown might be expected to make a habit of at least consulting financial advisers). These two cases, taken together, do not seem to bear out Lord Slynn's view that employers nowadays had a duty 'to care for the physical, financial and even psychological welfare of the employee'.[35] It does look very much as though, for the time being at least, the duty in *Scally* is not to be expanded into a general obligation to look after employees' financial well-being and ensure they are fully aware of how to maximize their benefits, **4.21**

---

32 Quoted by Hart J. at 439.
33 *Scally* [1992] 1 A.C. 294, 307.
34 [2004] E.W.C.A. Civ. 293; [2004] 4 All E.R. 447; [2004] I.R.L.R. 377, see above, paragraph **3.46**.
35 *Spring v. Guardian Assurance plc* [1995] 2 A.C. 296 at 335.

but is restricted to the circumstances enumerated by Lord Bridge and set out in the preceding paragraph.

2. Employer's duty not to require employee to commit unlawful acts

4.22 This may now be regarded as an aspect of the duty of trust and confidence. It seems tolerably clear, as a matter of common sense and logic, that requiring the employee to commit an unlawful act would be an act in itself calculated to destroy or damage trust and confidence between employer and employee, and to permit an employer to do this would be inconsistent with the employee's duty to indemnify the employer against the consequences of an employee's unlawful acts.

4.23 Treitel cites *Gregory v. Ford*[36] as an instance of this term.[37] In this case the employee drove a lorry without statutory insurance. Byrne J., sitting at the Nottinghamshire Summer Assizes, held that while the employers were not obliged to hold insurance to indemnify the driver, they were also not entitled to require him to drive without insurance. That they did so (because they did not have insurance) breached the implied term that they would not require him to commit an unlawful act. It was their breach of this term that left them with the liability to pay damages to the plaintiff, not the employee's unlawful act in itself. The distinction between this case and *Lister v. Romford* is a subtle one, but consists in the fact that in *Lister* the driver was insured, committed an unlawful act in driving negligently and the employer's loss was therefore attributable to his negligence, not the employer's actions. Similarly, in *Semtex Ltd v. Gladstone*,[38] Finnemore J. at the Birmingham Assizes held the employee driver liable for damage caused by his negligent driving because there was no implied term that the employers (who did hold insurance) would indemnify him for his own negligent acts.

3. Employer's duty to take care in giving references

4.24 In *Spring v. Guardian Assurance plc*,[39] the House of Lords (Lord Keith of Kinkel, Lord Goff of Chieveley, Lord Lowry, Lord Slynn of Hadley and Lord Woolf) held that employers owed to former employees a duty of care, in tort, in respect of providing references. Three of the panel (Lords Goff, Slynn and Woolf) also held that it was an implied term of the employment contract that

---

36   [1951] 1 All E.R. 121(Assizes).
37   Treitel, 206.
38   [1954] 1 W.L.R. 945; [1954] 2 All E.R. 206 (Assizes).
39   [1995] 2 A.C. 296; [1994] 3 All E.R. 129; [1994] 3 W.L.R. 354; [1994] I.C.R. 596; [1994] I.R.L.R. 460.

employers would ensure that reasonable care was taken in compiling and giving references.

Although there was some doubt whether there was a contract between Mr **4.25** Spring and Guardian Assurance, and that it was not necessary to find a contract, given the finding on negligence, Lord Goff on the question of whether such a contract would contain the implied term alleged by Mr Spring,[40] said:[41]

> Where the relationship between the parties is that of employer and employee, the duty of care could be expressed as arising from an implied term of the contract of employment, i.e. that, if a reference is supplied by the employer for the employee, due care and skill will be exercised by him in its preparation. Such a term may be implied despite the absence of any legal obligation on the employer to provide a reference (as I understand to have been accepted by the parties in the present case), and may be expressed to apply even after the employee has left his employment with the employer.

Adding, however:

> But in the present case this adds nothing to the duty of care which arises under the *Hedley Byrne* principle, and so may be applicable as a tortious duty, either where there is no contract between the parties, or concurrently with a contractual duty to the same effect.

Lord Slynn put the matter even more clearly: **4.26**

> There was undoubtedly a contract with Corinium as the judge found. Whether that was a contract of service or for services for present purposes in my view does not matter, though the title of the posts after the first appointment suggests that it was a contract of service. In the light of the relationship between these four companies I consider, on the judge's findings, (a) that it was an implied term of the contract of employment between the plaintiff and Corinium that Corinium would ensure that reasonable care was taken in the group of associated companies in the compiling and giving of the reference if it was asked for by a potential employer and (b) that Corinium was in breach of that implied term.
>
> The Court of Appeal did not express a view as to whether a contract also existed with Guardian Assurance although they found the argument that it did to be 'persuasive.' Since the issue of causation has to be remitted to the Court of Appeal, I would remit this question also on the basis that if there is found to be a contract with Guardian

---

40   To 'provide a reference which was full, frank and truthful and which was in any event prepared using reasonable care'.
41   At 320.

Assurance a term is to be implied into it that reasonable care would be taken in the giving of the reference.[42]

While Lord Woolf said:

Here, it is also possible to specify circumstances which would enable a term to be implied. The circumstances are: (i) The existence of the contract of employment or for services. (ii) The fact that the contract relates to an engagement of a class where it is the normal practice to require a reference from a previous employer before employment is offered. (iii) The fact that the employee cannot be expected to enter into that class of employment except on the basis that his employer will, on the request of another prospective employer made not later than a reasonable time after the termination of a former employment, provide a full and frank reference as to the employee.

This being the nature of the engagement, it is necessary to imply a term into the contract that the employer would, during the continuance of the engagement or within a reasonable time thereafter, provide a reference at the request of a prospective employer which was based on facts revealed after making those reasonably careful inquiries which, in the circumstances, a reasonable employer would make.[43]

4.27 Lord Keith expressly rejected the idea that there was an implied term to the effect alleged,[44] adopting the reasoning of Glidewell L.J. in the Court of Appeal that an implied term as to the provision of references would not need to go further than to say that the employer would provide a reference in accordance with Lautro rule 3.5(2), that is, one which made 'full and frank disclosure of all relevant matters which are believed to be true'.[45] Lord Lowry merely declined to make a finding on this point, since it was unnecessary in view of the decision regarding liability in negligence, observing:[46]

So far as concerns other matters which have been discussed, including in particular the defendants' liability in contract, I will be content, having regard to my conclusion on the negligence issue, to remind myself of the felicitous reference to obiter dicta and the proverbial chickens of destiny made by Bowen L.J. in *Cooke v. New River Co.*[[47]]

Though he did say that he thought that 'it might without difficulty be implied that, in the interests of the recipient, a reference should be a careful one as well as being full and frank'.[48]

---

42   At 340.
43   At 353–4.
44   At 315.
45   [1993] I.C.R. 412, 438–9.
46   [1995] 2 A.C. 296, 327.
47   (1888) 38 Ch.D. 56, 71.
48   [1995] 2 A.C. 296, 327.

With respect to Lord Keith and Glidewell L.J., the reasoning seems open to **4.28** question. Although Glidewell L.J. drew the proper distinction between implication in fact and implication in law, he went on to consider whether such a term as alleged could be implied in law and concluded not, as not being necessary, whereas he would have been open to argument that a term to meet Lautro requirements might meet the criteria for implication in law. That is then to take a very narrow view of the type of contract: that is, not a contract of employment generally, but a contract of employment to which Lautro regulations apply. In the latter case, surely a term based on trade custom would be more appropriate. Arriving at a term so specific to a very narrow kind of contract is barely going further than implication in fact and the approach to 'necessity' implicit in the finding tends to bear this out. It is a legitimate exercise to do as Lords Goff, Slynn and Woolf did and consider whether the generality of employment relations have as a necessary implication that employers, if providing references, will do so with reasonable care. Bearing in mind that few employments will be gained without the benefit of satisfactory references, this seems to go no further than is reasonably necessary, and would surely also meet the 'officious bystander' test also (though this is not strictly necessary for implication in law, of course), as it seems likely that if an officious bystander asked the parties to a contract of service whether there should be term that if at some future point the employee were to move on then any reference provided would be provided with reasonable care, the parties surely would say 'of course' rather than 'of course not'.

In summary, there is a duty of care in tort placed on employers and owed to **4.29** employees and former employees, to take reasonable care in providing references. Lord Goff's reasoning on such a duty as an implied obligation owed in contract is obiter, but arguably this is not the case with Lords Slynn and Woolf, since they both held that if it was found below that the alleged contracts existed then such a term was to be implied into them. Lord Lowry thought that such a term was to be implied but found it unnecessary to do so in the instant case, and this view is therefore also obiter. *Spring v. Guardian Assurance* is therefore doubtful as an authority, strictly speaking, on the implication of such a term, but if the issue were to arise in future, it would surely be likely that a lower court would feel that the views of three most distinguished law lords, expressed so clearly, ought to guide its determination. Whether the issue will ever need to be resolved, given the undoubted duty in tort, is far from certain. However, it is submitted that it is a shame their Lordships did not focus on the contractual obligation first, and place the obligation firmly on a contractual footing. To quote Lord Scarman in *Tai Hing Cotton Mill Ltd v. Liu Chong Hing Bank Ltd*:[49]

> Their Lordships do not believe that there is anything to the advantage of the law's development in searching for a liability in tort where the parties are in a contractual relationship. This is particularly so in a commercial relationship. Though it is possible as a matter of legal semantics to conduct an analysis of the rights and duties inherent in some contractual relationships including that of banker and customer either as a matter of contract law when the question will be what, if any, terms are to be implied or as a matter of tort law when the task will be to identify a duty arising from the proximity and character of the relationship between the parties, their Lordships believe it to be correct in principle and necessary for the avoidance of confusion in the law to adhere to the contractual analysis …[50]

4. Employer's duty not to endanger employee's health and safety

4.30   In view of the extensive requirements of health and safety legislation, it might be thought that an implied term on this would be otiose, but the legislation is regulatory and criminal in nature and an employee's rights against an employer are therefore still to be derived from contract and, of course, tort. The contractual duty on the employer not to endanger the employee's physical well-being is well established. It was recognized at least as early as 1845 when, in *Turner v. Mason* it was held that a servant might lawfully excuse herself from work when she apprehends a danger to life, or violence to her person, from the master, or when there is an infectious disease in the house and the servant needs to leave to preserve her life.[51] In *Ottoman Bank of Nicosia v. Chakarian*[52] a bank employee who had been posted from Smyrna to Constantinople informed his employers that in Constantinople his life was in danger from the Turkish authorities and asked to be transferred elsewhere. The bank declined, Chakarian fled, and the bank dismissed him. It was held that in the circumstances his actions did not amount to grave misconduct justifying dismissal.

---

49   [1986] A.C. 80.

50   At 170, cited with approval by Lord Bridge of Harwich in *Scally v. Southern Health and Social Services Board* [1992] 1 A.C. 294, 303.

51   (1845) 14 M. & W. 112; 2 Dow & L. 898; 14 L.J. Ex. 311. Applied in *Ottoman Bank v. Chakarian* [1930] A.C. 277 (P.C.) and approved in *Bouzourou v. Ottoman Bank* [1930] A.C. 271 (P.C.). Distinguished in *Laws v. London Chronicle (Indicator Newspapers) Ltd* [1959] 1 W.L.R. 698; [1959] 2 All E.R. 285 (C.A.).

52   [1930] A.C. 277 (P.C.). See also *Bouzourou v. Ottoman Bank* [1930] A.C. 271 (P.C.).

In *Matthews v. Kuwait Bechtel Corporation*,[53] in which a contractual right was **4.31** critical, it was held that the duty existed both in contract and in tort. The plaintiff, who had been injured falling into a trench while working on a pump, was domiciled in England but the defendant employer was a corporation domiciled in Panama. To bring proceedings against them for his work injury, the plaintiff had to obtain leave to serve the writ outside the jurisdiction. He obtained leave under R.S.C. Order 11, r.1(e), which relates to proceedings in contract. The writ was accordingly served in Panama and the defendant sought to have service set aside on the grounds that the claim had to be one in tort. This application was rejected by the Master and an appeal to the judge in chambers was also unsuccessful, whereupon the defendant company appealed further. The Court of Appeal (Sellers and Wilmer L.JJ.) dismissed the appeal, holding that there was an implied contractual duty on an employer to take all reasonable care for the safety of its employees in the course of their work. It was for the plaintiff to elect whether to bring an action in contract or tort and having elected to bring it in contract, the plaintiff here was entitled to apply for leave to serve outside the jurisdiction under O.13, r.1(e).

More recently, in *Johnstone v. Bloomsbury Area Health Authority*,[54] it was held **4.32** that there is a duty owed by an employer both in tort and in contract not to put at risk the health of an employee, in this instance by requiring him to work excessive hours, and that the duty was owed to an individual employee so that his state of health, resilience and so forth were the factors that should be taken into account, rather than that of an average or an ideal employee in that role. This duty was not overridden by a contractual entitlement of the employer to require the employee to work a given number of hours or in a given place, since this was a general entitlement of the employer not a requirement on the employer, whilst the duty not to endanger the employee's health did place an obligation on the employer.

D. MISCELLANEOUS

As already observed, a book of this length and scope must focus primarily on **4.33** general principles and cannot hope to supply a full account of specific terms. However, examples provide useful illustrations of the working out of the process in practice and the reader will be able to draw conclusions about policy in areas of law from consideration of detailed instances. The various instances

---

53 [1959] 2 Q.B. 57; [1959] 2 All E.R. 345; [1959] 2 W.L.R. 702 (C.A.). See also G.G. Webber, Note (1959) 22 M.L.R. 521 and J.A. Jolowicz, Note (1959) 17 C.L.J. 163.
54 [1992] 2 Q.B. 333; [1991] 2 All E.R. 293; [1991] 2 W.L.R. 1362 (C.A.).

from the law of employment contracts furnished above illustrate this. It would be unbalanced, however, to consider only employment, though this has certainly been a particularly fertile landscape for terms implied at common law. In this section we will consider a number of other instances of implied terms from different fields, by way of illustrating the breadth of the law's use of this device. The advice is repeated though, that the best sources for detailed and thorough information on implied terms in any field of law are the leading practitioner texts for each field.

1.   Fitness for habitation in contract to sell land and build house

4.34   It is trite law that there is no implied warranty of fitness for habitation in the case of the sale of an existing dwelling-house.[55] The case is different, however, where the contract concerns the purchase of a house to be built, or in the course of construction, with final completion occurring when the building is complete. In *Miller v. Cannon Hill Estates Ltd*,[56] a case concerning the building of new suburban residences in Raynes Park, Surrey, Swift J. held that there was an implied term that the building would be completed to a good and workmanlike standard using proper materials, a conclusion he reached because otherwise the consideration could be said to fail, as the purpose of such contracts is immediate occupation, rather than renovation.

4.35   *Miller v. Cannon Hill Estates* was referred to with approval and the principle followed by the Court of Appeal in *Perry v. Sharon Development Co. Ltd*.[57] This case also concerned a development of suburban houses, this time in Hendon. Like the house in *Miller*, it proved to be porous to the weather. Moreover, the walls of the dining room and drawing room were not fully plastered; no taps were installed, nor was the bath; and there was no lavatory-seat, there were no grates and no electric meter. All, in short, was far from well in Metroland, at least so far as Mr Perry was concerned. The defendant developer alleged that these were merely decorative niceties, that the house was complete and any deficiencies were Mr Perry's problem. The Court of Appeal (Sir Wilfred Greene M.R., Romer and Mackinnon L.JJ.) was bound by the judge's finding of fact as to the inadequacies of the construction and took the view that the building was not completed. The question then

---

55   See, for example, *Perry v. Sharon Development Co. Ltd* [1937] 4 All E.R. 390 at 393–3 per Sir Wilfred Greene M.R., 394 per Romer L.J. and 395 per Mackinnon L.J.

56   [1931] 2 K.B. 113; [1931] All E.R. Rep. 93 (Div. Ct).

57   [1937] 4 All E.R. 390 (C.A.). Applied in *Lynch v. Thorne* [1956] 1 All E.R. 744; [1956] 1 W.L.R. 303 (C.A.). As a matter of interest, the defendant developers were represented by Serjeant Sullivan K.C., the last of the Serjeants-at-Law, who died in 1951, and was perhaps best known for his defence on treason charges of Sir Roger Casement in 1916.

arose as to whether there was an implied term as to the standard to which the works ought to have been completed. The court unanimously held that there was an implied term. The Master of the Rolls stated that:

> [W]here the contract is a contract relating to a house which is still in process of being completed, where the vendor's workmen are still on the job, particularly where the completion is not to take place until the house has arrived at the contemplated condition – namely, complete finish and readiness for occupation – there must be implied in that contract an undertaking that the house shall be in that condition.[58]

Romer L.J., agreeing, said that 'In the case of the sale of a completed house, **4.36** there is to be implied on the part of the vendor no warranty as to the house being in any particular condition.'[59] The same would apply to an uncompleted house which has been made the subject matter of the sale, with the structure standing at the time of sale (meaning, presumably, that the contract is not for a house, currently uncompleted, but due to be completed by the vendor, at which time it will be handed over, but rather the sale of an incomplete house, as such). Where, however the contract is for the sale of a house when completed:

> [T]here is an implied contract on the part of the vendor, in the absence of there being any express contract as to the way in which the house is to be completed, that the house shall be completed in such a way that it is fit for human habitation.[60]

He went on to add, by way of clarification, that 'it matters not that the house has already been partly constructed'.[61]

The rule has been affirmed since, for example in *Hancock v. Brazier*.[62] An **4.37** express term inconsistent with the implied term, however, ousts the implied term in this case: *Lynch v. Thorne*.[63]

2. Duty to warn of defective building design

Furmston suggests that there may be implied obligation on a contractor to **4.38** warn an employer that designs forming the basis of a contract to erect a house are defective, so that the building constructed in accordance therewith will not

---

58 At 393.
59 At 394.
60 At 394–5.
61 At 395.
62 [1966] 2 All E.R. 901; [1966] 1 W.L.R. 1317 (C.A.), applying *Miller v. Cannon Hill Estates Co. Ltd.* The obligation in the building contract is not merged into the conveyance so as to be unactionable after conveyance: *Lawrence v. Cassel* [1930] 2 K.B. 83 (C.A.), also applied by the Court of Appeal in *Hancock v. Brazier.*
63 [1956] 1 All E.R. 744; [1956] 1 W.L.R. 303 (C.A.).

be fit for purpose.[64] The position has to be considered somewhat tentative as yet. He cites the 1974 Canadian case of *Nowlan v. Brunswick Construction Ltd*,[65] which concerned a house to be built to the client's specifications, which were faulty. But the language of the court, while couched contractually as to a general obligation to build something fit for habitation, an express term of the contract apparently, really suggests that the question is one of construction, where the obligation to build a house fit for habitation overrides the obligation to build in accordance with the plans provided, where the constructor is of sufficient experience to realize that following the plans will result in a defective house unfit to be occupied. The English case of *Equitable Debenture Corporation v. William Moss*,[66] certainly, does appear to support the existence of an implied term that defects in a building design should be pointed out to the employer, but this was a decision at first instance only and if it has been followed in the 25 years from decision to the time of writing, then this has not been reported in the main general series of reports.

4.39 There is also, of course, a duty of care placed on architects, engineers and the like to exercise due skill and care in producing their designs and supervising construction: *Greaves Co. (Contractors) Ltd v. Baynham Meikle & Partners*.[67] As to professional duties, see further, below at paragraphs 4.47ff.

3. Furnished property to be fit for habitation

4.40 A well-established implied term is that property let furnished is to be fit for habitation. In *Smith v. Marrable*[68] a house in Brighton was let furnished for five weeks at a rent of 8 gn. per week to Sir Thomas Marrable. The Marrables entered possession on Friday 16 September and on Saturday 17 September Lady Marrable wrote to Mrs Smith, the landlord's wife, that she intended to leave, paying one week's rent, as soon as alternative accommodation could be found, as all but one of the bedrooms being occupied were so infested with bugs as to be uninhabitable. Parke B. (with whom Lord Abinger C.B. and Alderson and Gurney BB. agreed) held that the tenants were entitled to do as they had done. He put it on the basis of an implied term:

> [I]f the demised premises are incumbered with a nuisance of so serious a nature that no person can reasonably be expected to live in them, the tenant is at liberty to throw

---

64   Cheshire, Fifoot and Furmston, 191.
65   [1974] Carswell N.B. 15 (Supreme Court of Canada).
66   (1984) 2 Con. L.R. 1; 1 Const. L.J. 131.
67   [1975] 3 All E.R. 99; [1975] 1 W.L.R. 1095; [1975] 2 Lloyd's Rep. 325 (C.A.).
68   (1843) 11 M. & W. 5; 152 E.R. 693. Applied in *Wilson v. Finch Hatton* (1877) 2 Ex.D. 336; 46 L.J.Q.B. 489 (Ex.D.) and *Bird v. Lord Greville* (1884) Cab. & L. 317 (Q.B.D.).

them up. This is not the case of a contract on the part of the landlord that the premises were free from this nuisance; it rather rests on an implied condition of law, that he undertakes to let them in a habitable state.[69]

Parke B. rested his conclusions on the cases of *Edwards v. Hetherington*[70] and **4.41** *Collins v. Barrow*,[71] but the Chief Baron, while 'glad that authorities have been found to support' the conclusion took the view that 'no authorities were wanted, and that the case is one which common sense alone enables us to decide' (which reminds us of Lord Wilberforce's dictum about common sense in *Liverpool C.C. v. Irwin*[72]) before continuing '[a] man who lets a ready-furnished house surely does so under the implied condition or obligation – call it which you will – that the house is in a fit state to be inhabited'.[73]

However, the report of *Collins v. Barrow* says nothing about whether the house **4.42** was furnished or not (it seems not) and there is no mention in the judgment (of Bailey B.) as to the dependence of the tenant's right to quit premises that the premises (which were prone to flooding due to lack of a sewer) were 'noxious and unwholesome to reside in, and that this state arose from no default or neglect of his own'[74] depended on the premises being let furnished. In *Edwards v. Hetherington* the premises were let from year to year, with rent payable quarterly, and no repairing obligation on the tenant. Lord Abbott C.J. in his summing-up observed that although a tenant was not generally entitled to throw up a tenancy in mid quarter or mid half-year, without proper notice, such serious circumstances may exist in respect of the state of the premises, where these were not the fault of the tenant and the tenant was not under an obligation to repair, that would entitle the tenant to an exception to the rule. The Chief Justice did not refer to any authority, but the report contains a footnote to *Baker v. Holtpzaffel*.[75] In that case, on appeal Lord Mansfield C.J. and Heath J. held in favour of the landlord in recovering rent from a tenant whose house had burnt down, on the basis that the land was still in existence, the tenant had not delivered up the land so that the landlord could rebuild, and that the tenant could have rebuilt if he wished.

Edwards v. Hetherington was overruled in *Hart v. Windsor*.[76] This concerned **4.43** the lease of a house and garden ground for cultivation. Counsel for the

---

69   At 8.
70   (1825) 7 Dow. & Ry. K.B. 117; Ry & M. 268; 171 E.R. 1016 (also known as *Edwards v. Etherington*).
71   (1831) 1 M. & Rob. 112; 174 E.R. 38.
72   [1977] A.C. 239, at 255. Above, 3.31.
73   (1825) 11 M. & W. 5, 9.
74   (1831) 1 M. & Rob. 112, 114.
75   (1811) 4 Taunt. 45; 128 E.R. 244.
76   (1843) 12 M. & W. 68; 152 E.R. 1114.

tenant argued that no distinction should be drawn between furnished and unfurnished lets, as *Edwards v. Hetherington* and *Collins v. Barrow* had been cases of unfurnished lets but stated that the tenant could leave where there was grievous disrepair. Counsel for the landlord argued that the habitability of a property was the business of the tenant except where the premises were let furnished, as in *Smith v. Marrable*. Parke B. held that if *Edwards v. Hethering-ton* and *Collins v. Barrow* were correctly reported, then they could not be supported. The rule was that where a lease was of real estate merely, then there was no implied term as to habitability, and that *Smith v. Marrable* was distinguishable as it concerned the temporary letting of a ready-furnished house.[77] An interesting point which can be seen from this judgment is that Parke B. considered that in cases such as *Smith v. Marrable* there was not only an implied term that the premises should be habitable, but to entitle the tenants to quit there must also be (and was) an implied term that the contract would be void if the premises were not in fact habitable.[78] We should say today, then, that Parke B. analysed the matter, in such a case, as one of frustration of the contract, on the implied term theory of frustration. (The distinction was an important one from a procedural point of view. In these cases the landlord had sued the tenant to recover unpaid rent, that is a debt, though pleaded in assumpsit. If the tenant raised the condition of the property as a defence, then he could only succeed if the contract or lease was void. Breach of an implied term simply that the property was not habitable, without the aspect of voidness, raised a counterclaim for damages for breach of the term, not a defence to the landlord's claim.)

4.44 What we can certainly draw from *Hart v. Windsor* is that there certainly is no implied term as to habitability in the case of unfurnished lettings, and that this rule is based on very old law indeed (Parke B. referred to Brooke's Abridge-ment title on 'Dette' (debt) and a number of other cases, old even then, in support of this view).

4.45 Before leaving this topic, it is worth noting the case of *Wettern Electric Ltd v. Welsh Development Agency.*[79] Although the court implied a term into a licence for use of factory premises, it did so not on the basis of a term implied in law. The court acknowledged the rule that no term of fitness was to be implied into leases of unfurnished premises (and the same should therefore be true of licences), but implied a term in fact in this particular instance, as the buildings had been specifically provided so that the plaintiffs could carry on and expand

---

77   At 87.
78   At 87.
79   [1983] Q.B. 796; [1983] 2 All E.R. 629; [1983] 2 W.L.R. 897; (1983) 47 P. & C.R. 113 (Q.B.D.).

their business while their existing premises were being enlarged. The contract would therefore have lacked business efficacy without a term of fitness for purpose (see Chapter 7, below).

4. Implied terms as to common parts and means of access

There is an implied term, at law, in the case of lettings of buildings in multiple **4.46** occupation, where common amenities and means of access remain in the control of the landlord, that the landlord will take reasonable care to maintain the same in reasonable working order. This term, and the authorities for it, have already been discussed extensively in Chapter 3, above. It should be noted, however, that where a letting specifically includes the use of a lift, there is a greater implied duty on the part of the landlord, to ensure that this lift is in working order save for the most temporary breakdowns and stoppages for maintenance et cetera, as otherwise the demise of the lift would not be given sufficient business efficacy and indeed amount to a derogation from grant: *De Meza v. Ve-Ri-Best Manufacturing Co. Ltd.*[80] A similar term is applicable in other cases where the use of a particular facility is provided for in the lease, for example the refrigerator in *Penn v. Gatenex Co. Ltd.*[81]

5. Professionals' duty to use skill and care

A professional person is under a special duty to a client to exercise due skill **4.47** and care in carrying out professional work for the client. This does not mean, however, that the professional warrants a particular result, unless he or she expressly warrants it. A surgeon, for instance, impliedly promises to carry out an operation with due skill and care, but does not impliedly warrant a successful outcome: *Eyre v. Measday*;[82] and *Thake v. Morris*.[83] A solicitor, of course, owes the equivalent duty,[84] but it is trite law that a barrister in private practice has no contract with either the professional or the lay client, and his duty is owed only in tort. No doubt, however, an employed barrister, who does have a contract with his employer will owe the contractual duty of care to the employer, not only on the basis of the warranty of competence but also on the same basic principle, enunciated in *Sim v. Rotherham M.B.C.*,[85] that a professional person in employment is still a member of a profession and owes professional duties in addition to the normal incidents of employment.

---

80 (1952) 160 E.G. 364.
81 [1958] 2 Q.B. 210; [1958] 1 All E.R. 712; [1958] 2 W.L.R. 606 (C.A.).
82 [1986] 1 All E.R. 488.
83 [1986] Q.B. 644.
84 And see dictum of Willes J. in *Harmer v. Cornelius*, above, paragraph **4.06**.
85 [1987] Ch. 126 (Ch.D.). See above, paragraph **4.09**.

4.48   In *Greaves & Co. (Contractors) Ltd v. Baynham Meikle & Partners*,[86] already alluded to above, it was held that there was an absolute warranty of fitness implied in fact, of which the defendants were in breach, but also that there was a term implied at common law that a professional person should exercise due skill and care, and this applied to engineers and architects in like manner to other professionals. Lord Denning M.R. said '[i]t seems to me that in the ordinary employment of a professional man, whether it is a medical man, a lawyer, or an accountant, an architect or an engineer, his duty is to use reasonable care and skill in the course of his employment'.[87] The Master of the Rolls cited *Bolam v. Friern Hospital Management Committee*,[88] now generally regarded as the *locus classicus* on professionals' duty to exercise due skill and care, wherein McNair J. said of the professional man's duty of care (in negligence) that, 'The test is the standard of the ordinary skilled man exercising and professing to have that special skill … It is well-established law that it is sufficient if he exercises the ordinary skill of an ordinary competent man exercising that particular art.'[89] The Master of the Rolls continued to note that in applying the test, the particular circumstances must be taken into account.[90]

6.   Commercial arbitrators

4.49   In *Chandris v. Isbrandtsen-Moller Co. Inc.*[91] the Court of Appeal held that an arbitration agreement in commercial cases includes an implied term that the arbitrator is expected to decide the case in accordance with the law of contract, and that any remedy that can be awarded by a court can be awarded by the arbitrator and is enforceable under the contract, subject to certain exceptions. As Tucker L.J. explained:

> I think that in mercantile references of the kind in question it is an implied term of the contract that the arbitrator must decide the dispute according to the existing law of

---

86   [1975] 3 All E.R. 99 (C.A.). See above, paragraph **4.39**.

87   At 104–5.

88   [1957] 2 All E.R. 118; [1957] 1 W.L.R. 582 (Q.B.D.). Applied by the House of Lords in *Sidaway v. Board of Governors of the Bethlem Royal Hospital and the Maudsley Hospital* [1985] A.C. 871; [1985] 1 All E.R. 643; [1985] 2 W.L.R. 480, *Re F.* [1990] 2 A.C. 1; [1989] 2 All E.R. 545; [1989] 2 W.L.R. 1025; [1989] 2 F.L.R. 376, and *Bolitho v. City & Hackney Health Authority* [1998] A.C. 232; [1997] 4 All E.R. 771; [1997] 3 W.L.R. 1151; [1998] Lloyd's Rep. Med. 26, and by other courts in around 40 reported cases at the time of writing.

89   At 121. Approved by the Privy Council in *Chin Keow v. Government of Malaysia* [1967] 1 W.L.R. 813.

90   [1975] 3 All E.R. 99 at 105.

91   [1951] 1 K.B. 240; [1950] 2 All E.R. 618 (C.A.). Applied in *Cosmos Bulk Transport Inc. v. China National Foreign Trade Transportation Corp. (The 'Apollonius')* [1978] 1 All E.R. 322; [1978] 1 Lloyd's Rep. 53 (Q.B.D.), and *President of India v. La Pintada Cie Navigacion S.A.* [1985] A.C. 104; [1984] 2 All E.R. 773; [1984] 3 W.L.R. 10; [1984] 2 Lloyd's Rep 9.

contract, and that every right and discretionary remedy given to a court of law can be exercised by him. To that there are, of course, certain well-known exceptions, such as the right to grant an injunction, which stand on a different footing; one of the reasons why an arbitrator cannot give an injunction is, of course, that he has no power to enforce it; but such an objection does not apply to the award of interest.[92]

This dictum was approved by the House of Lords in *Bremer Vulkan Schiffbau* **4.50** *und Maschinenfabrik v. South India Shipping Corp. Ltd*,[93] in which it was held that parties to a contract including an arbitration clause were under an implied duty to keep arbitration moving and both under an equal duty to apply to the arbitrator if necessary to prevent 'inordinate delay'. Furthermore, if a party had not itself applied to the arbitrator as appropriate, it would not be able to rely on the other party's failure to do so as a breach of contract bringing the obligation to arbitrate to an end.

7. Duty of co-operation

According to McMeel '[t]he duty of cooperation between contracting parties **4.51** which might be an aspect of a general duty of good faith in civil law systems finds its expression through the familiar vehicle of the implied term in English law'.[94] He goes on to cite Lord Blackburn's dictum in *Mackay v. Dick*:[95]

> I think I may safely say, as a general rule, that where in a written contract it appears that both parties have agreed that something shall be done, which cannot effectually be done unless both concur in doing it, the construction of the contract is that each agrees to do all that is necessary to be done on his part for the carrying out that thing, though there may be no express words to that effect.[96]

---

92 [1951] 1 K.B. 240, 262.
93 [1981] A.C. 909; [1981] 1 All E.R. 289; [1981] 2 W.L.R. 141; [1981] 1 Lloyd's Rep. 253. Applied in *Wilson (Paal) & Co. A/S v. Partenreederei Hannah Blumenthal (The 'Hannah Blumenthal')* [1983] 1 A.C. 854; [1983] 1 All E.R. 34; [1982] 3 W.L.R. 1149; [1983] 1 Lloyd's Rep. 103, *Abse v. Smith* [1986] Q.B. 536; [1986] 1 All E.R. 350; [1986] 2 W.L.R. 322 (C.A.), *Indescon Ltd v. Ogden* [2004] E.W.H.C. 2326 (Q.B.); [2005] 1 Lloyd's Rep. 31 (Tech. & Const. Ct), and *R.D.F. Media Group plc v. Clements* [2007] E.W.H.C. 2892 (Q.B.); [2008] I.R.L.R. 207 (Q.B.D.). Distinguished in *Atkinson v. Community Gateway Association* (E.A.T., 21st August 2014, unreported).
94 McMeel, 10.29.
95 (1881) 6 App. Cas. 251 (H.L.). Applied in *Shepherd v. Henderson* (1881) 7 App. Cas. 49 (H.L.), *Kleinert v. Abosso Gold Mining Co. Ltd* (1913) 58 Sol. Jo. 45 (P.C.), *Harrison v. Walker* [1919] 2 K.B. 453; (1919) 89 L.J.K.B. 105, [1918–19] All E.R. Rep. 572 (K.B.D.), *Sanders v. Ernest A. Neal Ltd* [1974] 3 All E.R. 327; [1974] I.C.R. 565; [1974] I.R.L.R. 236 (Nat.Ind.Rel.Ct), *General Trading Co. (Holdings) Ltd v. Richmond Corp. Ltd* [2008] E.W.H.C. 1479 (Comm.); [2008] 2 Lloyd's Rep. 475 (Q.B.D. Comm. Ct), *Hudson Bay Apparel Brands L.L.C. V. Umbro International Ltd* [2009] E.W.H.C. 2861 (Ch.), [2010] E.T.M.R. 15, and *Swallowfalls Ltd v. Monaco Yachting and Technologies S.A.M.* [2014] E.W.C.A. Civ. 186; [2014] 2 All E.R. (Comm.) 185; [2014] 2 Lloyd's Rep. 50. Dicta of Lord Blackburn at 263 applied in *Merton L.B.C. V. Stanley Hugh Leach Ltd* (1985) 32 B.L.R. 51; 2 Const. L.J. 189 (Ch.D.).
96 *Mackay v. Dick*, n. 95, above, at 263.

It is submitted, however, that this is not a term implied at common law at all, outside such specific types of contract, such as employment or partnership where such a term has been implied in law. In the general run of commercial contracts, in each and every case, it is necessary to demonstrate that such a term is necessary to give business efficacy to the contract in contention, and the term will be specific as to what is to be done, so that the term is implied in fact in each case. As Leggatt L.J. observed in *Yam Seng Pte Ltd v. International Trade Corporation Ltd*:

> [131] Under English law a duty of good faith is implied by law as an incident of certain categories of contract, for example contracts of employment and contracts between partners or others whose relationship is characterised as a fiduciary one. I doubt that English law has reached the stage, however, where it is ready to recognise a requirement of good faith as a duty implied by law, even as a default rule, into all commercial contracts. Nevertheless, there seems to me to be no difficulty, following the established methodology of English law for the implication of terms in fact, in implying such a duty in any ordinary commercial contract based on the presumed intention of the parties.[97]

4.52 The same can be said, to some extent, of the sort of term being referred to by Cockburn C.J. in *Stirling v. Maitland*[98] (in McMeel's words 'not to interfere in necessary pre-existing state of affairs'[99]), when he said that '[i]f a party enters into an arrangement which can only take effect by the continuance of a certain existing state of circumstances, there is an implied engagement on his part that he shall do nothing of his own motion to put an end to that state of circumstances …'.[100] Again, what we see is that in each case it has to be alleged that there is an implied term in the particular contract that one party or another will not allow a certain change of circumstances, as alleged but not found by the court in *Hamlyn v. Wood*,[101] and as found to exist by the court in *Shirlaw v. Southern Foundries (1926) Ltd*.[102] The rule is too general to be

---

97   [2013] E.W.H.C. 111 (Q.B.); [2013] 1 All E.R. (Comm.) 1321. See further, A.J. Bateson, 'The Duty to Co-operate' [1960] J.B.L. 187; J.F. Burrows, 'Contractual Co-operation and the Implied Term' (1968) 31 M.L.R. 390.

98   (1864) 5 B. & S. 840; 34 L.J.Q.B. 1; [1861–73] All E.R. Rep. 358 (Q.B.). Applied in *C.E.L. Group Ltd v. Nedlloyd Lines U.K. Ltd* [2003] E.W.C.A. Civ. 1716; [2004] 1 All E.R. (Comm.) 689; [2004] 1 Lloyd's Rep. 381.

99   McMeel, para. 10.30.

100   At 852.

101   [1891] 2 Q.B. 488; (1891) L.J.Q.B. 734; [1891–4] All E.R. Rep. 168 (C.A.). Applied in *Livock v. Pearson Bros* (1928) 33 Com. Cas. 188 (K.B.D.), and *Gaze (W.H.) & Sons Ltd v. Port Talbot Corporation* (1929) 27 L.G.R. 200.

102   [1939] 2 KB 206; [1939] 2 All E.R. 113 (C.A.). Affirmed by the House of Lords: [1940] A.C. 701; [1940] 2 All E.R. 445.

formulated into an implied term in the English tradition,[103] it is submitted, and will here be discussed in Chapter 7 on terms implied in fact.

E. CONCLUSIONS

We can, perhaps, draw three main lessons from the illustrations in this chapter. **4.53** First, that the technique of implication in law is one which has a very long history in English law. Secondly that the technique has proved highly flexible, though (as we saw in Chapter 3) it is not entirely clear what the principles are for first drawing the necessary inference that a term is necessary and will be implied into all contracts of a particular type. And, thirdly, that the boundaries between implication in law and implication in fact are not always easy to draw (see especially paragraphs **4.50** and **4.51**) and indeed, what started out as probably an *ad hoc* decision, which we would nowadays categorize as an implication in fact, may come to be treated as an implication in law. It might be added that, since terms may begin by implication in fact, be subsequently adopted in a perfectly analogous case, and then at some point be explained as an implication of law, not only would an attempt at a full exposition of terms implied in law have been unmanageable within the scope of this book, but such an attempt would be, in the final analysis, futile. The great practitioner works are certainly the best source for terms implied by law into the categories of contracts those works respectively treat, but it is quite impossible to draw a definitive and comprehensive list, however hard we try. The good news for the practising lawyer is that countless opportunities will still present themselves for arguing that a particular term their client would like to suggest is one that is implied in law: every such term has to be discovered for a first time.

---

103   See, below, paragraph 7.33.

5

TERMS IMPLIED BY CUSTOM, USAGE OR COURSE OF DEALING

A. INTRODUCTION

5.01 Terms may be implied into a contract from local custom, the usage or practice of a particular trade or market or from a course of prior dealing between the parties concerned. The first two of these are essentially the same conceptually, but it is convenient also to deal with the case of prior course of dealing here, as all these cases may be considered to belong to a residual category having features in common with each other and common differences from other types of terms implied other than by statute. In this chapter, 'custom' is used to refer to the case of a term implied in a particular locality while 'usage' refers to terms implied within a particular trade. The term 'trade practice' is probably as good as 'trade usage', but a distinction has been drawn between usages which may give rise to an implied term and 'mere trade practices' which will not suffice. It is important to note here, however, that custom as a source of implication is now seen very largely as a dead letter. As Sir Christopher Staughton has commented, '[i]t is rare in modern times to find that a contract is varied or enlarged by custom'.[1] He goes on there to instance the case of *The Litsion Pride*,[2] as being one in which 'it might be thought that [the judge] relied on market practice for the interpretation of a contract'[3] before commenting '[h]owever, it seems to me that this was a case of words used in a particular

---

1 Sir C. Staughton, 'How Do the Courts Interpret Commercial Contracts' (1999) 58 C.L.J. 303, 311.
2 [1985] 1 Lloyd's Rep. 437.
3 Ibid.

sense ("current war risks exclusions"), which it was permissible for market evidence to supply'.[4] Our consideration here will, therefore, be kept brief, and the reader should bear this caution in mind. However, by way of example of a local custom, we might cite the case of *Hutton v. Warren*,[5] concerning the agricultural tenancy of glebe land, in which it was proved at trial:

> [T]hat according to the custom of the country, a tenant was bound to cultivate the farm according to a certain course of husbandry, and was entitled, on quitting, to a fair allowance for seeds and labour on the arable land, and was bound to leave the manure on the land, if the landlord chose to purchase it.[6]

The Court of Exchequer of Pleas held that such a custom was incorporated into the tenancy by implication. Parke B., delivering the judgment of the court commented that 'it has long been settled, that, in commercial transactions, extrinsic evidence of custom and usage is admissible to annex incidents to written contracts, in matters in respect to which they are silent'.[7] Though Parke B. seems to have doubted the desirability of this rule, he thought that 'it is too late to pursue a contrary course; and it would be productive of much inconvenience if this practice were now to be disturbed'.[8]

5.02 Local customs and trade usages may potentially be of infinite variety, as, of course, can terms implied in fact, but there is no question of such terms being implied only if 'necessary' for business efficacy. Such terms may, indeed, be quite strange and an officious bystander will be unlikely (if not in the trade) ever to have thought of suggesting such a term. Alternatively, the term may be an extremely sensible and reasonable one that has grown up from long experience of traders and is implied into all contracts of that sort, but is not strictly necessary and therefore would not satisfy the requirements for transmutation into a term implied in law. Moreover, it is clear that a local custom can never satisfy the requirements for a term implied in law since, say, 'employment contracts made in the Northwich area' are not in themselves a generic type of contracts, as 'employment contracts' *simpliciter* might be.

---

4 Ibid.
5 (1836) 1 M. & W. 466; 5 L.J. Ex. 234; 2 Gale 71; 150 E.R. 517. Considered: *Johnson v. Blenkensopp* (1841) 5 Jur. 870, *Spartali v. Benecke* (1850) 10 C.B. 212; 19 L.J.C.P. 293; 138 E.R. 87, *Brown v. Byrne* (1854) 3 El. & Bl. 703; 23 L.J.Q.B. 313; 118 E.R. 1304, *Myers v. Sarl* (1860) 3 El. & El. 306; 30 L.J.Q.B. 9; 121 E.R. 457, *Re Constable and Cranswick* (1899) 43 Sol. Jo. 208. Explained: *Johnston v. Usborne* (1840) 11 Ad. & El. 549; 3 Per. & Dav. 236; 113 E.R. 524, *Vint v. Constable* (1871) 25 L.T. 324. Distinguished: *Gibson v. Small* (1853) 4 H.L. Cas. 353; 10 E.R. 499.
6 (1836) 1 M. & W. 466 at 468.
7 At 475.
8 At 476.

5.03 The same can be said of some terms implied from prior course of dealing between the parties, in which case the term is most unlikely to occur in its precise form to a stranger to the relationship. In other cases, however, the term might be an obvious one and the decision to categorize it as arising from prior course of dealing may be no more than one of judicial convenience or else the convenience or inspiration of the pleader.

5.04 Terms implied by custom, usage or course of dealing are different from other implied terms in an important respect. The basis of other implied terms is necessity. The basis of these terms is practice. Not only can these implied terms not oust an express term of the contract, but they are themselves ousted by any necessarily implied term or by something inherent in the nature of the contract. Chitty states the rule thus:

> If there is an invariable, certain and general usage or custom of any particular trade or place, the law will imply on the part of one who contracts or employs another to contract for him upon a matter to which such usage or custom has reference a promise for the benefit of the other party in conformity with such usage or custom; provided there is no inconsistency between the usage and the terms of the contract.[9]

It is also stated in the same place that 'the usage must be notorious, certain and reasonable, and not contrary to law; and it must also be something more than a mere trade practice'. The rules for implication from local custom do not appear to vary in any significant way from the rules in respect of trade usage, and it is clear from the second quotation from *Hutton v. Warren* in paragraph **5.01**, above,[10] that the courts in the early 19th century, at least, did not consider these to be two distinct categories. For that reason, we will consider trade usages in detail below and invite the reader to apply the same discussion to local custom.

5.05 In *Cunliffe-Owen v. Teather & Greenwood*,[11] which concerned the usages of the London Stock Exchange as to put-options, Ungoed-Thomas J. made clear the distinction between a usage and a practice and explained the basis upon which a usage could be established:

> 'Usage' is apt to be used confusingly in the authorities in two senses, (i) a practice, and (ii) a practice which the court will recognise. 'Usage' as a practice which the court will recognise is a mixed question of fact and law. For the practice to amount to such a recognised usage, it must be certain, in the sense that the practice is clearly established;

---

9   Chitty on Contracts, 27th edn., vol 1, para 13–014.
10   Text associated with n. 7, above.
11   [1967] 3 All E.R. 561; [1967] 1 W.L.R. 1421 (Ch.D.).

it must be notorious, in the sense that it is so well known in the market in which it is alleged to exist that those who conduct business in that market contract with the usage as an implied term, and it must be reasonable. The burden lies on those alleging usage to establish it, in this case, the defendants. The practice that has to be established consists of a continuity of acts, and those acts have to be established by persons familiar with them, although, as is accepted before me, they may be sufficiently established by such persons without a detailed recital of instances. Practice is not a matter of opinion of even the most highly qualified expert as to what it is desirable that the practice should be. However, evidence of those versed in a market, so it seems to me, may be admissible and valuable in identifying those features of any transaction that attract usage and in discounting other features which for such purpose are merely incidental and if there is conflict of evidence about this it is subject to being resolved like other conflicts of evidence. Arrangements or compromises to the same effect as the alleged usage do not establish usage; they contradict it. They may be the precursors of usage, but usage presupposes that arrangements and compromises are no longer required. It is, in my view, clearly not necessary that a practice should be challenged and enforced before it can become a usage as, otherwise, a practice so obviously universally accepted and acted on as not to be challenged could never be a usage. However, enforcement would be valuable and might be conclusive in establishing usage.[12]

B. TRADE USAGES

It is obviously not possible to consider all the possible trade usages. The **5.06** student, practitioner or jurist must work on the basis of the mixed question of fact and law referred to by Ungoed-Thomas J. in the extract reproduced above to determine the (likely) existence or not of any alleged usage and then to determine the question of whether an implied term exists, bearing in mind that it may be ousted by necessary implied terms, statutorily implied terms or, of course, the nature of the contract or its express terms. Nonetheless, a detailed illustration from case law will be useful for understanding the application of the rule.

1. *Danowski v. Henry Moore Foundation*

The case of *Danowski v. Henry Moore Foundation*[13] concerned the question of **5.07** ownership of 'artist's copies', in this case of sculptures created by the late Henry Spencer Moore O.M., C.H., F.B.A. It is illustrative of the courts' approach to both the question of the existence of a usage and the question of whether such a usage gives rise to an implied term in the particular contract

---

12   [1967] 3 All E.R. 561 at 572–3.
13   *The Times*, 19 March 1996; [1996] C.L.Y. 1282; (1996) 140 Sol. Jo. L.B. 101.

concerned. In this case Henry Moore, having reached the age of 78, was concerned with the protection of his artistic legacy. It was his wish that a foundation controlled by his family and others who understood his wishes should be responsible in the future for protecting the financial value of his works from depreciation owing to copying (easy in the case of sculpture, since any number of casts might be made), and to ensure that his work was appropriately exhibited after his death. In pursuance of this aim, he established a company limited by guarantee, with charitable status, the Henry Moore Foundation, to which he gave considerably in the way of money and a large collection of sculptures, lithographs, etchings and drawings. He also created a company (Raymond Spencer Co. Ltd,[14] later changed to HMF Enterprises Ltd) which was a wholly-owned subsidiary of the Foundation, and to which he transferred his equipment, working stock and the like. He took employment with this company as its managing director on terms that he gave up his 'profession' as a sculptor and in future would produce sculptures purely for the benefit of the company, which had the sole right to copy and sell his work. He carried on to produce an unexpectedly large number of works (at least 215, though evidence conflicted as to the exact number).

5.08 The executors and trustees of Mr Moore's estate included his daughter Mary Danowski. She became disenchanted with the running of the Foundation, apparently unhappy with the dominance of professional advisers on its board, which led to her leaving the board and moving to South Africa. A dispute arose over a large number of 'artist's copies'. These were copies of the works he created after the establishment of the Foundation and its subsidiary company (earlier ones were given to the Foundation, it seems). The consideration furnished by the company for Mr Moore's business was shares in the company, and for his employment, salary and benefits.

5.09 Artist's copies are copies of a work retained by the artist, who will typically wish to use them for future reference (seeing whether a technique used in the work was successful or needed amending in future, for instance), and for inclusion in exhibitions. The artist might also sell or otherwise dispose of these at some point. It is accepted practice that where an artist produces work that will be reproduced, for example, any number of sculptures might be cast from the original mould, any number of prints from the original plate, and the artist declares that the edition will be limited, he or she may make two additional copies beyond the declared number of the limited edition, to retain as artist's copies. These may later be sold without there being any breach of contract with the buyers of the limited edition. More than two, however, would be a

---

14   His father's name was Raymond Spencer Moore.

breach of contract and buyers of the limited edition would be entitled to damages for diminution in the value of their purchases and an injunction restraining further reproduction by the artist.

Mrs Danowski alleged that the artist's copies produced by her father after he **5.10** entered into the company's employment remained his and thus fell into the estate. The Foundation and the company argued that they belonged to the company (and thus to the Foundation). There were two relevant contracts: the 'sale contract', under which Mr Moore sold his 'business as a sculptor' to the company, and the employment contract of the same date, so far as relevant, these provided as follows:

(Sale Contract)

(C) … the Company is empowered inter alia to carry on the business of creating and dealing in sculptures and other works of art.

(D) The parties hereto have agreed that the Company shall purchase from [Mr Moore] … certain assets of the Business'.

(Employment Contract)

(B) … the Company is empowered inter alia to carry on the business of creating and dealing in sculpture and other works of art.

(C) The parties hereto have agreed that … Mr Moore shall discontinue his profession and the Company shall thenceforth employ Mr Moore and Mr Moore shall serve the Company …

8(i) DURING the continuance of this Agreement Mr Moore shall not carry on the business of a sculptor for or on behalf of any person other than the Company and unless the Board shall otherwise direct the ownership and sole right to copyright in any work of sculpture or design therefor executed by Mr Moore in pursuance of his employment shall vest in the company.

Expert evidence was given on both sides. All agreed that there was a **5.11** well-established convention relating to artist's copies. Witnesses for Mrs Danowski were of the view that this would have to apply in the case of an employed artist (though they could think of no comparable examples) unless this was expressly excluded. Witnesses for the Foundation could not think of any comparable instances either but thought it would turn on the employment contract (which is, of course, a matter of law, not for even expert witnesses).

The existence of the convention being beyond doubt, the real question facing **5.12** the Court of Appeal was whether this convention applied to employment contracts for artists and to this one in particular. The difficulty here was that only one witness knew of any such case, that of an artist employed by the

Royal Mint. He had retained the right to make artist's copies, but the witness did not know if his contract of employment made any express reference to this. The witnesses in general agreed that in the hypothetical case of an artist being employed exclusively to produce all his or her editions for a particular employer would probably retain the right to make artist's copies, though one witness was unsure whether this would need to be made express in the contract. One witness thought that it would automatically apply unless the artist made a specific act of giving up the right, for instance by assignment in writing. But all of this was hypothetical.

5.13 Nourse L.J. in the Court of Appeal agreed with the approach of the trial judge in the Chancery Division, Evans-Lombe J., that 'the existence of a general usage or custom of a particular trade is a question of fact upon which the court has to be satisfied on the evidence'. Upon this Evans-Lombe J., quoted by Nourse L.J., commented that 'I am satisfied, and there is no issue, that there is a custom or usage which is "notorious, certain and reasonable" as to the making of artist's copies. . .'. This suggests that it is not only the existence of a custom, or its notoriety but also its certainty and reasonableness that is a matter of fact and must be established by evidence. The question of whether a custom is a usage is a mixed question of law and fact in that once the facts of certainty, notoriety and reasonableness (the latter of which is a mix of fact and judicial judgment, but not a legal question), then it is a question of law as to whether it is not contrary to law and is consistent with the contract. Clearly once a superior court has held that a particular custom is a usage then the normal rules of precedent will dictate whether this is thus established as a matter of law, though the question of consistency with the contract will always need to be considered in each particular instance to determine whether the usage implies a term into the contract in question.

5.14 Nourse L.J. went on to say:

> With the exception of Mrs Davidson Davis' instance of the sculptor employed by the Royal Mint, none of the experts could speak to a case where the artist's copy convention had been treated as applying between employer and employee. Even in that instance the sculptor's right to his artist's copies may have been expressly conferred on him by the terms of his contract of employment. Both Mr Barker and Dr Farr thought that it might be something for which the contract would have to provide. The other evidence amounted to no more than expressions of opinion on hypothetical facts. The authorities establish that evidence which goes no further than that is not enough to support the existence of a general usage or custom of a particular trade.

He then turned to look at the authorities, albeit briefly, starting by citing *Chitty on Contracts*:

> If there is an invariable, certain and general usage or custom of any particular trade or place, the law will imply on the part of one who contracts or employs another to contract for him upon a matter to which such usage or custom has reference a promise for the benefit of the other party in conformity with such usage or custom; provided there is no inconsistency between the usage and the terms of the contract. To be binding, however, the usage must be notorious, certain and reasonable, and not contrary to law; and it must also be something more than a mere trade practice.[15]

After considering *Cunliffe-Owen v. Teather & Greenwood*, which we have **5.15** already discussed above, Nourse L.J. referred to the judgment of Jenkins J. in *London Export Corporation Ltd v. Jubilee Coffee Roasting Co. Ltd.*[16] As this deals with the question of consistency between the alleged custom and the express terms of the contract, however, we shall treat that below, under the next heading. McCowan and Thorpe L.JJ. delivered short concurring judgments.

2. Certain, notorious and reasonable

The burden of proving that an alleged usage is 'certain, notorious and **5.16** reasonable' rests on the party alleging its existence: *Cunliffe-Owen v. Teather & Greenwood*.[17]

The meaning of 'certain' seems, rather ironically, to be capable of raising some **5.17** confusion. In *Cunliffe-Owen* Ungoed-Thomas J. said a usage must be 'certain, in the sense that the practice is clearly established'.[18] But McMeel, in defining certainty[19] cites the dictum of Mance J. in *Roar Marine Ltd v. Bimeh Iran Insurance Co.* that '[f]or there to be any relevance in custom or practice, whether in a strict or informal sense, it must be possible to identify the particular custom or practice with certainty'.[20] It is the view of the present author, with respect, that McMeel errs in citing this in the way he does. The word 'certain' is being used here by Mance J. in a non-technical sense, that is to say it is not meant to be definitive of its meaning in the phrase 'certain,

---

15 *Chitty on Contracts*, 27th edn., vol. 1, para 13–014.
16 [1958] 2 All E.R. 411; [1958] 1 W.L.R. 661.
17 [1967] 3 All E.R. 561 at 573. Applied recently in *Goshawk Dedicated Ltd v. Tyser & Co. Ltd* [2005] E.W.H.C. 461 (Comm.); [2005] 2 All E.R. (Comm.) 115; [2005] Lloyd's Rep I.R. 379 (Q.B.D. Comm. Ct). Distinguished in *Crema v. Cenkos Securities plc* [2010] E.W.H.C. 461 (Comm.); [2010] 2 All E.R. (Comm.) (Q.B.D. Comm. Ct).
18 At 573.
19 McMeel, para. 12.15.
20 [1998] 1 Lloyd's Rep. 423 at 429.

notorious and reasonable'. Mance J.'s use of the words 'whether in a strict or informal sense' indicates that much, it is submitted. 'Certain' in the sense of 'certain, notorious and reasonable' only applies to usage in the strict sense of a usage that will be recognized and given effect to by a court. Whatever the learned judge may have intended by it, he must be taken, in the absence of some clear indication to the contrary, not to have been intending to substitute a new definition for that of Ungoed-Thomas J. in what is regarded as the leading case on the question. Ungoed-Thomas J. also defined 'notorious' in the passage quoted in paragraph **5.05**, above: 'it must be notorious, in the sense that it is so well known in the market in which it is alleged to exist that those who conduct business in that market contract with the usage as an implied term'.[21]

5.18 Ungoed-Thomas J. also discussed the sort of evidence that would tend to prove or disprove a trade usage:[22]

> The practice that has to be established consists of a continuity of acts, and those acts have to be established by persons familiar with them, although, as is accepted before me, they may be sufficiently established by such persons without a detailed recital of instances. Practice is not a matter of opinion of even the mostly highly qualified expert as to what it is desirable that the practice should be. However, evidence of those versed in a market, so it seems to me, may be admissible and valuable in identifying those features of any transaction that attract usage and in discounting other features which for such purpose are merely incidental and if there is a conflict of evidence about this it is subject to being resolved like other conflicts of evidence. Arrangements or compromises to the same effect as the alleged usage do not establish usage; they contradict it. They may be the precursors of usage, but usage presupposes that arrangements and compromises are no longer required. It is, in my view, clearly not necessary that a practice should be challenged and enforced before it can become a usage as, otherwise, a practice so obviously universally accepted and acted on as not to be challenged could never be a usage. However, enforcement would be valuable and might be conclusive in establishing usage. What is necessary is that for a practice to be a recognized usage it should be established as a practice having binding effect.[23]

5.19 A practice which is certain, notorious and reasonable will bind any party, even if that party has no knowledge of it. However, Ungoed-Thomas J. went on to observe that:

---

21 [1967] 3 All E.R. 561 at 572.

22 McMeel, for some reason, puts this under the heading of 'notoriety', but the present author does not take him to intend to suggest that this passage of the judgment refers specifically to proving the element of notoriety as distinct from certainty and reasonableness. Notoriety and certainty appear to be closely linked in the learned judge's analysis. This is natural given his definition of 'certain'.

23 [1967] 3 All E.R. 561 at 573.

If the practice, though certain and notorious, is unreasonable it follows that it cannot constitute a usage which the court will enforce as a usage. Nevertheless if a party knows of such a practice and agrees to it, then though unreasonable, he is bound by it.[24]

Authority for this proposition was found in *Perry v. Barnett*.[25] This case concerned instructions given by the defendant in 1884 to his stockbrokers in Bristol to buy shares in Oriental Bank. He knew that such shares could not be purchased on the Bristol Stock Exchange so he instructed them to buy the shares in London. The plaintiff stockbrokers accordingly instructed agents in London to buy the shares. The day after the purchase the bank stopped business. The defendant declined to pay his brokers who had paid the London brokers.

Now there was an Act of 1867, in force at the time, the purpose of which was **5.20** to prevent speculative dealing in bank shares, and which rendered void a contract for sale of bank shares which the seller did not already have in his possession.[26] The contract made for the purchase of the Oriental Bank was void under this Act. However, the majority of the business of the stock exchange was then as it is now entirely speculative and the rule was inconvenient (as it was intended to be) to the London Stock Exchange, which therefore ignored it and developed a custom of treating such contracts as valid. Any broker or jobber who failed to complete on the deal would be treated as in default and expelled from the exchange. The custom appears to have been both certain and notorious, though apparently not known to the defendant. Grove J. held at trial, and was unanimously upheld by the Court of Appeal (Brett M.R., Baggallay and Bowen L.JJ.), that the custom being contrary to law was unreasonable and did not bind someone who was in ignorance of it. So the defendant was not bound to pay his broker as he was not bound by the custom and had to be taken to have intended that a contractually valid purchase should be made on his behalf. There was therefore no question of implying a term into his contract with the plaintiffs that he would be bound to reimburse them for a purchase which was legally void but treated on the stock exchange as though it were valid. But it was accepted that had he known of the usage then he would have been bound by it even though it was unreasonable because it disregarded the Act.

This case is undoubtedly authority (because it has now been accepted as such) **5.21** for the proposition that unreasonable practices will bind someone who knows

---

24 At 573.
25 (1885) 15 Q.B.D. 388 (C.A.).
26 Known as Leeman's Act: 30 & 31 Vict. c. 29.

about them and chooses to contract anyway, but will not be usages in the sense of a recognized custom that is binding on all, whether they know about them or not. It is, however, illustrative of some of the conceptual difficulties in dealing with the area of trade usage. First, the analysis of all the judges depended on the fact that the defendant was purchasing the shares through agents, since only members of the stock exchange may trade on the exchange. Much of the analysis centred on the fact that he had given instructions to his agent (his stockbroker) which must be taken to have granted the agent authority only to enter into a legally valid contract. Thus, the agent was at fault in point of the principles of authority in the law of agency. So, was the result of the case dependent on the legal principles of implication of a term from a trade usage or market custom, or on discrete agency principles? In other words, would the result have been the same if the exchange was open to all and the defendant had personally bought the shares from a jobber, who did not own them at the time the contract was made? Quite possibly, it would, but this does not seem by any means certain. Secondly, the practice was deemed unreasonable because it was contrary to law. As we have already seen, these are now treated as two separate questions: an alleged usage has to be certain, notorious and reasonable and must not be contrary to law. In this case, then, the question of reasonableness has been treated not as a factual one but as a legal one, which gives rise, it is submitted, to natural confusion about the nature of the question whether a proposed usage is certain, notorious and reasonable, which, it has been argued above is essentially factual, since evidence about the reasons for, and convenience of, a practice is likely to be relevant to deciding whether or not it is reasonable. It would be helpful if the courts could clarify this matter.

5.22 There is reference in the passage from the *Cunliffe-Owen* case quoted in paragraph **5.18**, above, to participants in the trade. Obviously, whether or not a witness is a 'participant in the trade' is a matter for the commonsense of the judge. We would not feel the need to comment on this were it not for McMeel's discussion of the same point:

> In *Holt & Co. v. Collyear* [sic. for *Collyer*][27] the court rejected evidence that 'beerhouse' had a technical sense in the brewing trade when construing a restrictive covenant in a lease of commercial premises. It was held that a grocery business, which included sales of beer for consumption off the premises, did not infringe the covenant. Fry J. applied what he understood to be the 'ordinary usage and ordinary parlance', which would not label a grocery store, with an ancillary trade in beer for off-sales, as a 'beerhouse'. The case concerned an ordinary commercial lease and there was no evidence that the landlord was a brewer or connected to the beer trade. Accordingly the evidence of

---

27   (1881) 16 Ch.D. 718 (Ch.D.).

trade usage was rejected, presumably on the basis that neither party was concerned in the trade in which the alleged use was deployed.

This is a perfectly correct summary of the case, save that the word 'presumably' seems redundant, as Fry J.'s judgment is perfectly clear on the point. However, it has nothing whatever to do with the question of who is a participant in the trade nor has it anything at all to do with trade usage in the sense of terms implied from trade usage. The question was not one of whether there was a certain, notorious and reasonable practice within a trade which would give rise to an implied term that the contract should be thus interpreted. The question was simply one of the proper construction of the word 'beerhouse'. Fry J. declined to consider whether 'beerhouse' meant something particular in the brewing trade because neither the lessee nor the lessor were in the brewing trade: it was an ordinary commercial lease of retail premises (the plaintiff, Holt & Co. was indeed a brewer but not party to the lease itself, though the owner of the benefit of the restrictive covenant). It was therefore not legitimate in point of the technique of construction to consider a technical meaning which a word might possess in an irrelevant context (in this case, the beer trade). This case ought to be discussed with the ordinary rules of construction, not in the context of custom and usage in the technical legal sense of the term. It adds nothing to the question of who is a participant in the trade qualified to give evidence as to the existence and nature of a trade practice, nor does 'usage' in this sense mean the same thing as 'usage' in the sense of a 'trade usage' that can give rise to an implied term.

3.   Consistent with the contract

Consistency with the contract can bear the same meaning as it not being **5.23** contrary to law, as will be seen below. In such a case the law attaches certain legal incidents to the type of contract in question (in the cases discussed under the next subheading these are agency contracts). Consistency with the contract also of course involves non-contradiction of express terms; that is to say, any implied term alleged to be derived from a trade usage will be ousted by an inconsistent express term, or if the tenor of the contract as a whole is inconsistent with the alleged usage. We have earlier quoted *Chitty* to this effect and it will suffice here to do so again:

> If there is an invariable, certain and general usage or custom of any particular trade or place, the law will imply on the part of one who contracts or employs another to contract for him upon a matter to which such usage or custom has reference a promise

for the benefit of the other party in conformity with such usage or custom; provided there is no inconsistency between the usage and the terms of the contract.[28]

4. Not contrary to law

5.24   We shall follow the example of McMeel[29] in considering the cases of *Anglo-African Merchants Ltd v. Bayley*[30] and *North and South Trust Co. v. Berkeley*[31] to illustrate this point, though the present author respectfully departs from McMeel in considering that the requirement that such a term be not contrary to law is a separate consideration from reasonableness. The passages already cited from *Cunliffe-Owen v. Teather & Greenwood, Danowski v. Henry Moore Foundation* and from *Chitty* all treat the requirement that the term be not contrary to law as a discrete requirement in addition to reasonableness. This would seem to be the better view. It is not axiomatic that something being contrary to some rule of law is also unreasonable only for that reason: it may clearly be the case that two quite reasonable propositions may nonetheless contradict one another and one might venture to suggest also that some rules of law are unreasonable.

5.25   The difference is an important one, in that the fact that a usage is in conformity with law or not contrary to law will not of itself make it reasonable. Furthermore, although McMeel states that '[n]otoriety is essentially a threshold factual question' while '[c]ertainty and reasonableness have more of a legal tenor', the authorities discussed above indicate that all three are essentially questions of fact to be established by evidence (though the combined question was admittedly described by Ungoed-Thomas J. as a mixed question of fact and law), while conformity with law is necessarily a question of law. The present author would accept that there is a 'legal tenor' about reasonableness,[32] since judges are long used to treating this as a matter of judgment, but whether a practice is reasonable in the context of the particular market or trade is essentially factual. Certainly one might say that reasonableness, in particular, can be regarded as a matter of opinion in contradistinction to fact, but it is not

---

28   *Chitty on Contracts*, 27th edn., vol 1, para 13–014.

29   McMeel, 12.19.

30   [1970] 1 Q.B. 311; [1969] 2 All E.R. 421; [1969] 2 W.L.R. 686; [1969] 1 Lloyd's Rep. 268 (Q.B.D.). Applied in *Goshawk Dedicated Ltd v. Tyser & Co. Ltd* [2005] E.W.H.C. 461 (Comm.); [2005] 2 All E.R. (Comm.) 115; [2005] Lloyd's Rep. I.R. 379 (Q.B.D. Comm. Ct) and *Ward v. New India Assurance Co. (Trinidad & Tobago) Ltd* (2005) 70 W.I.R. 48 (Barb. C.A.).

31   [1971] 1 All E.R. 980; [1971] 1 W.L.R. 470; [1970] 2 Lloyd's Rep. 467 (C.A.).

32   Though the present author would not accept the same of 'certainty' in the context of a usage (as opposed to, say, whether the terms of a contract are sufficiently certain for the contract not to fail for uncertainty). Ungoed-Thomas J.'s definition of certain in the context of 'certain, notorious and reasonable' (above paragraph **5.17**) clearly indicates that it is a factual matter to be settled by evidence.

truly capable of being a question of law in contradistinction to fact, since there is no one legal definition, in the abstract, of what is reasonable.

This is not merely a matter of academic cavilling. It is important in practical **5.26** terms to bear in mind that a finding of fact by a trial judge that a usage is reasonable in a particular trade or market could only be challenged on appeal if it were perverse and contrary to evidence. A finding on the law is open to challenge at large on appeal. No evidence could be adduced as to whether the custom is contrary to law, but evidence as to certainty and reasonableness could be taken from appropriate witnesses who are experts in the relevant trade or market: what might be unreasonable in one trade or just generally might be reasonable in the relevant trade because of the particular circumstances of that trade, and this is certainly a matter for evidence.

Both of these cases concerned Lloyd's brokers. In the *Anglo-African* case, an **5.27** all-risks policy was effected through an intermediary for two firms of brokers, covering unused leather jerkins, described as government surplus and 'new', though they were in fact 20 years' old but unworn. The underwriters denied liability on a claim for loss of part of the consignment on the grounds of non-disclosure of their age and the fact that they were army surplus. It was held that although there was no misdescription there was a material non-disclosure and the underwriters were entitled to disclaim. However, it became apparent during the course of the hearing that the two firms of brokers involved had both made their files available to the underwriters. One of them, on discovery, refused to make their file, containing an assessor's report (obtained by them on the underwriters' instructions) available to the assured. The broker asserted that although a Lloyd's broker is the agent of the assured, the report was the property of the underwriters and could not be disclosed to the assured without the underwriters' consent. The suggestion that this was a custom of the market (and not only of Lloyd's but of the worldwide insurance market) was rejected by Megaw J. on the grounds that it was contrary to law, because it is a principle of agency law that an agent employed by one principal cannot accept an engagement from another principal inconsistent with his duties to the first principal, for which Megaw J. relied[33] on a passage from the judgment of Scrutton L.J. in *Fullwood v. Hurley*[34] and on *Bowstead on Agency*.

The *North and South Trust* case similarly raised the question of whether a **5.28** Lloyd's broker was liable to disclose an assessor's report to the assured in the course of discovery. Similarly, relying on *Fullwood*, Donaldson J. held on an

---

33   [1970] 1 Q.B. 311 at 322H–323B.
34   [1928] 1 K.B. 498; [1927] All E.R. Rep. 610 (C.A.).

interpleader summons that there was no valid custom of the market that a broker acted as agent for the assured in effecting the insurance but as agent for the underwriters where a claim was being doubted and an assessor's report requested. Certainly this was the practice in effect, but it was contrary to principles of agency law and therefore not a valid and enforceable custom of the market.

5. *British Crane Hire Corporation Ltd v. Ipswich Plant Hire Ltd* [35]

5.29 It seems convenient to deal here with this case separately from the rest of the discussion as it has special features and is open to more than one analysis. The case concerned the hiring of a dragline crane. Both plaintiff and defendant were companies engaged in hiring out plant, but on this occasion the defendant was carrying out civil engineering works on its own account and needed the use of specialist plant which it did not possess. An arrangement to hire the crane was made over the telephone and the hire and transport charges were expressly agreed. No express agreement was made in this conversation, however, about the other terms of the contract. The crane arrived and was put to use. A printed form also arrived from the plaintiff, setting out its terms and conditions, including a term that the defendant indemnify the plaintiff against any expenses connected with the hire of the crane. This form was the plaintiff's own, but its terms were to the same effect as the terms of the 'Contractors' Plant Hire Association form', which were standard throughout the industry.

5.30 When an accident occurred, causing the crane to sink deep into the ground, the plaintiff claimed recovery costs from the defendant. The defendant denied that the terms of the printed form were incorporated into the contract since it had never executed the document. The Court of Appeal (Denning M.R., Megaw L.J. and Sir Eric Sachs) held that because both parties were in the plant hire trade and a term such as the one the plaintiff sought to rely upon was standard within the industry, the parties were entitled to expect that such a clause would be incorporated into their oral contract. The reasoning of the Court of Appeal, however, is not rooted in trade usage as such. Denning M.R., with whom Megaw L.J. agreed, treated it as a case where the agreement was made with a common understanding that the plaintiff's terms would apply:

> It seems to me that, in view of the relationship of the parties, when the defendants requested this crane urgently and it was supplied at once – before the usual form was

---

35 [1975] Q.B. 303; [1974] 1 All E.R. 1059; [1974] 2 W.L.R. 856. Considered: *Scheps v. Fine Art Logistic Ltd* [2007] E.W.H.C. 541 (Q.B.); [2007] All E.R. (D) 290 (Mar.).

received – the plaintiffs were entitled to conclude that the defendants were accepting it on the terms of the plaintiffs' own printed conditions – which would follow in a day or two. It is just as if the plaintiffs had said: 'We will supply it on our usual conditions,' and the defendants said 'Of course, that is quite understood'.[36]

Sir Eric Sachs also thought that it amounted to a case of a common understanding between the parties, but also seems to have thought of it also in terms of a case of implication at common law. In this respect he inferred the presence of the term on the basis that had the defendant said to the plaintiff 'of course, if the machine sinks you take that risk and pay the costs of recovery' the plaintiff would have undoubtedly replied 'that is nonsense and you don't get the machine'.[37] He thought that to hold that there was such a term would be 'wholly unrealistic and contrary to the mythical officious bystander's views'.[38] **5.31**

Why it was dealt with in this way is not entirely clear, but may have to do with the way the case was pleaded. It seems natural to think that the invariable inclusion of such a term might be considered a usage of the trade and thus implied into the contract, but this seems not to have been expressly considered, though it is quite likely that Sir Eric Sachs was using the notion of implication by common law in a very loose sense and may have had in mind trade usage. **5.32**

6. Summary

We may summarize the above consideration of trade usage by saying that: **5.33**

(1) A practice of a particular trade or market which amounts to a usage will result in contracts connected with that trade having a term implied into them that the usage will apply, unless the usage contradicts the contract.
(2) Whether a practice amounts to a usage depends on a mixed question of fact and law.
(3) It needs to be established by evidence (or by prior authority) that the practice is certain, meaning clearly established in the relevant trade or market, notorious, meaning that it is well-known to those professionally engaged in the trade or market in question, and reasonable, in the ordinary sense of the word.
(4) It must not be contrary to law, which is a pure question of law.
(5) If a trade usage is thus established then it will bind all contracting in that trade or market regardless of their actual ignorance of the usage.

---

36 At 311D–E.
37 At 312F–G.
38 At 312G–H.

(6)   No term will be implied into a contract on the grounds of trade usage if it conflicts with the express terms of the contract or some necessarily implied term, nor if it conflicts with the tenor or purpose of the contract.

(7)   A practice which is certain, notorious but unreasonable will only bind those who enter into a contract in that trade or market in the knowledge of the practice and not dissenting from that practice. Such a practice is not, however, a usage, as a usage binds even the ignorant.

C. TERMS IMPLIED FROM PRIOR COURSE OF DEALING

5.34   A term may sometimes be implied from a prior course of dealing. This seems to arise in cases of oral contracts, where the parties had previously dealt on a number of occasions and where some sort of documentation had passed between them containing a clause to the same effect as the term the court is asked to imply.

5.35   In the case of *Hollier v. Rambler Motors (A.M.C.) Ltd*[39] the Court of Appeal (Salmon and Stamp L.JJ. and Latey J.) had to consider whether a term had been implied into a contract by course of dealing between the parties. The plaintiff had telephoned the defendant garage and spoken to the manager about the need to repair an oil leak. The manager told him that they could do nothing immediately but if the plaintiff would have it towed or sent on a conveyor to the garage the defendants would carry out the necessary repairs. To this the plaintiff agreed. Nothing else was agreed, though Salmon L.J. observed that there would 'obviously be an implied term that the defendants would carry out the repairs and look after his car with reasonable skill and care; and there would also be an implied term that the plaintiff would pay a fair and reasonable price for the repairs'.[40] The motor car was duly conveyed to the defendants, but while it was at their premises a fire broke out due to the defendants' negligence, resulting in substantial damage to the vehicle. Mr Hollier sued on the basis that the defendants had not discharged their duty of care as bailees. The trial judge (Judge Worthington-Evans in the Brentford County Court) found that the defendants had not discharged the burden of proof placed on them as bailees to prove they had taken reasonable care and further found that there was in fact positive evidence that they were indeed negligent.

---

39   [1972] 2 Q.B. 71; [1972] 1 All E.R. 399; [1972] 2 W.L.R. 401 (C.A.). Distinguished: *British Crane Hire Corp. Ltd v. Ipswich Plant Hire Ltd* [1975] Q.B. 303; [1974] 1 All E.R. 1059; [1974] 2 W.L.R. 856.
40   [1972] 2 Q.B. 71, 74F–G.

The defendants relied on an exemption clause in their standard terms. **5.36**
Mr Hollier had bought parts from them on a number of previous occasions
but had the repair work or servicing done elsewhere, but on three or four
occasions in the previous five years he had work done by the defendants and
on at least two of these occasions had signed a document described as an
'invoice', on one occasion very hurriedly in the rain. This 'invoice' contained
the relevant term. This had not happened on this particular occasion, but the
defendants argued that a term to the same effect should be implied into their
oral contract on this occasion on the basis of prior dealing. Salmon L.J. in his
judgment observed that:

> Mr Tuckey says that there was a course of dealing which constituted the three or four
> occasions over five years – that is, on an average, not quite once a year – from which it
> is to be implied that what he called 'the condition' at the bottom of the contract should
> be imported into the oral agreement made in the middle of March 1970. I am bound
> to say that, for my part, I do not know of any other case in which it has been decided or
> even argued that a term could be implied into an oral contract on the strength of a
> course of dealing (if it can be so called) which consisted at the most of three or four
> transactions over a period of five years.[41]

Salmon L.J. contrasted this with the course of dealing alleged and found in the **5.37**
Hardwick Game Farm case,[42] in which there had been three or four dealings a
month between the relevant parties over a period of about three years. (The
order would be made orally over the telephone, then on that day or the next a
'sold note' containing the clause was sent be the supplier to the purchaser.)
This clause, though the purchaser never read it, was held to be implied into the
oral contract by course of dealing, though it was held not effective to protect
the supplier by excluding s.14 of the Sale of Goods Act 1893. The Court of
Appeal in *Hollier* unanimously declined to imply a term based on course of
dealing between Mr Hollier and the garage.

Salmon L.J. also explained the case of *McCutcheon v. David MacBrayne Ltd*,[43] **5.38**
which had been cited in the *Hardwick Game Farm* case. In *McCutcheon* the
plaintiff's car was lost at sea on the way from Islay to the mainland, due to the
negligent navigation of the defendant's servants. The contract had been made

---

41 At 76A–C.
42 *Henry Kendall & Sons (A Firm) v. William Lillico & Sons Ltd & Ors* [1969] 2 A.C. 31 (H.L.).
43 [1964] 1 All E.R. 430; [1964] 1 W.L.R. 125 (H.L.). Applied: *Hollier v. Rambler Motors (A.M.C.) Ltd* [1972]
    2 Q.B. 71; [1972] 1 All E.R. 399; [1972] 2 W.L.R. 401 and *Jewo Ferrous B.V. v. Lewis Moore (A Firm)* [2001]
    Lloyd's Rep. P.N. 6; [2001] P.N.L.R. 12 (C.A.). Considered: *Thornton v. Shoe Lane Parking Ltd* [1971] 2 Q.B.
    163; [1971] 1 All E.R. 686; [1971] 2 W.L.R. 58, *Eastman Chemical International A.G. v. N.M.T. Trading Ltd
    & Anor* [1972] 2 Lloyd's Rep. 25, *White v. Blackmore* [1972] 2 Q.B. 651; [1972] 3 All E.R. 158; [1972] 3
    W.L.R. 296.

on behalf of Mr McCutcheon by his brother-in-law, Mr McSporran. The normal arrangement when things were sent by Mr McCutcheon, on behalf of his employer, or by Mr McSporran was that a 'risk note' would be signed when the goods were consigned, which included an exclusion clause. On this occasion the defendant's 'clerkess' had made out a risk note, but was not present when Mr McSporran attended the offices. He dealt with the ship's purser and was not given the note. Both Mr McCutcheon and Mr McSporran had signed such notes in the past, generally when sending goods on behalf of others, but had not read them. The House of Lords declined to imply a term into the contract of carriage on this occasion based on the risk note clause, apparently because the consignor and his agent were not aware of the actual terms. However, on Salmon L.J.'s reading, only Lord Devlin had considered knowledge of the terms as a critical factor. For the other Law Lords it had been one among a number of factors. In Salmon L.J.'s view the case can be viewed as one in which the course of dealing was simply insufficient, as in the instant case. Moreover, if Lord Devlin had meant that actual knowledge of the clause was essential, then the effect of the *Hardwick Game Farm* case was to show that this position was wrong.[44]

1. Summary

5.39 A term may be implied into an oral contract from a prior course of dealing where such a term had been consistently used in a document associated with those transactions, whether they were issued before or after each transaction. It does not matter that the other party did not read the clause and was not aware of its effect. However, the course of dealing must be quite significant: a few occasions over a period will not do, though it will clearly be a matter of judgment where the line is drawn between the extremes of *Hollier* on the one hand and *Hardwick Game Farm* on the other. Moreover, it appears that it should probably be consistent. The occasional lapse in delivering documentation is unlikely in itself to matter, but it seems necessary that it should usually have been issued and that the circumstances are similar (in *McCutcheon* some of the dealing between Mr McCutcheon and the carriers and between Mr McSporran and the carriers had been on their own behalf, but mostly on behalf of other consignors). A handful of prior dealings will clearly not suffice.

---

44 [1972] 2 Q.B. 71, 77G–78B.

D. CONCLUSIONS

Local custom seems to have been withering on the vine somewhat as a source **5.40** of implied terms. This is not to be wondered at, as our dealings become increasingly national and international in their nature. However, terms implied from the custom or usage of a particular market or trade are likely to continue to be of significance. They are efficient because they avoid the need to spell out and even negotiate terms on each occasion and allow business parties to deal with each other quickly on the basis of mutual understandings. Those who deal with a trade with which they are unfamiliar can consider themselves on notice to inform themselves of anything likely to be relevant and it would be prudent to do so. If the occasional case arises where someone outside a trade has his fingers burned, then it is submitted that this is a price worth paying for general business efficiency.

Terms implied from course of dealing can be understood as a sort of specially **5.41** localized custom between the parties. To demonstrate this, the course of dealing must be significant and sustained and this is most likely, perhaps only likely, to arise where both parties are businesses.

Local custom, trade usage and course of dealing can all be traced to the **5.42** supposed will of the parties or at least reasonable parties in the position of the actual parties. In so far as that is not the case, for instance with a local custom applying to an incomer, it represents a reasonable compromise as representing the presumable intentions of most parties dealing in that place or market or trade.

6

TERMS IMPLIED BY STATUTE

A. INTRODUCTION

6.01 Our examination so far has dealt with terms implied by the courts into particular kinds of contracts, or into contracts embedded in particular contexts. In this chapter we consider terms which are implied not by the courts but by statute. These terms have, on the whole, been derived from terms that once were implied by the courts, in the sense meant in Chapters 3 and 4, which subsequently underwent codification. Obvious examples of such terms are those in the Sale of Goods Act 1979. The implied terms in that Act were Sir Mackenzie Chalmers' codification of terms which had become well-established by the time of the first Sale of Goods Act in 1893. There have been modifications since,[1] which illustrate legislative activism through and about implied terms, as well as codification.

---

1 Particularly the substitution by the Sale and Supply of Goods Act 1994 of 'satisfactory quality' for the original 'merchantable quality' in s.14; but this is only one of a number of significant amendments.

For the consumer, the implied terms in sale of goods contracts and hire **6.02** purchase contracts probably represent (along with those in employment contracts) the most significant of all implied terms. For commercial parties, the significance is perhaps less marked, but clear all the same: most businesses are employers; all buy and many sell; and many sell through hire purchase.

In this chapter we will consider the principal examples of terms implied by **6.03** statute: those of the Sale of Goods Act 1979, the Supply of Goods and Services Act 1982, the Supply of Goods (Implied Terms) Act 1973, the Consumer Rights Act 2015 and the Marine Insurance Act 1906, and, where applicable, consider the origins of those terms prior to statutory codification, their significance for parties and some of the interpretative case law that has grown up concerning these terms, before reflecting also on the device of statutory implication of terms itself. We will not, however, attempt exhaustive detail. These provisions have generated considerable case law and comment and the best place to obtain detailed analysis and exposition is in the various specialist works treating of the areas of law involved.

B. IMPLIED TERMS AS TO SALE AND SUPPLY OF GOODS

The key implied terms regarding sale of goods are those in sections 12, 13, 14 **6.04** and 15 of the Sale of Goods Act 1979 ('SGA 1979' or 'SGA'). Since 1 October 2015, sale of goods contracts in cases where a 'trader' (as defined) sells to a 'consumer' (as defined), and in no other cases, are governed by corresponding and largely identical terms implied by various provisions of the Consumer Rights Act 2015 ('CRA 2015' or 'CRA'), with the addition of certain other implied terms. These will be discussed in context with the relevant terms implied by the SGA. Although the CRA does not mention the word 'implied', but instead refers to contracts being 'treated as including' specified terms, it does not appear to the present author that this has any significance beyond a desire in the draftsman to use the plainest possible language. Furthermore, these terms are not stated to be conditions, as is the case in SGA, nor as warranties. Rather, the remedy for breach is governed by separate sections on remedies. Finally, there are where relevant, corresponding terms in relation to digital content, which are new; and although digital content is not included in the definition of 'goods' in the CRA, it will be convenient to discuss them with their sale of goods analogues.

6.05   Goods may be supplied otherwise than by sale, in which case the key terms are drawn from the Supply of Goods (Implied Terms) Act 1973, the Consumer Credit Act 1974, which replaced the previous legislation on hire-purchase arrangements, and the Supply of Goods and Services Act 1982. Again, as regards contracts between traders and consumers, there are provisions of the CRA 2015 which now govern these implications. It may be observed, however, that many of these have much the same effect, mutatis mutandis, in the different contexts within which goods are supplied. We will, therefore, adopt the schematic order of the SGA and treat sequentially of terms as to ownership, terms as to conformity with description, terms as to quality and terms as to conformity with sample. The following table summarizes the distribution of coverage of these provisions. It should be noted that the principles are now the same for sales and hire-purchase, which was the effect of the Supply of Goods (Implied Terms) Act 1973, as slightly amended and re-enacted in the Consumer Credit Act 1974, schedule 4.

6.06   The different terms do often overlap in practice. That is to say, a claim might arise in which a single problem with the goods is alleged alternatively to be in breach of an implied term as to description and an implied term as to quality, for example. In relation to conformity of goods in general, in contracts to which the Consumer Rights Act 2015 applies, there is a mandatory rule that goods are non-conforming (according to whichever implied term as to conformity is relevant in the particular case) if either: (a) the goods are supplied under a contract which provides for installation and they are installed incorrectly by the trader or under the trader's responsibility: s.15 CRA; or (b) the goods are an item that includes digital content and that content does not conform with the contract for its supply, as to which the Act makes considerable provision: s.16. Section 15 is regrettably silent on what is to happen if the goods are supplied under a contract which includes installation but are installed not incorrectly but rather not at all.

1.   Implied terms as to ownership of goods

6.07   The common law position prior to the Sale of Goods Act 1893 was that the buyer was entitled to expect that a seller was entitled to sell the goods in question and pass a good title unless the seller stated that there was some defect in the title. In *Morley v. Attenborough*[2] a pawnbroker sold a harp at

---

2   (1848) 3 Exch. 500; 154 E.R. 943; [1843–60] All E.R. Rep. 1045. Applied in *Emmerton v. Matthews* (1862) 7 H. & N. 586; 31 L.J. Ex. 139, *Eichholz v. Bannister* (1864) 17 C.B.N.S. 708; 34 L.J.C.P. 105, *Bagueley v. Hawley* (1867) LR 2 CP 625; 36 LJCP 328 and *Raphael & Sons v. Burt & Co.* (1884) Cab. & El. 235. Distinguished in *Buddle v. Green* (1857) 27 L.J. Ex. 33.

Table 6.1   Corresponding provisions in sale and supply of goods

Nature of term	Sale of Goods Act 1979	Consumer Rights Act 2015 *(for goods)*	Consumer Rights Act 2015 *(for digital content)*	Supply of Goods (Implied Terms) Act 1973	Supply of Goods and Services Act 1982
Right to sell/supply	s.12	s.17	s.41(1)	s.8	s.2
Conformity with description	s.13	s.11	s.36(3)	s.9	s.3
Quality including general fitness	s.14(2)	s.9	s.34(1)	s.10	s.4
Fitness for a particular purpose	s.14(3)	s.10	s.35(3)	s.10(3)	s.4(5) (transfer) s.9(5) (hire)
Conformity with sample	s.15	s.13	N/A	s.11	s.5
Conformity with pre-contractual information	N/A	12(2)	37(2)	N/A	N/A

public auction. The pawnbroker had taken it as a pledge from one Poley, who had in fact hired the harp and did not own it. It was sold to the plaintiff with no warranty of title. Parke B., in giving the judgment of the Court of Exchequer Chamber made the following observation about the general law in sales cases:

> It is made a question whether there is annexed by law to such a contract, which operates as a conveyance of the property, an implied agreement on the part of the vendor, that he has the ability to convey. With respect to executory contracts of purchase and sale, where the subject is unascertained and is afterwards to be conveyed, it would probably be implied that both parties meant that a good title to that subject should be transferred in the same manner as it would be implied under similar circumstances that a merchantable article was to be supplied. Unless goods, which the party could enjoy as his own, and make full use of, were delivered, the contract would not be performed. The purchaser could not be bound to accept if he discovered the defect of title before delivery, and, if he did, and the goods were recovered from him, he would not be bound to pay, or, having paid, he would be entitled to recover back the price as on a consideration which had failed.[3]

---

3   (1848) 3 Exch. 500, 509.

Though the court held that in the case of a pawnbroker the only implication is that the goods are a pledge and irredeemable and that the seller knows of no defect of title. Had the pawnbroker known there was a defect in title, then an action would lie for fraud.

6.08 The position that the action should be for fraud where a seller sells knowing that the goods are not his to sell goes back a long way. In *Sprigwell v. Allen*[4] the plaintiff was nonsuited in his case where he had been sold a horse on the grounds that he had not alleged that the defendant knew he had no title to sell and that the law was that such a case must allege fraud. In *Medina v. Stoughton* Holt C.J. held that where a seller was in possession which had 'the colour of title', a mere affirmation that the goods were his own created a warranty of title.[5] A remedy was allowed even though the rightful owner had yet to reclaim them, since if the buyer waited for them to be reclaimed, he might for some reason lose his remedy.[6]

6.09 The basis for this seems to have been the doctrine of caveat emptor. That would only be displaced by a warranty of title. The warranty might be express or might be implied. Such a warranty would be implied, as we have seen, automatically in the case of future or unascertained goods, but would only be implied in the case of specific goods where the seller was in possession with the appearance of ownership and affirmed that he was the owner. However, by 1844 Pollock C.B. was able to say that 'the doctrine of caveat emptor applies not at all, as I apprehend, to the title of the plaintiff, but to the condition of the goods'.[7] The only inference, it is submitted, from this is that by this time it was beginning to be accepted that a seller impliedly warrants title to goods sold, unless he makes clear that he does not do so. The basis for this inference is that the old rule relied on the application of caveat emptor to questions of title, so that the abandonment of this application of the doctrine necessarily sweeps away the basis for saying that there is no implied warranty of title in the case of specific goods unless there is colour of ownership and affirmation. In the Sale of Goods Act 1893, section 12, the rule that there is an implied term that the seller has the right to sell the goods, or will have by the time the goods are to pass to the buyer, was enshrined in statute.

6.10 Section 12 SGA 1979 reads:

---

4 (1648) Aleyn 91; 82 E.R. 931.
5 (1700) 1 Ld Raym. 593; 1 Salk. 210; Holt K.B. 208; 91 E.R. 188. Approved in *Pasley v. Freeman* (1789) 3 Term Rep. 51; 100 E.R. 450; [1775–1802] All E.R. Rep. Applied in *Dobell v. Stevens* (1825) 3 B. & C. 623; 107 E.R. 864, and *Andrews v. Hopkinson* [1957] 1 Q.B. 229; [1956] 3 All E.R. 422; [1956] 3 W.L.R. 732.
6 *Furnis v. Leicester* (1618) Cro. Jac. 474; 79 E.R. 404.
7 *Allen v. Hopkins* (1844) 13 M. & W. 94, 103; 153 E.R. 39, 42.

(1) In a contract of sale, other than one to which subsection (3) below applies, there is an implied term on the part of the seller that in the case of a sale he has a right to sell the goods, and in the case of an agreement to sell he will have such a right at the time when the property is to pass.

(2) In a contract of sale, other than one to which subsection (3) below applies, there is also an implied term that –

    (a) the goods are free, and will remain free until the time when the property is to pass, from any charge or encumbrance not disclosed or known to the buyer before the contract is made, and

    (b) the buyer will enjoy quiet possession of the goods except so far as it may be disturbed by the owner or other person entitled to the benefit of any charge or encumbrance so disclosed or known.

(3) This subsection applies to a contract of sale in the case of which there appears from the contract or is to be inferred from its circumstances an intention that the seller should transfer only such title as he or a third person may have.

(4) In a contract to which subsection (3) above applies there is an implied term that all charges or encumbrances known to the seller and not known to the buyer have been disclosed to the buyer before the contract is made.

(5) In a contract to which subsection (3) above applies there is also an implied term that none of the following will disturb the buyer's quiet possession of the goods, namely –

    (a) the seller;

    (b) in a case where the parties to the contract intend that the seller should transfer only such title as a third person may have, that person;

    (c) anyone claiming through or under the seller or that third person otherwise than under a charge or encumbrance disclosed or known to the buyer before the contract is made.

(5A) As regards England and Wales and Northern Ireland, the term implied by subsection (1) above is a condition and the terms implied by subsections (2), (4) and (5) above are warranties.

(6) ...

The Supply of Goods and Services Act 1982, section 2, is in identical terms, **6.11** save that 'contract of sale' becomes 'contract for the transfer of goods', 'seller' becomes 'transferor', 'buyer' becomes 'transferee' and so on, that the subsections themselves specify condition or warranty, and that there is no subsection (5A) or (6). Section 8 of the Supply of Goods (Implied Terms) Act 1973 makes very similar provision in respect of hire-purchase agreements, with the principal implied terms couched as follows:

(1) In every hire-purchase agreement ... there is –

    (a) an implied term on the part of the creditor that he will have the right to sell the goods at the time when the property is to pass; and

    (b) an implied term that –

    (i)   the goods are free, and will remain free until the time when the property is to pass, from any charge or encumbrance not disclosed or known to the person to whom the goods are bailed …

    (ii) that person will enjoy quiet possession of the goods except in so far as it may be disturbed by any person entitled to the benefit of any charge or encumbrance so disclosed or known.

In hire-purchase agreements to which the CRA 2015 applies, section 17 of that Act implies the same term as to right to supply as it does into contracts for the sale of goods. Section 17(1)(a) CRA makes the same implication, *mutatis mutandis*, in relation to contracts of hire. In the case of each implied term, the relevant section of the CRA is couched in terms of 'every contract to supply goods', whether the supply is by way of sale, hire or hire purchase, with subsections and paragraphs dealing, where necessary, with differences depending on the legal form of the transaction.

6.12   It will be noticed that the present author has here used the vernacular expression 'ownership' rather than 'title', which latter is used in the section headings in the Acts. This is quite deliberate, as they deal with 'property' as much as title, which are two different things. In short, whilst property is good between the parties, a good title is good against the world. Section 12 needs to be read in tandem with s.2(1): 'A contract of sale of goods is a contract by which the seller transfers or agrees to transfer the property in goods to the buyer for a money consideration, called the price.' In turn, both need to be read together with s.61 which, so far as relevant, provides that 'property' means 'the general property in goods, and not merely a special property'. A 'a right to sell', then, means that the seller has (or will have at the time for performance) a right to transfer to the buyer the general property in the goods.

6.13   Some of the implied terms touch on title specifically, as in those dealing with encumbrances on title, and they might all be said to touch on title in the sense that they provide that only such rights as the seller or hirer or transferor has (or a specified third party has) are to be taken to be transferred: in that sense, they touch on title in that they make any transfer of property subject to the better title of any other person. Indeed, it is notable that s.12(1) does not refer to either title or property, only the seller's 'right to sell the goods', which is both narrower and wider, as will be seen below.

The s.12(1) right to sell has an additional meaning also, which can be seen **6.14** from the case of *Niblett v. Confectioners' Materials Co.*[8] in which it was held that a seller who sold tins of condensed milk in alleged breach of a third party's trade mark (the milk was branded 'Nissly' and the owners of the Nestlé trademark had objected in a previous instant involving other parties that similar branding was a colourable infringement of their mark and had the goods) had no right to sell the goods. It should also be noted that where a seller has a right to sell but cannot transfer the property expected, this may not be a breach of the term in s.12(1). For instance, where the owner of goods distrained but not removed by a sheriff sells the goods such a sale complies with s.12(1) but is subject to the sheriff's interest.[9] If the seller does not inform the buyer of the relevant circumstance then he will be in breach not of the term implied by s.12(1) but of that implied by s.12(2).

A fully detailed consideration of the terms implied in s.12 of the Sale of **6.15** Goods Act 1979 and of the corresponding provision in the 1973 Act would, as already pointed out, be out of place in a short book on implied terms in general, but can be sought from the usual works on the sale of goods, especially *Benjamin's Sale of Goods* or Atiyah, et al., *The Sale of Goods*. The same can be said of the other sales terms discussed in this chapter.

Section 2 of the Supply of Goods and Services Act 1982 refers specifically to **6.16** property. The Act does not apply to sales, hire-purchase agreements, exchanges for trading stamps, 'a transfer or agreement to transfer which is made by deed and for which there is no consideration other than the presumed consideration imported by the deed' or transfers 'intended to operate by way of mortgage, pledge, charge or other security'.

Section 8 of the Supply of Goods (Implied Terms) Act 1973 (see paragraph **6.17** **6.11**, above) is to the same effect, though it deals specifically with the question of the futurity essential to hire-purchase contracts, that is to say that the goods will not actually pass until some point probably years into the future, with the words in s.8(1)(b)(i) '… and will remain free until the time when the property is to pass of any charge or encumbrance not disclosed …', but this is no more than a necessary expansion of the terms of s.12 of the Sale of Goods Act to meet the circumstances of hire purchase.

---

8 [1921] 3 K.B. 387. Applied in *Microbreads A.G. v. Vinhurst Road Markings Ltd* [1975] 1 All E.R. 529; [1975] 1 W.L.R. 218, [1975] 1 Lloyd's Rep. 375. Distinguished in *Sumner, Permain Co. v. Webb & Co.* [1922] 1 K.B. 55; (1922) 91 L.J.K.B. 228.
9 *Lloyd's & Scottish Finance Ltd v. Modern Cars & Caravans (Kingston) Ltd* [1966] 1 Q.B. 764; [1964] 2 All E.R. 732; [1964] 3 W.L.R. 859 (Q.B.D.).

6.18 By section 6(1) of the Unfair Contract Terms Act 1977, any term in a contract of sale purporting to exclude the provisions of s.12 SGA 1979, is void. The same applies to the analogous terms in hire contracts.

2. Conformity with description

6.19 Even without having undertaken empirical research to establish the fact, it is probably safe to assume that the vast majority of sales are in part at least sales by description. This is made even more evident when one considers s.13(3) S.G.A. 1979: 'A sale of goods is not prevented from being a sale by description by reason only that, being exposed for sale or hire, they are selected by the buyer.' Thus, whilst it is obvious that any sale of future goods (not involving a sample), including any internet sale, catalogue sale, and so on, must necessarily be a sale by description (what else?), the typical instance of a person going into a shop and selecting goods from shelves or racks will often be a sale by description, too. If one buys in a supermarket a bundle of asparagus marked 'English asparagus', the asparagus-ness of the product will be obvious, and needs no description, but the Englishness of it will be an element of description to which the goods must conform: s.13(1) providing that: 'Where there is a contract for the sale of goods by description, there is an implied term that the goods will correspond with the description.' Even where a sale is made by sample, there may also be a description attached, in which case it may be both a sale by sample and a sale by description. In such cases, s.13(3) provides that: 'If the sale is by sample as well as by description it is not sufficient that the bulk of the goods corresponds with the sample if the goods do not also correspond with the description.'

6.20 The history of the implied term as to conformity with description is too straightforward, and too long, to go into in a book of this type and length. The plea in the old cases was that the seller sold goods described as so-and-so 'and *ubi re vera*[10] it was not' so-and-so. Such a plea if successfully made out, and the sale was one by description, was treated as a failure of consideration and the buyer was entitled to return of the price: see, for example, the cases of *Gompertz v. Bartlett,*[11] and *Gurney v. Womersley.*[12] Though in *Azémar v.*

---

10 *Ubi re vera*: 'whereas in reality'.

11 (1853) 2 El. & Bl. 849; 118 E.R. 985. This concerned a foreign bill of exchange: however, the basis for the decision was that being unstamped and unenforceable it did not meet description. The Queen's Bench Divisional Court in *Joliffe v. Baker* (1883) 11 Q.B.D. 255 per Watkin Williams J. at 271, referred to this as a case of non-existence of the subject matter, but this seems to be erroneous.

12 (1854) 4 El. & Bl. 133; 119 E.R. 51. Applied in *Hamilton Finance Co. Ltd v. Coverley Westray Walbaum and Tosetti Ltd and Portland Finance Co. Ltd* [1969] 1 Lloyd's Rep. 53 (Q.B.D.).

Casella, Martin B. rejected the terminology of 'warranty',[13] quoting Lord Abinger in *Chanter v. Hopkins*[14] thus:

> It would be better to distinguish such cases as a non-compliance with a contract which a party has engaged to fulfil; as, if a man offers to buy *peas* of another, and he sends him *beans,* he does not perform his contract; but that is not a warranty; there is no *warranty* that he should sell him peas; the contract is to sell peas, and, if he sends him anything else in their stead, it is a non-performance of it.[15]

The distinction did not really matter, though. The language of warranty and condition and so on was in flux, with the modern division of all requirements of a contract into conditions and warranties being derived from Pollock and adopted by Chalmers when drafting the 1893 Sale of Goods Act. Such points as Lord Abinger's were semantic rather than substantive.

3. Definition of 'sale by description'

Lord Wright in *Grant v. Australian Knitting Mills Ltd* defined sale by **6.21** description in the following terms:

> [a] thing is sold by description, though it is specific, so long as it is sold not merely as the specific thing but as a thing corresponding to a description, e.g., woollen under-garments, a hot water bottle, a secondhand reaping machine, to select a few obvious illustrations.[16]

This statement found favour with the English Court of Appeal in *Beale v. Taylor,* where Sellers L.J. applied it to the case of a second-hand motor car.[17] However, a particular description may or may not form part of the contract, and if it does not form a part of the contract then non-conformity with that particular description will not be a breach of the term implied by s.13.

A good illustration of this point is the case, well known to every student of **6.22** contract law, of *T. & J. Harrison v. Knowles and Foster.*[18] This case concerned the sale of two steamships. These were described in written particulars supplied to the plaintiffs as having dead-weight capacities in each case of 460

---

13   (1867) L.R. 2 C.P. 677, 679.
14   (1838) 4 M. & W. 399; 150 E.R. 1484.
15   (1838) 4 M. & W. 399, 404.
16   [1936] A.C. 85 (P.C.), 100. (The decision, however, was based on quality rather than description, though 'merchantable quality' as a concept did of course encompass the question of whether the goods could be resold under the description applied to them.)
17   [1967] 3 All E.R. 253, 255.
18   [1918] 1 K.B. 608 (C.A.).

tons. The particulars also stated that the defendants were 'not accountable for any errors in description'. The dead-weight capacity of the ships was, in the event, only 360 tons in each case. At trial,[19] Bailhache J. held that the description was only a warranty and that the 'not accountable' clause excused the defendants. The Court of Appeal (Pickford, Warrington and Scrutton L.JJ.) took a different approach, holding that the statement as to dead-weights was a mere representation (and innocent, not fraudulent), not a warranty, and it was clear that Scrutton L.J. doubted whether the mere fact of it being a warranty, coupled with the existence of the 'not accountable' clause would have excused the discrepancy in capacity had the statement as to capacities been a term of the contract rather than a representation.[20]

6.23 Other cases involving sales of goods also illustrate this point well. In *Oscar Chess Ltd v. Williams*[21] the central question was whether or not the statement that the motor car was a 1948 model was a term or merely a representation. It was not suggested at any point that a mere representation would amount to a description, raising the issue of a breach of the implied term in section 13. Similarly, the description of a painting as being by Gabriele Münter, in *Harlingdon & Leinster Enterprises Ltd v. Christopher Hull Fine Art Ltd*,[22] was found not to be a term of the contract, so there could be no question of a breach of the implied term as to conformity with description. The usual principles in determining whether a statement is or is not a term of the contract also determine whether (in relation to any given descriptive statement) the sale is by description, as Nourse L.J. observed in the *Harlingdon & Leinster* case: 'For all practical purposes, I would say that there cannot be a contract for the sale of goods by description where it is not within the reasonable contemplation of the parties that the buyer is relying on the description.'[23] The 'for all practical purposes' caveat presumably refers to cases where the description is indisputably a term of the contract, although there is no actual or likely reliance by the buyer; but, of course, tests of reliance (and contemplation of reliance) are only relevant in determining the status of statements as representations or terms where there is an element of doubt about the matter.

6.24 So, a sale is a sale by description if some description applied to the goods is a term of the contract, irrespective of whether the sale is of specific or unascertained goods, or whether the goods have been inspected and chosen by

---

19 [1917] 2 K.B. 606.
20 [1918] 1 K.B. 608, 610.
21 [1957] 1 W.L.R. 370.
22 [1991] 1 Q.B. 564.
23 At 574.

the buyer, and irrespective of whether a sample is also supplied. Whether the buyer relied on a description is irrelevant in itself, once it has been determined that the description is a term. Under s.13 SGA 1979 there is then also an implied term that the goods will be in conformity with such description.

4. Application of the implied term

In the case of *In re an Arbitration between Moore & Co Ltd and Landauer & Co*,[24] Moore & Co contracted to sell to Landauer & Co: **6.25**

> about 3,100 cases Australian canned fruits consisting of about 2,500 dozen 30/2½ nominal tins Vickar pears at 27s 6d per doz., 240 dozen 30/2½ nominal tins apricots at 27s 6d per doz., 2,358 dozen 30/2½, nominal tins plums at 27s 6d per doz., 964 dozen 30/2½ nominal tins Bartlett pears at 27s 6d per doz., 1,745 dozen 30/2½ nominal tins apples at 23s per doz., shipped per ss. *Toromeo*.

meaning that the tins of 2½ lb each would be packed in cases of 30. The tins as shipped were about half in cases of 30 and about half in cases of only 24 tins. Upon inspection, Landauer & Co. rejected the entire consignment. The umpire referred a special case to the High Court (Rowlatt J.),[25] as follows: 'whether in law under the contract of June 14, 1919, the buyers are bound to accept any goods packed twenty-four tins in a case …'. Rowlatt J.'s decision was subsequently appealed against by the sellers to the Court of Appeal (Bankes, Scrutton and Atkin L.JJ.). Rowlatt J. held in favour of the buyers on the basis that on the true construction of the contract the buyers had specified the way the goods were to be packed. Although, on the facts, the market value was unaffected, a buyer might have good reasons for wanting goods packed in a certain way. He held that the breach entitled the buyers to reject the whole consignment.

Bankes L.J., having stated the question put in the special case, continued: **6.26**

> That question of law, in my opinion, admits of a very simple answer. If it is true to say, as I think it is, that this is a sale of goods by description, and the statement in the contract that the goods are packed thirty tins in a case is part of the description, there is, under s. 13 of the Sale of Goods Act, 1893, an implied condition that the goods shall correspond with the description. The goods tendered did not as to about one-half correspond with that description.[26]

---

24 [1921] 2 K.B. 519 (C.A.).
25 [1921] 1 K.B. 73.
26 [1921] 2 K.B. 519, 522.

Going on to add the effect of s.30(3) that it was open to the buyer to reject the whole delivery where part of the delivery does not meet description.

6.27 The decision has been criticized, however. In *Reardon Smith Lines Ltd v. Hansen Tangen*[27] Lord Wilberforce described the decision in *Re Moore & Co. and Landauer & Co.* (or at least the way some other cases have interpreted it) as 'excessively technical and due for fresh examination in this House',[28] adding that:

> Even if a strict and technical view must be taken as regards the description of unascertained future goods (e.g. commodities) as to which each detail of the description must be assumed to be vital, it may be, and in my opinion is, right to treat other contracts of sale of goods in a similar manner to other contracts generally, so as to ask whether a particular item in a description constitutes a substantial ingredient of the 'identity' of the thing sold, and only if it does to treat it as a condition.[29]

This is consistent with the attitude of the House of Lords in the slightly earlier case of *Ashington Piggeries v. Christopher Hill Ltd.*[30] This case concerned the sale of animal feed to the plaintiff mink farmers, containing herring meal contaminated with a chemical called 'DMNA' which proved fatal to the mink, though it would not have harmed other animals. The House of Lords found in favour of the plaintiffs on grounds that the meal was unfit for purpose under s.14(3) S.G.A. 1893 and that the goods were unmerchantable under s.14(2). The House also found, however, that there was no breach of the term implied by s.13, as the presence of the contaminant did not mean that the goods were incorrectly described as 'herring meal', in spite of the contaminant.

6.28 The case of *Re Moore & Co. and Landauer & Co.* thus requires some explanation. The court supposed that the buyer may well have wished to have the tins in cases of 30 for good reasons of its own. It is not hard to suppose that this might be the case. But, putting aside sales law specifically for a moment, would a breach of this term have been a breach of condition (entitling the buyer to reject) or merely a breach of warranty, confining the buyer to

---

27 [1976] 3 All E.R. 570; [1976] 1 W.L.R. 989. Applied in *Sanko Steamship Co. Ltd v. Kano Trading Ltd* [1978] 1 Lloyd's Rep. 156 (C.A.), *Staffordshire Area Health Authority v. South Staffordshire Waterworks Co.* [1978] 3 All E.R. 769; [1978] 1 W.L.R. 1387 (C.A.), *Crittenden (Warren Park) Ltd v. Elliot* (1996) 75 P. & C.R. 20 (C.A.), *Clegg v. Andersson (t/a Nordic Marine)* [2002] E.W.H.C. 943 (Q.B.); [2009] All E.R. (D) 233 (Apr.), *Aung v. Parkway Hospitals Pte Ltd* [2008] S.G.C.A. 20; [2008] 1 L.R.C. 265 (Singapore C.A.), *Bashir v. Ali* [2010] E.W.H.C. 2320 (Ch.); [2010] 41 E.G. 127 (C.S.), and *Proteus Property Partners Ltd v. South Africa Property Opportunities plc* [2011] E.W.H.C. 768 (Q.B.).
28 [1976] 3 All E.R. 570, 576.
29 At 576. Lord Wilberforce's dictum was applied in *Earl of Lonsdale v. Attorney General* [1982] 3 All E.R. 579; [1982] 1 W.L.R. 887 (Ch.D.).
30 [1972] A.C. 441.

damages. It might well be found only to be a warranty. Damages might be hard indeed to prove, since the evidence was that there was no difference in the market values of tins of fruit packed in cases of 30 and tins of fruit packed in cases of 24. The obvious course must have seemed to be, therefore, to allege non-conformity with description, thus breach of the implied condition in s.13. This was clearly the way it was argued before the courts. If, as seems reasonable to conclude, the courts had sympathy with the buyer's position (perhaps in part because of the long delays in delivery of the goods), s.13 might well have offered a convenient peg on which to hang a decision in the buyer's favour. Given the approach of the Lords in the *Ashington Piggeries* and *Reardon Smith Line* cases, and particularly Lord Wilberforce's dictum in the latter case, discussed above, it is submitted that *Re Moore & Co. and Landauer & Co.* can be regarded as a high-water mark of the application of s.13, and probably not an approach likely to be followed in the future.[31]

6.29 In sum, in sales of goods between two parties acting by way of trade or two non-traders, it is an implied condition that goods sold by description shall conform to that description. In cases of a sale of goods by a trader to a consumer (both as defined in Consumer Rights Act 2015), it is an implied term that goods correspond with the description (s.11) and also match any 'model seen or examined' (s.14) (for instance a display sofa in a furniture shop, on the strength of which the consumer places an order for a new sofa). As pointed out in paragraph **6.04**, above, this is neither warranty nor condition, as such: the remedy for breach is governed primarily by the statute and is not affected at all by the categorization of the term. In other respects, it seems likely the courts will interpret cases under CRA 2015 in the same way as other cases on description. What counts as a sale by description depends upon whether the descriptive words form part of the contract, not a mere representation; a matter to be decided in accordance with ordinary principles of contract law. A description is only relevant for the purposes of the implied condition insofar as it forms what Lord Wilberforce called a 'substantial ingredient of the "identity" of the thing sold'.[32]

5. Quality and fitness

6.30 Outside the criminal law, the buyer's right to receive goods that are of satisfactory quality and 'fit for purpose' might well be the best known rule of

---

31   Of course, s.15A of the S.G.A. 1979, inserted by the Sale and Supply of Goods Act 1994, would mean that if the shortfall in delivery of the correct size of cases were small, then the buyer might have no right to reject. However, in *Re Moore & Co. and Landauer & Co.* the shortfall if the cases of 24 were rejected would be unlikely to be regarded as trivial.

32   *Reardon Smith Lines v. Hansen-Tangen*, above, paragraph **6.31**, [1976] 3 All E.R. 570, 576.

English law amongst lay-people in England. It can fairly be regarded as one of the cornerstones of consumer rights, though drafted originally with merchants, not consumers, in mind. The effects of this fact will be discussed further below. The historical common law origins of the statutory implied term are discussed in some detail in Chapter 1.[33]

6.31 The implied term as to quality represents not only a shift from caveat emptor but also, it is submitted, a distinctively modern approach. Mediaeval approaches involved the setting of specific standards relating to certain goods. The Assize of Bread and Ale (1266), regulating the quantities, contents and quality of bread and beer, not finally repealed until 1863,[34] is an English example. Living examples are common in Continental Europe: the *appellation d'origine controlée* system in France[35] and equivalent regulations in other Continental countries, the ranking of German wines into *Kabinett, Spätlese, Auslese, Beerenauslese* and *Trockenbeerenauslese,* based on ripeness of grapes, and the *Rheinheitsgebot,* regulating the contents of German beer, are particularly well-known instances. Britain has a good many statutory food standards, but they are concerned primarily with safety, rather than quality or supposed quality. Weights and measures legislation is a typical hangover from the past, but the scope is less than in the past: for example, if a loaf of bread is said to be 400 grammes, then it must be at least 400 grammes, but there is no law in England that says any given type of loaf must be 400 grammes and no other weight. The implied term, on the other hand, leaves the details to the market, but protects the buyer from receiving something rather less than he is promised or can reasonably expect to receive in all the circumstances.

6.32 The implied term as to quality also represents what Lord Wright described as a shift from *caveat emptor* to *caveat venditor,*[36] and Lord Steyn has observed that 'outside the field of private sales the shift from *caveat emptor* to *caveat venditor* in relation to the implied condition of fitness for purpose has been a notable feature of the development of our commercial law'.[37] Certainly, the position today is in startling contrast to that of the early 19th century. We have seen that in 1844 it was still being suggested that *caveat emptor* applied to all aspects of sales and that to displace it the buyer had to obtain a warranty or else allege and prove fraud. We have also seen in that year Pollock C.B. rejecting the suggestion that caveat emptor applied to title, and impliedly to description as such, and confining it to 'the condition of goods', that is to say,

---

33 See paragraphs **1.41 ff.**
34 By the Statute Law Revision Act 1863.
35 Albeit that this is as much, indeed mainly, aimed at producer rather than consumer protection.
36 *Grant v. Australian Knitting Mills Ltd* [1936] A.C. 85, 98 (P.C.).
37 *Slater v. Finning Ltd* [1997] A.C. 473, 488; [1996] 3 All E.R. 398, 410.

quality.[38] However, the concept of an implied warranty as to quality was not unknown by that time: the cases of *Laing v. Fidgeon*[39] and *Jones v. Bright*[40] are both early 19th century examples. However, this warranty did not extend to cases of sale by sample.[41] These cases are discussed in more detail in Chapter 1, above.[42]

Section 14 S.G.A. also implies a term as to fitness for purpose. This, too, has **6.33** common law origins: see, for example, *Randall v. Newson*.[43]

Originally, the term implied by section 14 extended to goods being of **6.34** 'merchantable quality' and that they be fit for any one purpose for which goods of that type were normally sold. If a special purpose was intended and made known to the vendor, then fitness for that special purpose was also implied where the vendor sold the goods on the understanding that they would be fit for that purpose. This provision might be expected to work well for sales between merchants, since often the purpose of the purchase will be resale, but from the point of view of a consumer buyer the provision clearly had its limitations.

These limitations come down essentially to two matters. First, a consumer, or **6.35** any end user, wants goods of appropriate quality for enjoyment, not goods which can be resold as goods of that description. Merchantability is not a relevant concept for an end user since they do not wish to market the goods. Second, a consumer will want goods for a particular purpose. This purpose may be one of the common purposes for which goods of that description are used, but there may be other common purposes which the consumer or end user does not wish to put the goods. If they are merely fit for some purpose the buyer does not want them for, then they might be resold to someone who does wish to obtain goods for that purpose; but an end user is not interested in selling the goods, rather in using them. Fitness for any purpose for which goods of that description are commonly sold is not, then, an end-user-relevant consideration.

The authors of Atiyah's *Sale of Goods* comment that: **6.36**

---

38 *Allen v. Hopkins* (1844) 13 M. & W. 94, 103; 153 E.R. 39, 42. See paragraph **6.13**, above.
39 (1815) 6 Taunt. 108; 128 E.R. 974.
40 (1825) 5 Bing. 533.
41 See *Parkinson v. Lee* (1802) 2 East 314; 102 E.R. 389.
42 See paragraphs **1.41–1.44**.
43 (1876) 2 Q.B.D. 102.

Under the 1893 Act no attempt to define the concept of 'merchantable quality' was made, and the matter was left entirely to case law. Probably the word 'merchantable' seemed sufficiently precise and appropriate to most lawyers and judges of the time, especially when the cases coming to their attention were mostly commercial contracts between businessmen. But to many, it appeared less appropriate in modern times when applied to consumer sales. But despite this the word did service for some 80 years without any statutory definition. A very large body of case law eventually developed … Not surprisingly no simple or single judicial *definition* ever emerged.[44]

6.37 Eventually, a statutory definition was supplied by the Supply of Goods (Implied Terms) Act 1973, in due course incorporated into the Sale of Goods Act 1979 as s.14(6):

> Goods of any kind are of merchantable quality within the meaning of subsection (2) above if they are as fit for the purpose or purposes for which goods of that kind are commonly bought as it is reasonable to expect having regard to any description applied to them, the price (if relevant) and all the other relevant circumstances.

After the Sale and Supply of Goods Act 1994 the requirement changed to 'satisfactory quality' and something similar to s.14(6) became s.14(2A):

> For the purposes of this Act, goods are of satisfactory quality if they meet the standard that a reasonable person would regard as satisfactory, taking account of any description of the goods, the price (if relevant) and all the other relevant circumstances.

The fitness for purpose aspect of quality became part of s.14(2B):

> For the purposes of this Act, the quality of goods includes their state and condition and the following (among others) are in appropriate cases aspects of the quality of goods–
>
> (a) fitness for all the purposes for which goods of the kind in question are commonly supplied,
> (b) appearance and finish,
> (c) freedom from minor defects,
> (d) safety, and
> (e) durability.

But fitness for purpose is in no sense a distinct term from 'satisfactory quality' and was not a distinct term from 'merchantable quality'. Subsection (2C) provides for exemption of certain matters making the goods unsatisfactory:

---

44 P.S. Atiyah, J.N. Adams, H. MacQueen, *The Sale of Goods*, 10th edn. (Longman: London, 2001) p. 156. (Emphasis in original.)

(2C) The term implied by subsection (2) above does not extend to any matter making the quality of goods unsatisfactory–

    (a) which is specifically drawn to the buyer's attention before the contract is made,

    (b) where the buyer examines the goods before the contract is made, which that examination ought to reveal, or

    (c) in the case of a contract for sale by sample, which would have been apparent on a reasonable examination of the sample.

However, subsection (3) of s.14 may fairly be regarded as a separate instance, **6.38** since it provides that where a special purpose is made known to the seller (or, in a sale on instalment payments, to a credit-broker who sold the goods to the seller), 'there is an implied term that the goods supplied under the contract are reasonably fit for that purpose, whether or not that is a purpose for which such goods are commonly supplied', unless it is shown that the buyer does not reasonably rely on the skill or judgement of the seller or credit-broker. Note that the buyer's reliance must be *both* actual *and* reasonable for this term to be implied.

The 1994 Act was introduced as a private member's Bill but substantially put **6.39** into effect the recommendations of the Law Commission's final report on *Sale and Supply of Goods* of 1987, save that the recommended term 'acceptable quality' was substituted with 'satisfactory quality'.

The old terminology continued to provide challenges of interpretation, even **6.40** after the 1973 definition. As the authors of Atiyah's *Sale of Goods* note, 'for some years, the case law proceeded in the old way, despite the statutory definition. Former editions of this book continued to discuss the case law at some length, before even considering the statutory definition.'[45]

Two cases in 1987 took quite different approaches to the interpretation of **6.41** 'merchantable quality'. The Court of Appeal in *Aswan Engineering Establishment Co. v. Lupdine Ltd*[46] (Fox, Lloyd and Nicholls L.JJ.) exhaustively examined the old case law on merchantable quality[47] before considering the 1973 definition in s.14(6); but a differently constituted Court of Appeal (Mustill and Woolf L.JJ. and Sir Edward Eveleigh) in *Rogers v. Parish (Scarborough) Ltd*[48] held that s.14(6) should be applied without reference to the old case law, as Mustill L.J. explained:

---

45   Above, n. 44, at p. 157.
46   [1987] 1 All E.R. 135; [1987] 1 W.L.R. 1.
47   As to which, see Chapter 1, above, at paragraphs **1.41ff**.
48   [1987] Q.B. 933; [1987] 2 All E.R. 232. Applied, *Shine v. General Guarantee Corp.* [1988] 1 All E.R. 911.

The Act of 1973 was an amending Act and it cannot be assumed that the new definition was included simply because the draftsman saw a convenient opportunity to reproduce in more felicitous and economical terms the gist of the speeches and judgments previously delivered. The language of section 14(6) is clear and free from technicality, and it should be sufficient in the great majority of cases to enable the fact-finding judge to arrive at a decision without exploring the intricacies of the prior law.[49]

Woolf L.J. adding that:

I firmly endorse what has been said by Mustill L.J. with regard to the fact that those provisions are best applied directly where there is a dispute as to whether or not goods are merchantable, without having recourse to authorities which were dealing with the different provisions of section 14 of the Act of 1893 before that Act was amended.[50]

6.42 There seems not to have been generated a particularly large amount of case law either on the 1973 definition of merchantable quality or on the current definition of satisfactory quality found in s.14(2A), (2B) and (2C) of the S.G.A. 1979. Nonetheless, it appears clear that the statutory definition of satisfactory quality is largely to be applied case-by-case without reference to the old merchantable quality case law. This is an obvious approach, because the standard is a new one and meant to be distinct from merchantable quality, though cases concerning merchantable quality are not entirely irrelevant, since they may be relevant in having set standards in relation to special types of contract.

6.43 The definition has, we might say, an odour of case law about it. That is to say that the legal part of the question 'are these goods of satisfactory quality?' is taken care of within the section, in much the same way that the criteria for determining the difference between penalties and liquidated damages clauses are set out in the speech of Lord Dunedin in *Dunlop Pneumatic Tyre Co. Ltd v. New Garage and Motor Co. Ltd*:[51] all the judge need do is answer factual questions regarding fitness for purpose, appearance and finish, freedom from minor defects, safety and durability, and any issue raised by subsection (2C) and subsection (3), where relevant. If the judge finds as a fact that the goods are not safe, or not durable, or not free from minor defects, then the legal question is automatically answered by the provisions of s.14.

---

49 [1987] Q.B. 933, 942.
50 At 947.
51 [1915] A.C. 79, 86.

It also seems to be the case that these several factors do not merely contribute **6.44** to painting an overall picture of satisfactoriness. It is of no avail to the seller that the goods are fit for purpose, of perfect appearance and finish, have no minor defects and are safe if it is found that they are not durable so far as would be expected for the type of goods in question (including factors such as price). Failure of goods to be satisfactory in any one aspect renders the goods unsatisfactory. For example, in the case of *S. W. Tubes Ltd v. Owen Stuart Ltd (t/a O.S.L. Technical Services)*[52] the Court of Appeal (Aldous L.J. and Sir Christopher Slade) held that a second-hand circular saw was not of satisfactory quality because the lack of a guard made it unsafe. Aldous L.J., with whom Sir Christopher Slade agreed, stated in the course of his judgment that:

> [37] The evidence as to guards was given by Mr Hobson of Strange, Strange and Gardner. He said:
>
>> 'It is necessary to have some part of a circular saw blade exposed to allow it to function. However, in the situation in question it is practicable to design and construct an enclosure to nullify the dangers of the cutting head. It would also be reasonably practicable to arrange safety switches on the front and rear cabinet panels. The arrangement we saw appears to allow these panels to be easily removed without affecting the saw cycle.'
>
> [38] Mr Hobson believed that operation of the saw without guards would be likely to make Tubes liable under the Health and Safety Regulations and at common law. However, he accepted that that was a decision for legal opinion.
>
> [39] Mr Baker emphasised that the saw was second-hand and that it had been operated in the past without guards. But that does not mean that it was safe. In my view it was not safe to operate the saw without guards. That conclusion is supported by the photograph on p 106 of the bundle which shows guards on an old machine. The sort of guards involved are simple structures. As safety is an aspect of quality under the 1979 Act, I conclude that the saw was not of satisfactory quality and its supply breached the term implied by s 14 of the 1979 Act.

(Mr Baker was the proprietor of the vendor company and represented the company in the Court of Appeal.)

More recently, Field J. considered the satisfactoriness of gasoil sold f.o.b. in the **6.45** case of *K.G. Bominflot Bunkergesellschaft für Mineralöle m.b.h. & Co. K.G. v.*

---

52 [2002] E.W.C.A. 854; [2002] All E.R. (D) 243 (May).

Petroplus Marketing A.G. (The Mercini Lady)[53] Reference was made to merchantability, but this was to assist in considering the point at which satisfactoriness needs to be judged in the case of an f.o.b. contract (where property and risk passes when the goods pass the ship's rail):

> [38] In my judgment, in the absence of any term inconsistent therewith, there is to be implied into an FOB contract a term under s.14(2) of the 1979 Act that the goods will be of satisfactory quality not only when the cargo is delivered on to the vessel but also for a reasonable time thereafter. Such a term is also to be implied at common law with the additional dimension that the goods should not only be of satisfactory quality for a reasonable time but also should remain in accordance with the contractual specification (if any) for such a period. I reach this conclusion for the same reasons that Diplock J. gave in *Mash and Murrell* [54] for upholding the buyer's alternative claims under s.14(2) of the 1893 Act and at common law. At the heart of that reasoning was the acceptance of Atkin J.'s view based on *Beer v. Walker* [55] that the condition that the goods must be merchantable means that they must be in that condition when appropriated to the contract and that they will continue so for a reasonable time. Hence Diplock J.'s words quoted in para. 16 above:
>
> > "[M]erchantability in the case of goods sold c.i.f. or c.&f. means that the goods must remain merchantable for a reasonable time and that in the case of such contracts a reasonable time means time for arrival and disposal upon arrival." [39] So far as the term to be implied under s.14(2) of the 1979 Act is concerned, my conclusion is fortified by the fact s.14(2B) makes 'durability' an aspect of 'satisfactory quality'. And in respect of the term to be implied at common law, if the seller has bound himself to supply goods of a particular specification, I think it plain that in the absence of any inconsistent term he is to be taken to have agreed that the goods should remain on specification for a reasonable time after delivery.

6.46 Section 9 of the Consumer Rights Act implies a term as to quality into contracts to which that Act applies. It is in very similar terms except that 'relevant circumstances' in s.14(2A) S.G.A., becomes 'all other relevant circumstances (see subsection (5))' in C.R.A. Subsections (5) to (7) introduce as relevant circumstances public statements 'about the specific characteristics of the goods made by the trader, the producer or any representative of the trader or producer' (subsection (5)), which 'includes, in particular, any public statement made in advertising or labelling' (subsection (6)).[56] Subsection (7) excludes liability for statements the trader was not and could not reasonably

---

53 [2009] E.W.H.C. (Comm.) 1088; [2009] 2 All E.R. (Comm.) 827.

54 *Mash and Murrell Ltd v. Joseph I. Emanuel Ltd* [1961] 1 All E.R. 465 (Q.B.); [1961] 1 W.L.R. 862; [1961] 1 Lloyd's Rep. 46. The decision was reversed on the facts by the Court of Appeal: [1962] 1 All E.R. 77n.; [1962] 1 W.L.R. 16n.; [1962] 2 Lloyd's Rep. 326.

55 (1877) 46 L.J.Q.B. 677; [1874–80] All E.R. Rep. 1139.

56 This provision consolidates the effect on this point of the Sale & Supply of Goods to Consumers Regulations 2002.

have been aware of and statements withdrawn or corrected before the contract was made (paragraphs (a) and (b)). Subsection (7)(c) excludes such statements that could not have influenced the consumer's decision to contract for the goods. This latter is presumably directed at 'mere puffs' of the 'Sudso washes whiter than white' or 'the ultimate driving machine' type. Notably, however, subsection (7) places the burden of proving that these exceptions, including that in paragraph (c) on the trader.

It might conveniently be noted here that whereas s.14 Sale of Goods Act 1979 **6.47** includes in subsection (2) fitness for common purposes as part of the standard of satisfactoriness and in subsection (3) fitness for a particular purpose in appropriate circumstances, the CRA deals with fitness for particular purposes in a separate section (s.10), while retaining fitness for usual purposes as an aspect of quality in s.9(3). Similarly, the provision in SGA s.14(1) that there are no implied terms as to quality save for the one in s.14, in the CRA is replicated in its effect by s.18, though s.9(8) allows inclusion of an implied term as to quality as a matter of custom.

6. Fitness for special purposes

Where a buyer notifies the seller of the need for the goods to be fit for a **6.48** particular purpose which is not one of the usual purposes to which such goods are put and the buyer is relying on the seller's expertise, then the goods must be fit for that specific purpose. This is expressed as follows in s.14(3) S.G.A. 1979:

> Where the seller sells goods in the course of a business and the buyer, expressly or by implication, makes known
>
> (a) to the seller, or
> (b) where the purchase price or part of it is payable by instalments and the goods were previously sold by a credit-broker to the seller, to that credit-broker, any particular purpose for which the goods are being bought,there is an implied term that the goods supplied under the contract are reasonably fit for that purpose, whether or not that is a purpose for which such goods are commonly supplied, except where the circumstances show that the buyer does not rely, or that it is unreasonable for him to rely, on the skill or judgment of the seller or credit-broker.

What is notable here is that fitness for purpose is a concept playing two roles **6.49** in section 14. First, in s.14(2), it is an aspect of quality to be considered by the court in determining whether the goods are of satisfactory quality and thus in conformity with the implied term as to quality, then, in s.14(3) it is in its own right the subject of an implied term. It is important to note, also, that these are not exclusive terms, but concurrent. It is obvious that goods may satisfy the tests of satisfactory quality in s.14(2) yet breach the implied term in s.14(3), as in the case of *Ashington Piggeries Ltd v. Christopher Hill Ltd*,[57] in which animal food was supplied which was quite suitable for its normal uses, but not as food for mink, to which it was fatal. Less obvious is the fact that goods may be fit for a special purpose and thus conform with the implied term in s.14(3) yet nonetheless be supplied in breach of the implied term as to quality inserted by s.14(2), either because they are not fit for all usual purposes of the type of goods in question, or because they fail to satisfy some other criterion of quality in s.14(2) or derived from elsewhere.

6.50   Sir Roy Goode has criticized the situation in the following terms:

> It is unfortunate that when the Supply of Goods (Implied Terms) Act was enacted opportunity was not taken to remove the overlap of the implied conditions of quality and fitness. Because of the differences between the criteria laid down in s. 14(2) and those enunciated in s. 14(3), the possibility is created of goods being fit for their normal purpose so as to be of satisfactory quality within s. 14(2) yet being unfit for their normal purpose within s. 14(3), and vice versa.[58]

He explains that the problem arises because s.14(2) excludes defects disclosed to the buyer, while s.14(3) provides for no such exclusion. Is this 'unfortunate', however? It is submitted that a satisfactory rationale can be found for this apparent anomaly. It arises naturally from the circumstances in which s.14(3) is employed. Defects disclosed might or might not affect the goods' fitness for all ordinary uses of that type of goods. If defects are disclosed affecting fitness for an ordinary purpose, the buyer might decide to take them anyway as he does not wish to use them for the purpose so affected. Or, he may take them with knowledge of the defects and the intention of himself remedying those defects, thus rendering the goods fit for the purpose in question. In either case, the buyer is relying on his own skill and judgement, not that of the seller. Section 14(3), however, only applies where the buyer reasonably relies on the seller's skill and judgement as to the goods' fitness for a particular purpose. Now if the seller discloses to the buyer some defects rendering the goods unfit either for one of the ordinary purposes of such goods, *where the seller knows the goods are intended for that use*, or for a special use for which such goods are not ordinarily bought and sold, again with knowledge that this is the intended use, and the goods are unfit for that use, then it becomes incumbent on the seller to make clear that he is unable to say that the goods will be fit for the specified purpose. If he does so then the buyer clearly cannot be considered to be

---

57   [1972] A.C. 441.
58   Sir R. Goode, *Commercial Law,* 3rd edn. (Butterworths: London, 2004) p. 316.

reasonably relying on the seller's skill and judgement but is clearly relying on his own skill and judgement, so the implied term in s.14(3) would not operate. If, however, the seller does not make such a disclaimer and the buyer reasonably relies on the seller's skill and judgement to the effect that any defects disclosed do not affect the fitness of the goods for the specified purpose, then it does not seem at all unreasonable that the seller should be liable in spite of having disclosed the defects. Equally, in the ordinary case where no reliance is being placed on the seller's skill and judgement, or no specific purpose is disclosed, it seems reasonable that disclosure of any defects that operate to render the goods unfit for purpose, leaving the buyer to exercise his own skill and judgement, should relieve the seller of liability in respect of unfitness.

In contracts to which the Consumer Rights Act 2015 applies, the situation **6.51** where goods are required for a particular purpose which is not one of the usual purposes for which such goods are supplied, contained in section 10. This is in essentially identical terms to s.14(3) SGA 1979. One difference in terminology which might be noted is in subsection (5) CRA, which reads '(5) In a contract to supply goods a term about the fitness of the goods for a particular purpose may be treated as included as a matter of custom.' The corresponding provision in SGA is s.14(4) reads '(4) An implied term about quality or fitness for a particular purpose may be annexed to a contract of sale by usage.' However, the present author is at this stage of the opinion that Parliament is unlikely to have intended to draw a distinction between 'custom' in CRA and 'usage' in SGA and the courts are unlikely to do so. The natural conclusion to draw is that the law will continue to be the same as in the past, save as to the question of remedies, in trader-consumer transactions.

7. Correspondence of bulk with sample

Section 15 Sale of Goods Act 1979, as amended, reads as follows in the first **6.52** two subsections:

(1) A contract of sale is a contract for sale by sample where there is an express or implied term to that effect in the contract.
(2) In the case of a contract for sale by sample there is an implied term –
    (a) that the bulk will correspond with the sample in quality;
    (b) [repealed]
    (c) that the goods will be free from any defect, making their quality unsatisfactory which would not be apparent on reasonable examination of the sample.

Subsections (3) and (4) make the term a condition in England and Wales and in Northern Ireland and applies a provision in a schedule in relation to contracts made before 18 May 1973.

6.53 A sale by sample is one in which a sample is intended to form part of the contractual basis of the sale. So, as Sir Roy Goode has observed: '[t]he mere fact that a sample is exhibited during negotiations for a sale does not make it a sale by sample'.[59] He goes on to say that:

> [a]s a working rule, it may be said that a sale is unlikely to be considered a sale by sample unless the sample is released by the seller to the buyer … for the purpose of providing a means of checking whether the goods subsequently tendered correspond with the sample.[60]

6.54 As to the function of a sample, Goode cites Lord Macnaghten in *James Drummond & Sons v. E.H. Van Ingen & Co*[61] and the passage from that speech will repay reproduction here:

> After all, the office of a sample is to present to the eye the real meaning and intention of the parties with regard to the subject-matter of the contract which, owing to the imperfection of language, it may be difficult or impossible to express in words. The sample speaks for itself. But it cannot be treated as saying more than such a sample would tell a merchant of the class to which the buyer belongs, using due care and diligence, and appealing to it in the ordinary way and with the knowledge possessed by merchants of that class at the time. No doubt the sample might be made to say a great deal more. Pulled to pieces and examined by unusual tests which curiosity or suspicion might suggest, it would doubtless reveal every secret of its construction. But that is not the way in which business is done in this country. Some confidence there must be between merchant and manufacturer. In matters exclusively within the province of the manufacturer, the merchant relies on the manufacturer's skill.[62]

This has two corollaries. First, that the bulk need only conform to the sample in respect to those qualities which reasonable observation and testing, rather than exhaustive testing (usually) would disclose. Secondly, that aspects of quality that would not be disclosed by such reasonable examination may still be the liability of the seller under s.14(2).

6.55 For contracts for supply of goods to which the Consumer Rights Act 2015 applies, there is a slightly different implied term inserted by s.13, which is worded as follows.

---

59   Goode, above, p. 324.
60   Ibid.
61   (1887) 12 App. Cas. 284.
62   At 297.

13 Goods to match a sample

(1) This section applies to a contract to supply goods by reference to a sample of the goods which is seen or examined by the consumer before the contract is made.

(2) Every contract to which this section applies is to be treated as including a term that–

    (a) the goods will match the sample except to the extent that any differences between the sample and the goods are brought to the consumer's attention before the contract is made, and

    (b) the goods will be free from any defect that makes their quality unsatisfactory and that would not be apparent on a reasonable examination of the sample.

If one compares this with s.15 of the Sale of Goods Act 1979, it will be seen that s.13(2)(a) appears different from s.15(2)(a) S.G.A. 1979 which reads 'the bulk will correspond with the sample in quality'. The dual references to 'before the contract is made' are not significant, as this would follow necessarily in S.G.A. 1979 s.15 cases and is just a feature of the drafting of the CRA, but whether there is any significance in goods being required to 'match the sample' that goes beyond corresponding in quality remains to be seen and will only be really apparent once there is sufficient case law, if ever such a body of case law arises, since sales by sample to which the Consumer Rights Act would apply are likely to be relatively few in number. One supposes that a consumer might buy a case of wine, for instance, after sampling the wine at a tasting, and find that the wine delivered, though of satisfactory quality and apparently matching description, differs in some way in character from that sampled at the tasting. The chances of this complete set of circumstances arising seem slim, however, and consumer cases are far more likely to arise in relation to quality or description (or non-correspondence with a model, see paragraph **6.56**, below).

8.   Goods to match a model

The Consumer Rights Act 2015 introduces a novel implied term into the law **6.56** of England and Wales, though not altogether new in the common law. Section 14 provides that:

(1) This section applies to a contract to supply goods by reference to a model of the goods that is seen or examined by the consumer before entering into the contract.

(2) Every contract to which this section applies is to be treated as including a term that the goods will match the model except to the extent that any differences between the model and the goods are brought to the consumer's attention before the consumer enters into the contract.

[...]

This may be compared with the Uniform Commercial Code from the United States, section 2–313 of which provides:

> **§ 2–313 Express Warranties by Affirmation, Promise, Description, Sample.**
>
> (1) In this section, '**immediate buyer**' means a buyer that enters into a contract with the seller.
> (2) Express warranties by the seller to the immediate buyer are created as follows:
>   (a) ...
>   (c) Any sample or model that is made part of the basis of the bargain creates an express warranty that the whole of the goods shall conform to the sample or model.
> (3) It is not necessary to the creation of an express warranty that the seller use formal words such as 'warrant' or 'guarantee' or that the seller have a specific intention to make a warranty, but an affirmation merely of the value of the goods or a statement purporting to be merely the seller's opinion or commendation of the goods does not create a warranty.
>
> [...]

Original or not, the provision in s.14 C.R.A. 2015 seems plain on its face. The only difficulty is whether the contract needs to be made wholly by reference to the model, as the most literal reading might suggest, or if it suffices that it was only partly on the basis of the model. The latter case would clearly fall within the wording of the U.C.C. and it is submitted that it would be regrettable if the courts in England and Wales took a more restrictive approach, as it is unlikely that many consumer contracts would be made solely on the basis of a model without any description at all being applied.

9. Delivery to consumer

6.57 Section 28 of the Consumer Rights Act 2015 implies a term that, in the absence of contrary agreement, the trader must deliver the goods to the consumer (s.28(2)) and another that, in the absence of express agreement as to a particular time or period for delivery, such delivery must be without undue delay (s.28(3)(a)) and in any event not more than 30 days after the day on which the contract is made (s.28(3)(b)). The implied term as to timeliness of delivery applies to each individual instalment if goods are to be delivered on an instalment basis. The remainder of s.28 sets out remedial provisions. The s.28 terms are applicable even in the event that the goods are second-hand goods purchased at a public auction and the consumer had the opportunity to attend in person: s.2(6) CRA 2015.

'Delivery' is defined in s.59 CRA 2015 and means, in line with existing sales **6.58** law, 'voluntary transfer of possession'. Quite why the mechanism of an implied term is adopted for this particular aspect rather than adopting the default rule approach of s.29 Sale of Goods Act 1979, is not absolutely clear. The delivery provisions in the Consumer Rights Act, indeed, appear less clear than those of the SGA, since, for instance, no default position is specified as to *place* of delivery. (Under s.29 SGA 1979 the default place of delivery is the seller's place of business (or residence if he has no place of business) unless the sale is of specific goods and the parties know them to be in some other place, in which case that other place is the default place of delivery.) The Act is silent on this as far as the present author can see and nothing is said about it in the Explanatory Notes to the CRA 2015 either. It remains to be seen, therefore, whether the courts will fill the apparent gap by analogy with s.29 SGA 1979.

10. Passing of risk

The Consumer Rights Act 2015 implies terms to the effect that goods remain **6.59** at the trader's risk until they come into the 'physical possession' either of the consumer himself or of 'a person identified by the consumer to take possession of the goods': s.29(2). But if the goods are placed into the hands of a carrier chosen by the consumer (and not from a list proffered by the trader), risk passes to the consumer upon delivery to the carrier: s.29(3) and (4). Subsection (5) provides, perhaps rather unnecessarily, that this latter provision does not affect any liability of the carrier to the consumer. The s.29 terms are applicable even in the event that the goods are second-hand goods purchased at a public auction and the consumer had the opportunity to attend in person: s.2(6) CRA 2015.

11. Contracts to which these sections apply

Sections 12, 13 and 15 of S.G.A. and the related sections of other legislation **6.60** apply to all contracts of sale other than ones to which the Consumer Rights Act 2015 applies. Section 14 only applies to sales where the seller sells in the course of business.

The implied terms cannot be excluded as against a consumer buyer: s.6(1) and **6.61** (2) Unfair Contract Terms Act 1977. This remains relevant even for contracts made since the coming into force of the Consumer Rights Act 2015, as that Act does not apply to contracts made between a consumer buyer and a non-trader seller; though naturally it is no longer relevant in the case of s.14 SGA 1979 as the implied term in that section applies only where the seller deals by way of trade and would thus be a 'trader' within the meaning of CRA

2015. The amendment to UCTA 1977 in the form of the insertion of s.6(5) states that section 6 does not apply to consumer contracts, but 'consumer contracts' here means contracts to which the CRA 2015 applies, not all contracts which involve a consumer. The implied term in s.12 (and s.8 Supply of Goods (Implied Terms) Act 1973) cannot be excluded against any buyer. The implied terms in ss.13, 14 and 15 may be excluded in a sale to a non-consumer, but only so far as the excluding term satisfies the requirements of reasonableness: s.6(3) Unfair Contract Terms Act 1977. For cases concerning the meaning of a consumer for these purposes, the reader should see any of the standard works on sale of goods law. None of the implied terms in the Consumer Rights Act 2015 may be excluded.

C. IMPLIED TERMS IN SUPPLY OF DIGITAL CONTENT

6.62 The Consumer Rights Act 2015 breaks wholly new ground in making statutory implications into contracts to supply 'digital content', which apply whether such content is essentially a working component of goods sold or otherwise supplied (e.g., a portable telephone's operating system) or is supplied as a product in its own right. The relationship between the different provisions of the CRA in respect of goods and of digital content respectively are shown in Table 6.1, above.

1. Trader to have right to supply digital content

6.63 Section 41 CRA 2015 makes equivalent provision to that made in s.17 CRA for supplies of goods (s.12 SGA, s.8 SG(IT)A) in relation to the trader's right to supply digital content and provides as follows:

> (1) Every contract to supply digital content is to be treated as including a term –
> (a) In relation to any digital content which is supplied under the contract and which the consumer has paid for, that the trader has the right to supply that content to the consumer;
> (b) In relation to any digital content which the trader agrees to supply under the contract and which the consumer has paid for, that the trader will have the right to supply it to the consumer at the time when it is to be supplied.

It is only notable that there is a reference in each case to the consumer having paid for the content.

2. Digital content to be as described

Section 36 CRA 2015 implies a term that 'the digital content will match any **6.64** description of it given by the trader to the consumer', which corresponds with that of s.11 CRA 2015 and s.13 Sale of Goods Act 1979. And the correctness of pre-contract information in relation to digital goods is implied as a term by s.37 CRA 2015.

3. Quality and fitness of digital content

Implied terms as to quality and fitness of goods are extended to digital **6.65** content, as far as applicable, by s.34 the Consumer Rights Act 2015, and in respect of fitness for a particular purpose by s.35. One of the tests of satisfactoriness in relation to goods is that of 'durability' (see s.14(2) Sale of Goods Act 1979 and s.9 CRA 2015). With digital content that is unlikely to be an issue in relation to the content itself. However, provision is made for an implied term that where digital content is made available to a consumer via access to a 'processing facility' (see s.39(4) for definition) then if no period is stipulated in the contract during which the consumer is to have access to that facility, access is to be made available for a reasonable time: s.39(5). Further, every fresh transmission of digital content to the consumer must comply with the implied terms as to description, quality and fitness and fitness for a particular purpose: s.39(6). However, as regards conformity with description, if the contract specifies that content may be modified by the trader or a third party, then improvements to features of the content or the addition of new features do not prevent the goods conforming to the description, provided 'the digital content continues to match the description of it given by the trader to the consumer' at the time the original contract was made: s.40 CRA 2015. It will be interesting to see whether any case law develops about this section in relation to the matter of whether 'improvements' are such as to render the content no longer in conformity with the description (and any other relevant information) given at the time the contract was made. It may be wise for traders supplying digital content to confine themselves to fairly vague and general descriptions of digital content, and likewise with other pre-contractual information (see s.37 CRA 2015), to avoid claims that what they may see as 'improvements' but some users might not view in quite that light, would not fall outside such original description and information.

D. IMPLIED TERMS AS TO SUPPLY OF SERVICES

6.66 Statutory implication of terms into contracts for supply of services dates to the Supply of Goods and Services Act 1982 ('SGSA 1982'). We have already seen in this chapter how that Act applies to supply of goods otherwise than by sale or hire purchase and the bulk of the Act deals with such supplies. The brief Part II of the Act, consisting only of sections 12 to 16, deals with contracts for supply of services. Since 1 October 2015, these provisions do not apply to contracts to which the Consumer Rights Act 2015 applies.

6.67 The SGSA 1982 implies three terms into relevant contracts for services (for 'relevant contracts' see paragraph **6.69**, below), *viz.* that: (a) a supplier of services who supplies them in the course of business will exercise reasonable skill and care in doing so (s.13); (b) a supplier of services who supplies them in the course of business will do so within a reasonable time if no time is specified in the contract (s.14); and (c) irrespective of whether supply is in the course of business or not, if no consideration is otherwise established under the contract then a reasonable amount will be payable by the recipient (s.15).

6.68 In the case of s.15, the statutory term takes effect in the absence of either: (i) a specification as to the charges payable; or (ii) a provision in the contract for how the charges are to be determined; or (iii) the existence of a course of dealing between the parties (see paragraphs **5.34–5.39**, above). So in this case not only is the implied term to be ousted by any express terms, as might reasonably be expected, but also by another (specified type of) implied term.

6.69 Contracts to which Part II of the Act applies are described in s.12, which is set out in full here:

> **12 The contracts concerned.**
>
> (1) In this Act a 'relevant contract for the supply of a service' means, subject to subsection (2) below, a contract under which a person ('the supplier') agrees to carry out a service, other than a contract to which Chapter 4 of Part 1 of the Consumer Rights Act 2015 applies.
> (2) For the purposes of this Act, a contract of service or apprenticeship is not a relevant contract for the supply of a service.
> (3) Subject to subsection (2) above, a contract is a relevant contract for the supply of a service for the purposes of this Act whether or not goods are also—
> (a) transferred or to be transferred, or
>   (b) bailed or to be bailed by way of hire, under the contract, and whatever is the nature of the consideration for which the service is to be carried out.

(4) The Secretary of State may by order provide that one or more of sections 13 to 15 below shall not apply to services of a description specified in the order, and such an order may make different provision for different circumstances.

(5) The power to make an order under subsection (4) above shall be exercisable by statutory instrument subject to annulment in pursuance of a resolution of either House of Parliament.

The main exceptions, then, are apprenticeships (in which, presumably, the service is provided by the master to the apprentice, through the training intended to be provided, rather than the other way around) and contracts to which the Consumer Rights Act applies. The Act is, in short, inclusive and a contract which involves both supply of services and supply of goods is not by that fact to fall outside the operation of these sections.

The parties are free to exclude the operation of these implied terms by express **6.70** terms in the contract which either specify that they are to be excluded or which are inconsistent with the implied terms: s.16 SGSA 1982. Nothing in the Unfair Contract Terms Act 1977 prevents the use of contractual terms to exclude the implication of terms under the SGSA 1982 since in relation to breaches of contract s.3 of that Act prevents exclusion of liability arising under the contract and if the terms are excluded from the contract in the first place then that would not be liability arising under the contract. If, however, the terms are not excluded then an attempt to restrict or exclude liability for their breach would, under s.3 UCTA 1977, be required to satisfy the requirement of reasonableness. This leaves the nice question of whether or not a term seeking to restrict liability for breach of the implied term in s.13 SGSA 1982 would be an express term of the contract that was inconsistent with the implied term in s.13 and therefore takes effect to oust the implication.

There is nothing of which this author is aware that would prevent a party **6.71** arguing that a term which the *proferens* argues ousts the implications of the SGSA 1982 either does not do so on the normal rules of interpretation (on the grounds that the proffered express term is not inconsistent, see paragraphs **1.30** and **1.31,** above) or is not incorporated, for example under the 'red hand' rule.[63]

Breach of the term clearly requires fault and is analogous to negligence **6.72** liability. As Burnett J. put it in *Abramova v. Oxford Institute of Legal Practice*:

---

63 See, especially, *J. Spurling Ltd v. Bradshaw* [1956] 1 W.L.R. 461; [1956] 2 All E.R. 121 (C.A.) and *Interfoto Picture Library Ltd v. Stiletto Visual Programmes Ltd* [1989] Q.B. 433; [1988] 2 W.L.R. 615; [1988] 1 All E.R. 348 (C.A.).

Section 13 of the Supply of Goods and Services Act 1982 implied a term that the educational services would be provided with reasonable care and skill. The effect of that term was to imply a term that the educational services would be provided without negligence. [...] This is not to open the door to claims based on poor quality of teaching. It is one thing for the law to provide a remedy in damages when there is manifest incompetence or negligence comprising specific identifiable mistakes. It would be an altogether different matter to countenance claims of a more general nature, to the effect that the child did not receive an adequate education at the school, or that a particular teacher failed to teach properly. Proof of under-performance by a child is not by itself evidence of negligent teaching.[64]

It is also important to ask whether the carelessness complained of relates to a contractual commitment by the offending party. So in *Finch v. Lloyds T.S.B. Bank plc*[65] the claimant's action against the bank alleging a breach of the term implied by s.13 through the bank's failure to draw the claimant's attention to a clause in a fixed-interest loan which would make the borrower liable for around £1.5 million of the bank's costs in cancelling a hedging contract designed to protect it against rate variability, failed because the contract was for a loan, not for advice about the terms of the loan. The Act, however, preserves a claimant's right to sue on the basis of any existing rule of law imposing stricter liability on the party supplying services: s.16(3) SGSA 1982.

6.73 Unlike the implied terms of the Sale of Goods Act, those of Part II of SGSA 1982 are not conditions. Neither do they appear to be warranties. Terms implied by the Act into contracts involving the transfer or hire of goods are described as 'conditions' or 'warranties' but these are merely described as 'terms', which presses us to the conclusion that they are innominate or indeterminate terms, a view held by the author of Treitel[66] with which the present author respectfully agrees.

6.74 The Sale and Supply of Goods Act 1982 no longer applies to consumer contracts within the meaning of the Consumer Rights Act 2015, which is to say in essence, business-to-consumer transactions, but still applies to business-to-business contracting and between parties neither of whom is a 'trader' within the meaning of the 2015 Act. In contracts governed by CRA 2015, there are similar implied terms. Section 49 implies a term that the service be performed with reasonable care and skill. Section 50 implies a new term that information supplied or representations made by the trader to the consumer

---

64   [2011] E.W.H.C. 613; [2011] E.L.R. 385 (Q.B.) at [58] and [59].
65   [2016] E.W.H.C. 1236 (Q.B.).
66   E. Peel, *Treitel, The Law of Contract*, 14th edn. (Sweet & Maxwell: London, 2015) at para. 18–050.

prior to the contract being made are to be treated as included as terms of the contract if the consumer took them into account in deciding to enter the contract. Section 51 implies a term that a reasonable price is payable if one is not fixed by the contract and the contract does not specify a mechanism for doing so, as with s.15 SGSA 1982, but only applies if the consumer has not already paid a 'price or other consideration for the service'. On the face of it this is not very clear, but the Explanatory Notes assume that if a price has already been paid prior to the delivery of the service then this means the price is known to the consumer. In other words, the provision involves looking at the contract for terms as to price before implying one, but this is only necessary if the services have not already been paid for. Section 52 provides for the service to be provided within a reasonable time if not otherwise specified.

The implied term that a service must be provided with reasonable care and **6.75** skill cannot be excluded against a consumer in a contract to which the Consumer Rights Act 2015 applies: s.57(1) CRA 2015. Similarly, subject to the qualifications in s.50(2) (contract information qualified by the trader on the same occasion and changes subsequently expressly agreed to by the consumer before entering into the contract), the implied term about information cannot be excluded: s.57(2). Nor can the consumer's rights where applicable under ss.51 and 52 be excluded: s.57(3). It is probably easiest simply to say that it is unlikely ever to be possible to exclude any of these terms to the detriment of the consumer, nor to have any term restricting the consumer's remedies or preventing particular liabilities arising (s.57(5)), though an arbitration clause is permissible provided it is in writing: s.57(6). The same saving as in s.16 SGSA 1982, that the implied terms do not oust enactments or rules of law imposing stricter duties on the trader is found in s.53(1).

E. IMPLIED TERMS IN MARINE INSURANCE

The Marine Insurance Act 1906 implies a number of terms. In some cases **6.76** these are described as conditions and in other cases as warranties. However, the warranties are in fact conditions in the normal sense in that breach discharges the performance liability of the non-breaching party. Section 33 provides as follows.

33 Nature of Warranty

(1) A warranty, in the following sections relating to warranties, means a promissory warranty, that is to say, a warranty by which the assured undertakes that some particular thing shall or shall not be done, or that some condition shall be fulfilled, or whereby he affirms or negatives the existence of a particular state of fact.

(2) A warranty may be express or implied.

(3) A warranty, as above defined, is a condition which must be exactly complied with, whether it be material to the risk or not. If it be not so complied with, then, subject to any express provision in the policy, the insurer is discharged from liability as from the date of the breach of the warranty, but without prejudice to any liability incurred by him before that date.

6.77 Warranties are not, however, absolute. Section 34 sets out circumstances when non-compliance might be excused, and when it is not excused. These circumstances do not, however, concern us directly here, as they apply to all warranties, express or implied.

6.78 Section 36(2) provides that: 'An express warranty does not exclude an implied warranty, unless it be inconsistent therewith.' This presumably means that there may be an express warranty dealing with a particular issue but this does not exclude the application of an implied warranty also dealing with that issue which is different in scope but otherwise consistent so far as it applies to the actual scope of the express warranty.

1. The implied terms

6.79 There are seven implied terms in the Act. Six are described as warranties and two as conditions. All are in fact conditions, in the normal sense of the term, as discussed in paragraph **6.76**, above. The five implied warranties, so called, are set out in Table 6.2.

6.80 There is no implied term that goods or other moveables insured should in themselves be seaworthy: s.40(1).

2. Voyage policy on vessel

6.81 Voyage policies are distinct from time policies. Time policies give insurance, usually of the ship's hull, for a specific period of time. Voyage policies insure the vessel and/or cargo from A to B. Both time and voyage policies may be comprised in one contract of insurance: s.25 Marine Insurance Act 1906. The implied warranties as to seaworthiness relate to voyage policies.

6.82 The duty is strict (unlike in time clauses, where due diligence by owners and managers excuses), though in relation to hulls it is likely that the policy will include an '*Inchmaree*' (or the similar but wider, and misnamed, 'Liner'

Table 6.2   Statutory implied warranties in marine insurance

Voyage policy on vessel	Voyage policy on goods	The adventure generally
s.39(1): '… at commencement of the voyage the ship shall be seaworthy for the purpose of the particular adventure insured' **s.39(2):** where the policy attaches while the ship is in port, 'she shall, at the commencement of the risk, be reasonably fit to encounter the ordinary perils of the port' **s.39(3):** where the voyage is to be undertaken in stages requiring different preparation or equipment 'at the commencement of each stage the ship is seaworthy in respect of such preparation or equipment for the purposes of that stage'	**s.40(2):** in respect of goods or other moveables: 'at the commencement of the voyage the ship is not only seaworthy as a ship, but also that she is reasonably fit to carry the goods or other moveables to the destination contemplated by the policy'	**s.41:** '. . .the adventure insured is a lawful one, and that, so far as the assured can control the matter, the adventure shall be carried out in a lawful manner'

Negligence) clause specifically insuring against negligence of master, officers, crew or pilots in respect of perils covered by the policy.[67]

'Seaworthiness' is not a purely general notion but depends on the nature of the   **6.83** voyage. Specific instances include whether Danube river barges had been suitably altered for a Black Sea voyage,[68] and whether a shrimp-drying factory vessel was seaworthy for a towage voyage.[69] However, it is outside the scope of this work to discuss the question of seaworthiness in detail, for which recourse should be had to specialist works.

As is typically the case with statute implied terms, the seaworthiness impli-   **6.84** cation had its origins in the common law well before the passage of the Act. As long ago as 1839 the case of *Dixon v. Sadler*[70] dealt with the question of seaworthiness prior to the commencement of each leg of a journey to be completed in stages. The general principle of seaworthiness was considered, and decided along very strict lines, in 1870 in *Quebec Marine Insurance v.*

---

67   See R.J. Lambeth, *Templeman on Marine Insurance*, 5th edn (Macdonald & Evans: Plymouth, 1981) pp. 444–52.
68   *Harocupus v. Mountain* (1934) 49 Ll.L. Rep. 267.
69   *Neue Fischmehl Vertriebsgesellschaft Haselhorst v. Yorkshire Insurance Co.* (1934) 50 Ll.L. Rep. 151.
70   (1839) 8 M & W 895; 151 E.R. 1303. See also *Thin & Sinclair v. Richards & Co.* [1892] 2 Q.B. 141.

Commercial Bank of Canada,[71] in which it was held that a vessel which had been insured for a voyage from Montreal to Halifax, Nova Scotia, had turned back to Montreal, had her boilers repaired, set out once more and then been lost in bad weather, was not seaworthy at commencement, so the insurers were not liable. There is, by the way, no implied warranty of seaworthiness at any stage of the adventure in a time policy: s.39(5) Marine Insurance Act 1906.[72]

3. Voyage policy on goods

6.85 Here the implied term attaches not to the seaworthiness of the goods, as to which there is no implied term (s.40(1) Marine Insurance Act 1906) but to the ship itself, which must at the commencement of the voyage be seaworthy in itself and reasonably fit to carry the goods insured: s.40(2) Marine Insurance Act 1906.

4. Lawfulness of adventure

6.86 Section 41 of the Act implies a term that '… the adventure insured is a lawful one, and that, so far as the assured can control the matter, the adventure shall be carried out in a lawful manner'. This means lawful under English law and, where relevant, under the law of *friendly* foreign nations under the general principle of comity of nations: *Regazzoni v. K.C. Sethia (1944) Ltd*.[73] The term clearly relates to two different things. First, the legality of the adventure in itself,[74] so that a voyage to export illegal ivory, for instance, will clearly be illegal from its outset. Secondly, the voyage must be conducted in a lawful manner, so that if, for instance, a ship refuels at a port in a country which is an enemy of the Crown (whether or not it was so at the time the voyage began), this would be a breach of the term since it is illegal to trade with an enemy.

6.87 It also, in respect to the first of these aspects, affects adventures which are lawful at the outset but become unlawful. In *Sanday v. British & Foreign Marine Insurance Co. Ltd*,[75] two British vessels, the *St Andrew* and the *Orthia*, sailed from the River Plate in 1914, but prior to the outbreak of the Great War, bound for Hamburg with cargoes of linseed totalling £44 000 contracted

---

71 (1870) L.R. 3 P.C. 234.
72 Though American time policies do include an implied term of seaworthiness at the inception of the policy and that the insured will not knowingly permit, through neglect or bad faith allow the ship to break ground in unseaworthy condition during the term of the policy: see the decision of the U.S. Court of Appeals in *Saskatchewan Government Insurance Office v. Spot Pack Inc.* AMC 655 (1957).
73 [1958] A.C. 301; [1957] 2 Lloyd's Rep. 289. Per Viscount Simonds [1958] A.C. 301 at 309.
74 See, e.g., *Parkin v. Dick* (1809) 11 East 502; 103 E.R. 1097.
75 [1915] 2 K.B. 781 (K.B.D. and C.A.).

for sale in Hamburg on c.i.f terms but with a term that property would not pass to the purchasers until delivery. The *St Andrew* additionally carried £800 of wheat which it was intended should be sold in Germany. While they were at sea war was declared and proclamation issued by The King forbidding trade or communication with any part of the German Empire. The two adventures were insured on voyage policies in identical terms save as to the value of their cargoes. The *Orthia* received a cable from her owners when she called at St Vincent for bunkering, directing her to divert to Glasgow. The *St Andrew* was signalled in the Channel by a French cruiser and diverted to Falmouth for safety, from whence she was directed to sail to Liverpool to discharge her cargo. Notice of abandonment was given in respect of the cargoes and a claim made for constructive total loss. One of the underwriters' defences was that the adventure became illegal while at sea and the contract was therefore avoided, in accordance with the implied term. However, since they had at first opportunity been diverted to a lawful adventure and the illegality had arisen from 'restraint of princes', which was covered in the policies, the defence was disallowed and the claim allowed under the cover provided for restraints of princes. The judgment was upheld in the Court of Appeal and subsequently on appeal to the House of Lords,[76] where, however, the illegality argument was not raised.

5. Warranty of neutrality

Two implied conditions attach where a ship is expressly warranted neutral. **6.88** This protects the underwriter in cases where a ship and/or cargo is declared by the insured to be 'neutral'; that is to say that they ought not to be at risk of seizure or destruction by belligerent parties and therefore a lower premium should apply than if the converse were the case. The warranty is set out in s.36 of the Act, as follows:

(1) Where insurable property, whether ship or goods, is expressly warranted neutral, there is an implied condition that the property shall have a neutral character at the commencement of the risk, and that, so far as the assured can control the matter, its neutral character shall be preserved during the risk.

(2) Where a ship is expressly warranted 'neutral' there is also an implied condition that, so far as the assured can control the matter, she shall be properly documented, that is to say, that she shall carry the necessary papers to establish her neutrality, and that she shall not falsify or suppress her papers, or use simulated papers. If any loss occurs through breach of this condition, the insurer may avoid the contract.

---

76 [1916] A.C. 650.

6.89 Lambeth describes this section as calling for 'no special comment'.[77] The nationality of the ship, of course, might be changed during the period of cover and this could be done to maintain neutrality. Changing nationality to that of a belligerent party would clearly be in breach of the plain meaning of s.36, though there is no implied term as to maintenance of nationality of the ship.[78] Clearly an express term to retain nationality might be included in the policy, in which case the assured may have some difficulty as regards maintaining neutrality.

6.90 Ivamy gives a number of examples of the application of the warranty of neutrality.[79] For instance, a Dutch ship is warranted neutral at and from A to B. After she sails war breaks out between England and Holland. There is held to be no breach of the warranty of neutrality.[80] The carrying of proper papers seems to have given rise to a number of disputes. *Bell v. Bromfield*[81] is a rather intriguing case in which the complaint was not that the papers were false – the underwriter had given leave for false papers to be carried with the intention of showing the ship and cargo to be American rather than British – but that they were bad fakes and that this increased the risk of them being condemned as prize (as they were, by a Danish prize court in favour of a privateer). The Court of King's Bench dismissed the underwriter's case on the grounds that all that could be told from the verdict of the prize court was that the ship had been condemned on the basis that it was carrying false papers, not on the basis that the false papers were bad ones.

F. GENERAL OBSERVATIONS

6.91 Three observations occur to the present author. The first is that implication of terms by statute is an exceedingly uncommon device in English law insofar as the incidence in statute law is concerned, but these implications are numerically common in civil litigation, since sales, the various types of lease and hire-purchase (and similar) transactions are common sources of litigation. Marine insurance law likewise affects a very large number of business transactions involving a country which is primarily a trading nation and a maritime trading nation at that (with over 90 per cent of imports and exports transported by sea) and a world centre of marine insurance markets.

---

77 R.J. Lambeth, *Templeman on Marine Insurance*, 5th edn. (Macdonald & Evans: Plymouth, 1981), p. 410.
78 Section 37 Marine Insurance Act 1906.
79 E.R.H. Ivamy, *Chalmers' Marine Insurance Act 1906*, 8th edn. (Butterworths: London, 1976).
80 Citing *Eden v. Parkison* (1781) 2 Dougl. 732; 99 E.R. 468 per Lord Mansfield
81 (1812) 15 East 364; 104 E.R. 882.

The second is that every one of these statute-implied terms is a codification of **6.92** terms already implied at common law. That said, Parliament has, through amendments subsequent to the original legislation, reformed the law through some of these implied terms: specifically, s.14 of the Sale of Goods Act 1979 and its corresponding provisions in the Supply of Goods (Implied Terms) Act 1973 (namely, s.10) and the Supply of Goods Services Act 1982 (namely, s.4). Where Parliament has sought to codify what might be called 'commercial best practice' it has turned not to the device of implied terms but to that of default rules, as can be seen throughout the rest of the Sale of Goods Act 1979.

Thirdly, terms implied by statute are treated differently from terms implied by **6.93** other means. They are not excluded simply because there is an express term in the contract dealing with the issue. If the statutory implied term is wider, then the statutory implied term deals with such matters as fall beyond the express term. In the case of s.12 of the Sale of Goods Act 1979, even an express term stipulating that the implied term does not apply will not exclude it, as it is invalid under s.6(1)(a) of the Unfair Contract Terms Act.[82] The implied terms in ss.13, 14 and 15 S.G.A. 1979 cannot be ousted by an express term in any contract where the buyer is a consumer (s.6(2) U.C.T.A. 1977) and only if reasonable in business-to-business sales contracts: (s.6(3) U.C.T.A. 1977). In this sense, these implied terms are a special case amongst implied terms in general.

---

82   UCTA 1977, s.6(1)(b) contains a corresponding provision in relation to hire purchase.

7

TERMS IMPLIED IN FACT

A. INTRODUCTION

7.01 Up until this point, we have dealt with terms that are naturally implied by operation of law. We began consideration of the substantive law with terms that are implied by the courts into all contracts of a given, identifiable, type: we have designated these 'terms implied at common law'. We continued with terms implied by the courts not as a necessary incident of contracts of the type in question, but on the basis that they are customary in the trade or locality, or (in the case of prior course of dealing) have become the 'localized' expectation of the parties involved. We then considered terms that are implied into contracts by statutes, some of which were formerly implied at common law. Some of these terms can be excluded by express terms, some cannot. Except for the prior course of dealing category, all of these terms are 'out there' and, with sufficient care and skill and patience, can be discovered. They apply to contracts of a type, or within a trade or locality, or involving categories of parties, in which any number of contracting parties might find themselves engaging.

7.02 In this final chapter, we will consider the process known as implication in fact. This process is fundamentally different from other processes of implication of terms in that it involves only the particular contract, the exact transaction, under consideration by the court. All implication of terms is, in a way, an aspect of construction of contracts, in the sense that in order to discover the true meaning and effect of the contract in question we need to see what all the terms are, including those not mentioned. But implication in fact is construction *par excellence*: construction in the sense of interpretation, yes, but also construction in the sense of the making of the contract for the parties *eo instante*.

The law has developed a shorthand term for terms implied in fact into one **7.03** particular contract: they are often called '*Moorcock* terms' after the Court of Appeal case in which the basis for such implication seems first to have been made explicit, namely *The Moorcock*.[1] Any consideration of this category of implication must begin with a thorough examination of *The Moorcock* and proceed to consider the leading cases in light of that. The influence of *The Moorcock*, moreover, has not been confined to implication in fact. As we saw in Chapter 3, it has been much discussed in relation to terms implied at common law, both as a discourse on 'necessity' and as a means of differentiation: terms implied at common law have sometimes been defined in terms of being *other* than *Moorcock* terms.

B. *THE MOORCOCK*

In November 1887, after a course of correspondence and meetings between **7.04** the defendants, operators of St Bride's Wharf, Wapping and the plaintiffs, owners of a steamship, the *Moorcock*, it was agreed that the plaintiffs would use the defendant's services as wharfinger to load, unload and store cargoes carried on the *Moorcock* between London and Antwerp. There were no mooring charges, but the plaintiffs were to pay for the use of the defendants' cranes and for landing and storing goods, and shipping of goods from the wharf. The defendants controlled the wharf and the jetty at which ships were moored, but control of the riverbed was the responsibility of the Thames' Board of Conservators.

Because the Thames is a tidal river at Wapping, the water level at the jetty **7.05** dropped considerably when the tide went out, meaning that vessels moored there would necessarily be grounded every low tide. The plaintiffs sought assurances that the berth would be safe for their vessel. At first instance,[2] Butt J., sitting with two assessors from Trinity House, found that no express assurance had been given, but that the plaintiffs or their agents had been

---

1   (1889) 14 P.D. 64; [1886–90] All E.R. Rep. 530 (C.A.).
2   (1888) 13 P.D. 157 (P.D.A.).

shown a similar sized vessel lying safely at the mooring, and had been thereby satisfied that the *Moorcock*, too, could safely be moored there.[3]

7.06 The other vessel, however, was a bit different from the *Moorcock* and when the latter moored at St Bride's Wharf, and settled on the riverbed when the tide went out, a crack or loud noise was heard: she had, in effect, broken her back. This calamity was a result of a ridge in the riverbed, which could have been, but was not, discovered by the defendants through taking soundings at low tide. The court also learned that, although the riverbed was the sole responsibility of the Conservators, a neighbouring wharfinger had in 1877 obtained permission from the Conservators to level out a section of the riverbed due to problems with snagging propellers.

7.07 Butt J. held that there had been no express warranty of the suitability of the jetty for mooring the vessel;[4] nor did he find, as alleged by the shipowners, an express representation.[5] He did, however, hold that there was an implied representation that the defendants 'had taken reasonable care to ascertain that the bottom of the river at the jetty was in such a condition as not to endanger the vessel …'[6] and that the defendants had not in fact done so. Thus, the basis of the decision at first instance appears to have been misrepresentation rather than breach of contract.

7.08 The defendants appealed to the Court of Appeal, where the case was heard in February 1889 by Lord Esher M.R. and Bowen and Fry L.JJ. Counsel for the appellant wharfingers argued that as the riverbed was vested in the Conservators, who had responsibility for the state of it, the wharf should be regarded as analogous to a warehouse next to a public highway, in which case the warehouseman would have no liability for the state of the road, or to ascertain the state of the road, but was only under a duty not to invite someone to come there if he knew it to be dangerous.[7] As there had been a vessel of 'fully the same length'[8] as the *Moorcock* lying at the jetty and taking no harm, there was nothing to alert the appellants to any danger.

7.09 In the Court of Appeal the respondents repeated their argument at first instance: that the jetty could not be used in the ordinary course of business without the vessel lying at it being grounded at low tide, and it must therefore

---

3 At 159.
4 At 159.
5 At 159.
6 At 160.
7 (1889) 14 P.D. 64, 65.
8 At 65.

have been a term of the contract that the wharfinger had taken care to ascertain that the riverbed was reasonably safe, or else would warn shipowners if it was not safe.[9]

Although the Master of the Rolls expressed himself in terms of agreement **7.10** with Butt J., he actually put the matter on a different footing: not implied representation, but an implied term in the contract. As this judgment is seldom referred to, it is worth quoting from it at some length:

> What, then, is the reasonable implication in such a contract? In my opinion honest business could not be carried on between such a person as the respondent and such people as the appellants, unless the latter had impliedly undertaken some duty towards the respondent with regard to the bottom of the river at this place. If that is so, what is the least onerous duty which can be implied? In this case we are not bound to say what is the whole of the duty. All we have got to say is whether there is not at least the duty which the learned judge in the court below has held does lie on them and to be implied as part of their contract. The appellants can find out the state of the bottom of the river close to the front of their wharf without difficulty. They can sound for the bottom with a pole, or in any way they please, for they are there at every tide, and whether they can see the actual bottom of the river at low water is not material. Supposing at low water there were two feet of water always over the mud, this would make no difference. Persons who are accustomed to the water do not see the bottom of the water with their eyes, they find out what is there by sounding, and they can feel for the bottom and find out what is there with even more accuracy than if they saw it with their eyes, and when they cannot honestly earn what they are desiring to earn without this, it is implied that they have undertaken to see that the bottom of the river is reasonably fit, or at all events that they have taken reasonable care to find out that the bottom of the river is reasonably fit for the purpose for which they agree that their jetty should be used, that is, they should take reasonable care to find out in what condition the bottom is, and then either have it made reasonably fit for the purpose, or inform the persons with whom they have contracted that it is not so. That I think is the least that can be implied as their duty …[10]

It seems, then, that the Master of the Rolls thought that there was an implied **7.11** term in the contract, and that the basis for its implication was that it was the least onerous one necessary, consistent with doing business honestly.

Bowen L.J., however, put the matter somewhat differently:

> Now, an implied warranty, or, as it is called, a covenant in law, as distinguished from an express contract or express warranty, really is in all cases founded on the presumed intention of the parties, and upon reason. The implication which the law draws from

---

9   At 66.
10   At 67.

what must obviously have been the intention of the parties, the law draws with the object of giving efficacy to the transaction and preventing such a failure of consideration as cannot have been within the contemplation of either side … In business transactions such as this, what the law desires to effect by the implication is to give such business efficacy to the transaction as must have been intended at all events by both parties who are businessmen; not to impose on one side all the perils of the transaction, or to emancipate one side from all the chances of failure, but to make each party promise in law as much, at all events, as it must have been in the contemplation of both parties that he should be responsible for in respect of those perils or chances.[11]

The Court of Appeal held that the term to be implied was that the wharfingers warranted that they had taken reasonable care to ascertain the state of the river bed at the jetty (not, as is quite often but quite erroneously stated, that the wharfingers warranted a safe berth for the vessel).[12]

7.12 It is interesting, perhaps, to speculate as to why it has been the judgment of Bowen L.J., not the leading judgment of the more senior judge that has usually been cited by counsel, judges and academics. It is submitted that it simply fits better with the intellectual habits, and the traditional stance, of the common law. The law of contract is 'about' doing business. The idea that a term can be implied in circumstances where it is necessary to give 'such business efficacy to the transaction' as business parties to the contract must have intended, and no more, is not an unattractive one: enterprise is facilitated, one of the key 'uses' of contract,[13] but the intervention is the minimum required to do this. The approach of Lord Esher M.R., however, is broader: the minimum term required to make the contract work assuming that the parties wish to do business *honestly*. The suggestion, then, is that a term will be implied to the extent that it would be expected in a contract made in good faith, a concept that (while a feature of the law of insurance contracts) is, and has been, and was then, essentially alien to the common law of general contracts.[14] However,

---

11 At 68. The reference to '… the presumed intention of the parties, and upon reason' may be considered ambiguous and be taken as the basis for arguments such as Lord Denning's in *Liverpool City Council v. Irwin* [1976] QB. 319 (C.A.) at 329–30 (also reported at [1975] 3 All E.R. 658; [1975] 3 W.L.R. 663) for implication of such terms as are 'reasonable'. Taken in its original context, however, it seems tolerably clear that this is surplusage, and it should always be borne in mind that Bowen L.J. says '*and* upon reason', not '*or* upon reason'. That is to say, the basis for implication is the presumed intention of the parties and, naturally, be a logical inference.

12 See, for example, McMeel, 11.13.

13 See generally H.C. Havighurst, *The Nature of Private Contract* (Northwestern UP: Evanston, Illinois, 1961).

14 Long since then, a requirement of good faith has been imported into the American law of contract by the Uniform Commercial Code, but this is a require ment of performing and enforcing in good faith (U.C.C. §1–203, which should be read together with §1–102(3)), not of making agreements in good faith. The Unfair Terms in Consumer Contracts Regulations 1994 (now 1999) imported a requirement of good faith in the making of agreements into English law, but it only applies where one party contracts as a consumer, the other party contracts otherwise than as a consumer, and the contract is made on the latter's terms, not

that may be, this is not the principle that has been derived by English lawyers from *The Moorcock*. Perhaps the idea was so unlikely that it was not even noticed.

1. The *Moorcock* principle

The principle which can and has been drawn from *The Moorcock* is taken from **7.13** the judgment of Bowen L.J. and can, it is submitted, be expressed in either of two ways:

1. a term will be implied into a contract when it is necessary in order to give the contract business efficacy; or
2. a term will only be implied into a contract if it is necessary to give business efficacy to a contract.

Logically, these two versions are indistinguishable from one another; necessity for business efficacy being the crucial concept; but on a different level they are quite different in the degree of willingness to imply a term: the former seems permissive, the latter restrictive. For example, Greer L.J. in *Foley v. Classique Coaches Ltd*,[15] was clearly emphasizing the permissive element when he said that: 'I think the words of Bowen L.J. in *The Moorcock* are clearly applicable to a case of this kind, and that in order to give effect to what both parties intended the Court is justified in implying that in the absence of agreement as to price a reasonable price must be paid, and if the parties cannot agree as to what is a reasonable price then arbitration must take place.'[16] Maugham L.J. was clearly also thinking that way in his judgment in the same appeal,[17] as had been Lord Hewart C.J. at first instance, as the headnote from the Court of Appeal report shows:

> The Lord Chief Justice, in the course of his judgment, said: '[…] In *The Moorcock* Bowen L.J., in reference to implied terms in contracts, said: "The implication which the law draws from what must obviously have been the intention of the parties, the law draws with the object of giving efficacy to the transaction and preventing such a failure of consideration as cannot have been within the contemplation of either side. … In business transactions such as this, what the law desires to effect by the implication is to

---

individually negotiated. This is a very restricted consumer provision, best regarded, for the time being, as standing outside the English general law of contracts.

15 [1934] 2 K.B. 1; (1934) L.J.K.B. 550; [1934] All E.R. Rep. 88. Applied in *National Coal Board v. Galley* [1958] 1 All E.R. 91; [1958] 1 W.L.R. 16 and *Beer v. Bowden* [1983] 3 All E.R. 662. Distinguished in *Grow With US Ltd v. Green Thumb (UK) Ltd* [2006] E.W.C.A. Civ. 1201, [2006] All E.R. (D) 435 (July).

16 [1934] 2 K.B. 1, 11.

17 At 15.

give such business efficacy to the transaction as must have been intended at all events by both parties who are business men.' The Lord Chief Justice accordingly held that there was a valid and binding contract for the purchase and sale of petrol in accordance with the terms of clauses 1 and 7. If nothing had been said, or if the parties failed to agree the price of the petrol the law would imply that a reasonable price should be paid …[18]

7.14 Here the emphasis is clearly on the desirability of avoiding 'such a failure of consideration as cannot have been within the contemplation of either side',[19] in other words to preserve the contract in being and in sense. It should be noted that in *Foley* the contract would have failed altogether for uncertainty had not a term as to price been implied; so that one can readily assume that the parties must have intended that there be *some* provision, as they surely cannot have intended to make no contract at all at the time they made the contract, whatever they might feel about it by the time it comes into dispute; and so something has to be implied, and a term that the price be agreed at the time of delivery or else be settled by arbitration is clearly a reasonable and indeed not a wholly improbable one, had the parties been asked to direct their minds to it by a wise friend or adviser at the time.

7.15 As will be seen below, we also do not want for examples of Bowen L.J.'s words being used in a restrictive sense, that is, with the emphasis on 'necessary'; such examples can therefore wait their turn.

7.16 Few authorities are cited in *The Moorcock* itself, either in argument or in the judgments. The main cases relied upon seem to have been *R. v. Williams*[20] and *Mersey Docks and Harbour Board Trustees v. Gibbs*.[21] These are both cases sounding in tort; founded on alternative counts of breach of statutory duty, alternatively negligence. They are not contracts cases and although they may have assisted the court in *The Moorcock* so far as they relate to expectations as to the care to be taken by those maintaining docks and harbours (and by analogy, wharves and jetties), they offer little assistance in understanding the legal grounding for the implication of terms into contracts generally. Bowen L.J. also referred to *Coggs v. Barnard*,[22] a leading case on bailments and particularly the duties of a bailee, to cite the dictum of Lord Holt C.J. in that

---

18 At 5–6.
19 (1889) 14 P.D. 64 at 68.
20 (1884) 9 App. Cas. 418, 53 L.J.P.C. 64; [1881–5] All E.R. Rep. Ext. 1313 (P.C.).
21 (1866) L.R. 1 H.L. 93; 11 H.L.C. 686; 35 L.J. Ex. 225; 11 E.R. 1500; [1861–73] All E.R. Rep. 397. Applied in *Re Winding-up of the Christian Brothers of Ireland in Canada* (2000) 3 I.T.E.L.R. 34.
22 (1703) 2 Ld Raym. 909; 91 E.R. 25; 92 E.R. 107; [1558–1774] All E.R. Rep. 1 (Q.B.).

case that 'it would be unreasonable to charge persons with a trust, farther than the nature of the thing puts it in his power to perform it'.[23]

However, there are appellate cases from earlier in the 19th century directly on the question of implied terms, which would have been available to the court as authority had it chosen to refer to them. In *Stirling v. Maitland*,[24] Cockburn C.J. held that it was a necessary implication into a contract between an insurance company and an agent that the company would not do anything to prevent itself from performing its commitments to the agent under the contract, in this case transferring its undertakings to another company and dissolving itself. The Chief Justice said: 'I look upon the law to be that, if a party enters into an arrangement which can only take effect by the continuance of a certain existing state of circumstances, there is an implied engagement on his part that he shall do nothing of his own motion to put an end to that state of circumstances, under which alone the arrangement can be operative.'[25] The same judges as heard that case had also heard *Whittle v. Frankland*,[26] in which it was held that a contract of service included an implication that the employer would find the appellant work and would not discharge him from his service before a certain time.[27] The reason being that the contract, as a contract of service 'would be perfectly illusory [if the court were] to hold otherwise'.[28]

7.17

In *Whittle* reference was made[29] to the case of *Valpy v. Gibson*,[30] which concerned a contract for sale of goods, in which Wilde C.J., giving the judgment of the court, said that:

7.18

> [I]t appears that the price was agreed on, but that the mode and time of payment were not at first specified. But the omission of the particular mode or time of payment, or even of the price itself, does not necessarily invalidate a contract of sale. Goods may be sold, and frequently are sold, when it is the intention of the parties to bind themselves to a contract which does not specify the price or the mode of payment, leaving them to be settled by some future agreement, or to be determined by what is reasonable under the circumstances.[31]

---

23 (1703) 2 Ld Raym. 909, 918.

24 (1864) 5 B. & S. 840; 34 L.J.Q.B. 1; [1861–73] All E.R. Rep. 358. Applied in *C.E.L. Group Ltd v. Nedlloyd Lines U.K. Ltd* [2003] E.W.C.A. Civ. 1716; [2004] 1 All E.R. (Comm.) 689; [2004] 1 Lloyd's Rep. 381.

25 At 852.

26 (1862) 2 B. & S. 49; 121 E.R. 992.

27 At 59, per Cockburn C.J.

28 At 59.

29 At 56.

30 (1847) 4 C.B. 837; 136 E.R. 737. Applied in *Kendall v. Marshall, Stevens & Co.* (1883) 11 Q.B.D. 356; 52 L.J.Q.B. 313 and *Re Isaacs, ex p. Miles* (1885) 15 Q.B.D. 39; 54 L.J.Q.B. 566.

31 At 864.

This dictum clearly suggests that the basis for implication is the presumed intention of the parties, making it a case of implication of terms in fact rather than as an invariable matter of law. Moreover, it is also clear that judges in 1847 were prepared to imply quite a wide range of terms into contracts in order to validate common business practices that might be considered very sloppy (and where, indeed, failure to imply terms would in many cases probably lead to the contract being held void for uncertainty).

7.19 Perhaps the clearest 19th century antecedent for the approach taken in *The Moorcock* is, however, the case of *M'Intyre v. Belcher*.[32] This concerned the sale and purchase of a medical practice, which involved payments continuing to be made from the earnings of the practice in each of the years 1860, 1861, 1862 and 1863 to the vendors, to the extent of one quarter of the earnings in each year.[33] A strong court (Erle C.J. and Williams, Willes and Byles JJ.) held unanimously that a term should be implied that the purchaser should not by his own wilful actions or default, prevent the accumulation of such earnings (in fact, by ceasing to practice). Erle C.J. held that the defendant purchaser had 'wilfully chosen to destroy the goodwill … I think it is necessarily implied from the stipulations in the agreement that the defendant would take common and ordinary care so to carry on the business as to realize receipts. And a wilful omission so to do renders him liable to an action.'[34]

Williams J., concurring, added that:

> In cases of this sort, the court should be cautious not to infringe the golden rule, that contracts are to be construed, not by what one feels would be right, but by what is expressed in or is necessarily to be implied from the language of the parties. Looking at this agreement, although it is true there is no express contract on the part of the defendant to carry on the business for the four years, I think such a contract may be fairly implied.[35]

---

32 (1863) 14 C.B.N.S. 654; 33 L.J.C.P. 254; [1861–73] All E.R. Rep. Ext. 1569. Applied in *Brown & Co. v. Brown* (1877) 35 L.T. 54. Distinguished in *Re English and Scottish Marine Insurance Co. ex p. Maclure* (1870) 5 Ch. App. 737; 39 L.J. Ch. 685 (C.A.), *Rhodes v. Forwood* (1876) 1 App. Cas. 256; 47 L.J.Q.B. 396; [1874–80] All E.R. Rep. 476 (H.L.) and *Hope v. Gibbs* (1877) 47 L.J. Ch. 82 (Ch.D.).

33 Provided that the purchaser was still living at 31 December in each of these years.

34 (1863) 14 C.B.N.S. 654, 664.

35 At 664.

Willes J. concurred,[36] while Byles J., agreeing, said that 'it seems to me that a contract on the defendant's part that he will not wilfully incapacitate himself from carrying on the business so as to earn the profits, is necessarily implied'.[37]

The judgments of Williams and Byles JJ. find particular resonance in that of **7.20** Bowen L.J. just a quarter of a century later, even though *M'Intyre* is not mentioned in *The Moorcock*. It is clear, at least, that the court in *The Moorcock* was not in any sense revolutionary in its approach.

C. IMMEDIATE SUCCESSORS TO *THE MOORCOCK*

The Moorcock has been cited in a good many cases: a Lexis citation search by **7.21** the present author produced nearly 400 citations of reported cases in the courts of England and Wales, and there must be many times that number of occasions when the case has been cited in cases not reported, both in the superior courts and in the county courts. There are still other cases where the principle has been applied without *The Moorcock* being mentioned by name.

It is, of course, quite unnecessary to explore all of these instances. The case has **7.22** been cited so many times in just the Court of Appeal and the House of Lords that we may safely ignore all the instances of its citation in the High Court. Furthermore, it has often been cited in certain categories of case which need not concern us here, inasmuch as they do not really advance our inquiry into the general principles of implication of terms by the courts. For instance, there are very many cases involving specifically duties in relation to moorings, docks, harbours and wharves.[38] It has also come up from time to time in master and servant cases.[39] A particular application has been in cases where frustration has been alleged and argued on the basis of the now somewhat disfavoured

---

36 At 664. Here, Byles J. is using 'contract' to mean 'covenant' or 'term'; he is not referring to 'implied contracts' as such. The terminology is common throughout at least the 19th century.

37 At 665. As noted in Chapter 4, above, McMeel (paragraph 10.30) treats this sort of case as a species of terms implied at common law, that is, 'not to interfere with a necessary pre-existing state of affairs'. This author respectfully disagrees for the reasons given above at paragraphs **4.52–4.53**.

38 See, for example, *The 'Empress'* [1923] P. 97, *The 'Grit'* [1924] P. 246, *The 'Crossbill'* (1928) 30 Lloyd's Rep. 271, *B. Jacob & Sons Ltd v. Bennets Haulage, Warehousing & Wharfage Co. Ltd* (1928) 31 Lloyd's Rep. 284, *S. & R. Steamships Ltd v. Sutton Harbour Improvement Co. (The 'Presto')* (1940) 67 Lloyd's Rep. 398, *The 'Jessmore' (Owners) v. Manchester Ship Canal Co.* [1951] 2 Lloyd's Rep. 512, *Cawood, Wharton & Co Ltd v. Samuel Williams & Sons Ltd (The 'Cawood III')* [1951] P. 270; [1951] 1 Lloyd's Rep. 350.

39 See, for example, *Easton v. Hitchcock* [1912] 1 K.B. 535; (1912) L.J.K.B. 395 (Div.Ct), *Browning & Ors v. Crumlin Valley Collieries Ltd* [1926] 1 K.B. 522, *Howman & Son v. Blyth* [1983] I.C.R. 416; [1983] I.R.L.R. 139.

implied term theory of frustration.[40] (Indeed, Bowen L.J.'s approach makes this theory of frustration perhaps far more satisfactory than current orthodoxy allows.)

7.23 The first cases which help to shed light on our topic are the decisions in *Hamlyn & Co. v. Wood & Co.*[41] and *Miller v. Hancock*.[42] Both of these cases were heard by the Court of Appeal and in both instances Lord Esher and Bowen L.J. formed the panel together with Kay L.J. (the only one of the three who was not on the panel in *The Moorcock*).

1. *Hamlyn v. Wood*

7.24 In *Hamlyn* a brewer had agreed to sell waste products of the brewing process to the plaintiffs, at market price, in preference to other buyers for the next ten years. However, the defendants sold their business to Watneys, who did not adopt the contract. The plaintiffs contended that a term should be implied to the effect that the defendants would not wilfully cease to do business within the ten-year life of the contract. The Court of Appeal unanimously declined to imply any such term. Lord Esher M.R. did not refer to his earlier suggestion that honesty had anything to do with the matter, but expressly adopted Bowen L.J.'s analysis in *The Moorcock*: 'In the case of *The Moorcock*, Bowen, L.J., laid down the principle upon which such implications must be made in terms which seem to me to be really an expansion of the terms I have used, and with which I entirely agree.'[43] What Lord Esher had said was the following:

> I have for a long time understood [the] rule to be that the Court has no right to imply in a written contract any [implied in fact] stipulation, unless, on considering the terms of the contract in a reasonable and business manner, an implication necessarily arises that the parties must have intended that the suggested stipulation should exist. It is not enough to say that it would be a reasonable thing to make such an implication. It must be a necessary implication in the sense that I have mentioned.[44]

---

40   See, for example, *Krell v. Henry* [1903] 2 K.B. 740; (1903) 72 L.J.K.B. 794; [1900–3] All E.R. Rep. 20, *In Re An Arbitration between Shipton, Anderson & Co. and Harrison Brothers & Co.* [1915] 3 K.B. 676; (1915) 84 L.J.K.B. 2137, *F.A. Tamplin Steamship Co. Ltd v. Anglo-Mexican Petroleum Products Co. Ltd* [1916] A.C. 397; (1916) 85 L.J.K.B. 1389; [1916–17] All E.R. Rep. 104, *Re an Arbitration between Comptoir Commercial Anversois and Power, Son & Co* [1920] 1 K.B. 868; (1916) 89 L.J.K.B. 849; [1918–19] All E.R. Rep. 661 (C.A.).

41   [1891] 2 Q.B. 488; (1891) 60 L.J.Q.B. 734; [1891–4] All E.R. Rep. 168 (C.A.). Applied in *Livock v. Pearson Bros* (1928) 33 Com. Cas. 188 (K.B.D.) and *W.H. Gaze & Sons v. Port Talbot Corporation* (1929) 27 L.G.R. 200 (Ch.D.).

42   [1893] 2 Q.B. 177 (C.A.).

43   [1891] 2 Q.B. 488, 491 per Lord Esher M.R.

44   At 491.

Bowen L.J. added practically nothing beyond saying that he agreed with the Master of the Rolls as to declining to imply a term in the instant case, and as to the reasons for so doing.[45]

Lord Esher's terminology here is, it is submitted, significant. The necessity of **7.25** implication arises '… on considering the terms of the contract in a reasonable and business manner … '. An echo of this is found in the words of Scrutton L.J. in *Reigate v. Union Manufacturing Co (Ramsbottom) Ltd*:[46] 'A term can only be implied if it is necessary in the business sense to give efficacy to the contract …'[47] It seems to be meant that in order for a term's implication to be permitted, that term must be 'necessary in a business sense' to give efficacy to the contract, rather than logically necessary to give the contract business efficacy. That is to say, 'necessary' is linked to 'business'. Something could be 'necessary' in the way the word is used by business people, without being a logical necessity as it might be meant by a philosopher (or a lawyer). That Bowen L.J. does not dissent from this – the contrary, in fact – is also significant, naturally.

Also significant are the words 'no right [to imply a term] … unless …'[48] This **7.26** prefigures Scrutton L.J.'s 'only … if' in *Reigate*. Both Lord Esher M.R. and Scrutton L.J. clearly think of the rule as a restrictive rather than an enabling one: not 'if necessary' but *only* if necessary'. This is not, however, necessarily implicit in the judgments in *The Moorcock* itself, and perhaps especially not implicit in Lord Esher's judgment in that case, rooted as it was in the notion of doing business honestly.[49] Lord Esher M.R., in his judgment in *The Moorcock*, did refer to '… the least that can be implied as their duty …',[50] but this has to be read in conjunction with the remainder of the sentence, to the effect that he believed this is what Butt J. had implied at first instance, and his foregoing remark that the Court of Appeal was '… not bound to say what is the whole of the duty. All we have got to say is whether there is not at least the duty which the learned judge in the court below has held does lie on them …'[51] That is to say that Lord Esher's reference to the 'least that can be implied' is not a

---

45 At 493–4.
46 [1918] 1 K.B. 592; (1918) 87 L.J.K.B. 724; [1918–19] All E.R. Rep. 143 (C.A.). Applied in *Re Gramophone Records Ltd* [1930] W.N. 42 (Ch.D.), *Fowler v. Commercial Timber Co. Ltd* [1930] 2 K.B. 1; (1930) 99 L.J.K.B. 529; [1930] All E.R. Rep. 224 (C.A.), *Wettern Electric Ltd v. Welsh Development Agency* [1983] Q.B. 796; [1983] 2 All E.R. 629; [1983] 2 W.L.R. 897, (1983) 47 P. & C.R. 113 (Q.B.D.) and *Nicholson v. Markham* (1997) 75 P. & C.R. 428 (C.A.).
47 At 605.
48 *Hamlyn*, n 41, above, per Lord Esher M.R. at 491.
49 See above, paragraph **7.10**.
50 *The Moorcock*, n 1, above, at 67.
51 Ibid.

statement about the law of implied terms, but about the necessary scope of the appellate court's review being limited in this instance to asking whether the judge went too far, not to establishing the full extent of what can be implied if that was not *less* than what Butt J. had implied.

2. *Miller v. Hancock*

7.27 *Miller v. Hancock*[52] is really a case of implication at common law, and has certainly been treated as such in subsequent cases. However, it will be discussed here because it is evidence for the proposition that, *contra* Mackinnon L.J. in *Shirlaw v. Southern Foundries (1926) Ltd*, who said that 'I fancy that [Bowen L.J.] would have been rather surprised if he could have foreseen that these general remarks of his would come to be a favourite citation of a supposed principle of law,'[53] Bowen L.J. did in fact regard his statement in *The Moorcock* as a general statement of the law. It also illustrates the haziness that can be found at the dividing line between implication in fact and implication at common law, since this implication at common law case was decided using *Moorcock* principles, a difficulty that, as we saw in Chapter 3, stayed with the law over a considerable period of time, resulting in much confusion as to the proper principles for implication at common law.

7.28 *Miller v. Hancock* was an action for personal injuries, brought by a collector for the Midland Railway Company. On making a visit to Messrs Gwynne & Co., tenants of the defendant, in order to collect money owing to the railway company, he fell through the stairs due to a defectively maintained step. The building was let in chambers or office suites, with the stairs, which were the only means of access to the upper floors (Gwynne & Co.'s office was on the second floor), being retained in the control of the landlord. The tenants had an easement over the stairs and it was accepted by both parties that as a matter of law, unless agreed otherwise between the dominant and servient owners, the owner of the dominant tenement must maintain the easement if he wished to use it. The central issue in the case was whether there was such an

---

52 [1893] 2 Q.B. 177; [1891–4] All E.R. Rep. 736 (C.A.). Applied in *Liverpool C.C. v. Irwin* [1977] A.C. 239; [1976] 2 All E.R. 39; (1976) 32 P. & C.R. 43. On the question of liability of the landlord to the visitor, this case was subsequently guidance on implication as between the parties involved (in that case landlord and tenant), as Lord Cross of Chelsea observed in *Liverpool C.C. v. Irwin*: 'Certainly that case, as a decision concerning a claim by a visitor, has been overruled ... But I cite the passage for its common sense as between landlord and tenant, and you cannot overrule common sense' [1977] A.C. 239 at 255. *Miller v. Hancock* may be a case regarding the obligation of landlords of blocks of flats generally, thus a case of implication in law, but it is clear that the court was proceeding on *Moorcock* principles (though without citing *The Moorcock*), as Lord Edmund-Davies made clear in his judgment in *Irwin* at 265–6. Moreover, as the court included both Lord Esher M.R. and Bowen L.J., it is valuable here as providing an insight into their thinking about implied terms, tending to rebut Mackinnon L.J.'s statement in *Shirlaw*.
53 [1939] 2 K.B. 206, 227.

agreement between tenants of the building and the landlords. There being no such term in writing, the plaintiff relied upon the allegation of an implied term in the agreement between the landlords and Gwynne & Co., who had invited him onto the premises, in order to place upon the defendant landlord a duty to maintain, breach of which would give the plaintiff a right of action against the landlords in respect of his injuries.

As noted in our discussion of the case in Chapter 3[54] the Court of Appeal **7.29** went to some trouble in this case to ensure that the clearly meritorious plaintiff did not fail and have to begin a new action against Gwynne & Co. The case boiled down to whose duty it was to keep the staircase in repair. If it was Gwynne & Co.'s responsibility, then the plaintiff's must inevitably fail, but if it was the landlord's duty, then the plaintiff must succeed. The landlord therefore needed to demonstrate that maintenance of the staircase was not its respons- ibility, arguing that the staircase was not demised to the tenant but retained by the landlord, but that the tenants had an easement over the staircase, making them responsible, as a matter of trite law, for the maintenance, citing *Pomfret v. Ricroft*[55] and *Gale on Easements*.

Lord Esher emphasized the relationship between the parties, and his judg- **7.30** ment centred around the case of *Smith v. London & St Katharine Docks Co*[56] and addressed himself to the question of whether the landlord was necessarily responsible for the safety of visitors using the stairs, rather than on the question of responsibility as between landlord and tenant. Bowen L.J., how- ever, did focus on the landlord-tenant relationship:

> It appears to me obvious, when one considers what a flat of this kind is, and the only way in which it can be enjoyed, that the parties to the demise of it must have intended by necessary implication, as a basis without which the whole transaction would be futile, that the landlord should maintain the staircase, which is essential to the enjoyment of the premises demised, and should keep it reasonably safe for the use of the tenants, and also of those persons who would necessarily go up and down the stairs in the ordinary course of business with the tenants; because, of course, a landlord must know when he lets a flat that tradesmen and other persons having business with the tenant must have access to it. It seems to me that it would render the whole transaction inefficacious and absurd if an implied undertaking were not assumed on the part of the landlord to maintain the staircase so far as might be necessary for the reasonable enjoyment of the demised premises.[57]

---

54 See above, paragraphs **3.04–3.05**
55 (1666) 1 Wm Saund. 322
56 (1868) L.R. 3 C.P. 326; 37 L.J.C.P. 217; [1861–73] All E.R. Rep. 580.
57 [1893] 2 Q.B. 177 at 181.

7.31 What seems clear from the approach of the 19th century judges generally, and, of particular significance here, that of the judges in *The Moorcock* themselves, when considering similar cases, is that a pragmatic stance was adopted. The courts at this time, whilst eschewing the suggestion that they introduce reasonable terms in order to secure what would seem to them a 'fair' outcome, nonetheless seem to arrive at what was probably the same result. Moreover, in spite of Mackinnon L.J.'s suggestion that Bowen L.J. would have been surprised at the use being made of his extempore judgment,[58] it appears that Bowen L.J. himself (and Lord Esher M.R.) were happy themselves to do exactly this in subsequent cases, so that Mackinnon L.J.'s remark seems somewhat less than thoroughly well-founded.

D. 20TH CENTURY APPLICATION AND THE 'OFFICIOUS BYSTANDER'

7.32 There have been a good many cases on the matter of terms implied in fact during the century or so following *Hamlyn* and *Miller*, and many possible combinations might be chosen for discussion, while only one combination can be, and a choice must be made. In this section the cases of *Reigate v. Union Manufacturing (Ramsbottom) Ltd*,[59] *Shirlaw v. Southern Foundries (1926) Ltd*,[60] and *Philips Electronique Grand Public S.A. v. British Sky Broadcasting Ltd*,[61] which might fairly be said to be representative of 20th century authorities on terms implied in fact, will be considered in turn in relation to the statement of the law in *The Moorcock*, with a view to establishing the degree of separation or influence that can be discerned. It would probably be fair to say, also, that whatever difficulties there might be in making this selection, no such discussion could fairly or reasonably be had without at least *Reigate* and it is also probably impossible to ignore *Shirlaw*, if not for its own merits, then at least because it is so frequently cited in the textbooks.

1. *Reigate v. Union Manufacturing*

7.33 McMeel treats terms of the type found in *Reigate v. Union Manufacturing Co (Ramsbottom) Ltd and Elton Cop Dyeing Co Ltd*[62] as terms implied at common law: an 'implied term not to interfere in necessary pre-existing state of

---

58   See above, paragraph **7.27**.
59   [1918] 1 K.B. 592; (1918) 87 L.J.K.B. 724; [1918–19] All E.R. Rep. 143 (C.A.).
60   [1939] 2 K.B. 206; [1939] 2 All E.R. 113 (C.A.)
61   [1995] E.M.L.R. 472.
62   [1918] 1 K.B. 592; (1918) 87 L.J.K.B. 724; [1918–19] All E.R. Rep. 143 (C.A.).

affairs'.[63] It is submitted, however, that this is not really a correct categorization. Terms implied at common law have to be terms which relate to an identifiable 'generic' category of contracts: see, for example, *Clarion Ltd v. National Provident Association*.[64] A 'contract in which a pre-existing state of affairs must be maintained to give the contract the efficacy intended by the parties' is not a generic type of contract. Furthermore, a term implied in law is specific to an extent: 'employee to serve faithfully', 'employer not to endanger employee's health', furnished premises 'to be fit for human habitation' and so on. 'Not to interfere with necessary pre-existing state of affairs' is too unspecific, since the question remains 'what state of affairs is necessary and must not be interfered with?' Such terms as these are implied into specific contracts in such form as 'not to wind up X Ltd' or 'not to dispose of asset Y'. They are terms implied in fact, not at common law.

Mackinnon L.J. in *Shirlaw v. Southern Foundries (1926) Ltd*,[65] is often credited **7.34** with the so-called 'officious bystander test', which is supposed to be a different test to that in *The Moorcock*. In fact, while he may well have been the first to refer to an 'officious bystander', the test was not at all new. Scrutton L.J. laid down this test in *Reigate* some 21 years previously. What Scrutton L.J. said on that occasion, which presaged Mackinnon L.J.'s more famous dictum, was no more than a means of explaining the test of *The Moorcock,* as is quite apparent from the following passage from Scrutton L.J.'s judgment:

> A term can only be implied if it is necessary in the business sense to give efficacy to the contract; that is, if it is such a term that it can confidently be said that if at the time the contract was being negotiated some one had said to the parties, 'What will happen in such a case,' they would both have replied, 'Of course, so and so will happen; we did not trouble to say that; it is too clear.' Unless the Court comes to some such conclusion as that, it ought not to imply a term which the parties themselves have not expressed.[66]

There is no hint here that Scrutton L.J., one of the most distinguished commercial lawyers of his, or any other, generation, thought that he was creating an alternative to Bowen L.J.'s test, still less replacing it. This was merely an explanatory gloss as to how one determines whether or not the *Moorcock* test had been met.

---

63   McMeel, para. 10.30.
64   [2002] 2 All E.R. 265; [2000] 1 W.L.R. 1888 (Ch.D.), per Rimer J. at 273.
65   [1939] 2 K.B. 206; [1939] 2 All E.R. 113 (C.A.).
66   [1918] 1 K.B. 592, 605.

7.35   *Reigate* concerned what we would now term a 'commercial agent'.[67] Albert Reigate had been dealing in fabric products from Germany until the outbreak of war in 1914. He approached the Union Manufacturing Company in Manchester and suggested the manufacture of a range of products for which he would be the exclusive agent in Britain, India and the colonies (save for one product, for which he would be sole agent in those areas, except for Manchester). He invested £1000 in the company through a share purchase. The agency was to last for seven years (should he live so long), and thereafter continue until determined by either party on six months' notice. The agreement provided that he was not to accept orders firmly, but only subject to confirmation by the company. However, such confirmation was not to be withheld unreasonably. In 1915 the company was experiencing financial difficulties and asked Mr Reigate to invest some more money to keep them afloat. He tried but was unable to raise the necessary money. The company then told him that the only way forward was for him to give up his agency in respect of the valuable Manchester district. This he declined to do, and the company entered voluntary liquidation. The business was subsequently sold. Mr Reigate sued on the basis that the company had breached the contract by demanding that he step down and then entering liquidation.

7.36   The argument seems to have revolved around whether or not the agreement fell into the *Rhodes v. Forwood* category,[68] in which there was no real commitment to the agent at all, therefore no term, express or implied, to the effect that the principal was not to put itself out of business, and also on some technical points regarding the effect of voluntary as against involuntary liquidation on the employment status of servants of a company.

7.37   The first judgment was given by Pickford L.J., who held that although the company need not accept any order, it could only reject for a good reason, so that even though they might currently have a good reason for rejecting orders at given prices, on the basis that these orders would be uneconomic to fulfil, that state of affairs might not last, so that at some time before termination in accordance with contractual terms, there might be orders secured by Mr Reigate which they would not be entitled to decline, so that he might earn a substantial commission. On that basis, Pickford L.J. held that the company was in breach of an express term of the contract, namely that 'during the term of the agency the company will execute the orders obtained by the plaintiff, which he on his part is bound to use his best endeavours to obtain, subject to a

---

67   Within the meaning of the Commercial Agents (Council Directive) Regulations 1993.
68   (1876) 1 App. Cas. 256; 47 L.J.Q.B. 396; [1874–80] All E.R. Rep. 476. This refers to an agency where although there is a period specified for the agency to last, the only undertaking by the principal is to use the agent for relevant sales it makes, without commitment to making sales at all.

right in the company reasonably to refuse to execute them'.[69] Bankes L.J. agreed with this approach.

Scrutton L.J. looked at the question of an implied term from what we might **7.38** call the other direction. That is to say, having canvassed the express terms of the agreement, and come to the same conclusion as Pickford and Bankes L.JJ., he asked whether there was an implied term to end the contract in certain circumstances other than as provided:

> Is there an implied condition 'that the contract is to remain in force only so long as a certain state of things continues to exist,' and if so, what state of things is to exist which is the condition of the contract remaining in force? As I understand it, it is suggested that the contract is only to remain in force so long as the company carry on their business. Is that a necessary implication? If this matter had been mooted at the time when the contract was being negotiated, I expect that the parties would at once have disagreed as to what the position was. Unless we are satisfied that it is an implication which must necessarily have been in the minds of both parties, we cannot imply a term …[70]

It is clear, however, when we read this passage together with the one already quoted above, that this was a gloss on 'necessary', not a whole new test. *The Moorcock*, interestingly, was not mentioned at all in the case, though the language in discussing implied terms clearly echoes Bowen L.J., as where Scrutton L.J. states that 'a term can only be implied if it is necessary in the business sense to give efficacy to the contract …'[71] The terminology of implication in fact adopted by Bowen L.J. in *The Moorcock* appears, then, to have come to be regarded as standard and, by implication, the *Moorcock* test as trite law, as early as 1918.

2.   *Shirlaw v. Southern Foundries*

This case really is only significant in that it is frequently cited in the textbooks. **7.39** It concerned the employment of a managing director. Mr Shirlaw was taken on by Southern Foundries Limited for a fixed period of ten years. At the time he was taken on this was an independent company, essentially owned by one individual. Its articles of association provided that managing directors could have their directorships terminated like any other director, except that in their case the termination of directorship was subject to their contracts as managing directors. Since Mr Shirlaw's contract gave him a job for ten years (no doubt

---

69   [1918] 1 K.B. 592, 601.
70   At 605.
71   At 605.

terminable for good cause, such as misconduct or incapacity), in effect he could not be removed from his directorship for ten years. If, however, at any point he did cease to be a director, he *ipso facto* and immediately would cease to be a managing director also, since it is inherent in the role of managing director, as opposed to a mere manager, that the individual also be a director of the company. After about three years, the owner sold out to a new company called Federated Foundries Ltd, which was essentially a holding company for a new combination of several smaller companies like Southern Foundries. It had been agreed that all the companies would adopt similar articles of association, and the new articles did not make the termination of directorships subject to contract in the case of managing directors: any director could be removed by lodging at the registered office a document to that effect signed by two directors and the company secretary. At some point Federated decided it wanted to be rid of Mr Shirlaw, but he refused to go, so Federated removed him as a director via the three signature rule and, *ipso facto* and immediately, he of course ceased to be managing director as well.

7.40 Arguments followed as to his terminability and whether he had a 'guaranteed' job for ten years. The case contains much learned discussion of company law rules and concepts, but the key point was whether he could be terminated as managing director within ten years and without either his consent or else the incurring of liability in damages to him. The trial judge, Humphreys J., held that he could not, and a majority of the Court of Appeal agreed. The majority included Mackinnon L.J., who made both his famous remark about the officious bystander and also the remark about the overworking of Bowen L.J.'s remarks in *The Moorcock*.

7.41 Prefacing his statement of the officious bystander test, Mackinnon L.J. referred to 'an essay I wrote some years ago',[72] from which the officious bystander test was a quotation. Andrew Phang has identified the essay as the text of a lecture given by Mackinnon J., as he then was, to the London School of Economics on 3 March 1926 and entitled 'Some Aspects of Commercial Law'.[73] It was not until the slightly later case of *Broome v. Pardess Co-operative Society of Orange Growers (Est. 1900) Ltd*,[74] that Mackinnon L.J. referred to Scrutton L.J.'s judgment in *Reigate* (remaining silent as to the 'officious bystander' who seems to have been displaced by an 'imaginative friend'[75]).

---

72 [1939] 2 K.B. 206, 227.
73 A. Phang, 'Implied Terms, Business Efficacy and the Officious Bystander – A Modern History' [1998] J.B.L. 1, 14. The lecture, of course, came some six years after *Reigate*.
74 [1940] 1 All E.R. 603; (1940) 109 L.J.K.B. 571 (C.A.).
75 At 612.

Phang has also pointed out[76] that the then Mackinnon J. had not been deprecatory of reliance on *The Moorcock* when himself applying it a few years prior to *Shirlaw* in the case of *Wallems Rederij A/S v. Wm H. Muller & Co, Batavia*:

> Applying the principles which were laid down in *The Moorcock* and in similar cases, which one has to apply in order to ascertain whether there is or is not an implied term of the contract, I think that it is an implied term of this and every other charter that if the charterer fails to fulfil his duty in shipping the cargo that he is bound to ship, the shipowner is at liberty to fill up the space in the ship which the charterer has left vacant, if in doing so he is acting reasonably.[77]

7.42 However that may be, Mackinnon L.J. found an implied term that the company would do nothing of its own motion that would terminate the managing directorship contract. Whether that was a necessary implication is debatable. It is at least arguable that any action by Southern Foundries which would lead automatically to the termination of the contract would necessarily be a breach of contract. Although there was some suggestion by counsel that Federated had in fact taken the action terminating the contract, the fallacy of this is obvious: the termination was forced by Federated's actions in having Mr Shirlaw removed as a director, but Southern Foundries was under a contractual obligation to employ him for 10 years that was nowhere made subject to the actions of third parties. Contractual obligations are strict ones and it simply does not matter that Southern had no realistic choice in the matter.[78] Thus, Southern was in breach of an express term of the contract and an implied term was unnecessary.

7.43 The decision of the Court of Appeal was upheld, again by a majority, in the House of Lords,[79] where, however, no reference was made to Mackinnon L.J.'s remarks.

---

76 n. 72, above, at 17.

77 [1927] 2 K.B. 99, 106–7.

78 The strictness of contractual obligations is obvious from cases such as *The Super Servant Two*, in which the sinking of a ship before the commencement of the charter did not excuse the shipowner from performance (in spite of the owner being in no way at fault), since the owner could have chosen to breach another contract by diverting the remaining ship to the instant contract (which could have been performed by either ship): *J. Lauritzen A.S. v. Wijsmuller B.V. (The 'Super Servant Two')* [1990] 1 Lloyd's Rep. 1.

79 [1940] A.C. 701; [1940] 2 All E.R. 445; (1940) 109 L.J.K.B. 461, Lords Atkin, Wright and Porter (Viscount Maugham and Lord Romer dissenting).

3. *Philips Electronique v. British Sky Broadcasting*

7.44 The appeal in *Philips Electronique Grand Public S.A. & Anor v. British Sky Broadcasting Ltd*[80] was heard by Sir Thomas Bingham M.R., Stuart-Smith and Legatt L.JJ., with a single judgment given for the court by the Master of the Rolls. The case concerned agreements between British Satellite Broadcasting[81] ('B.S.B.') and various parts of the Philips electronics empire. These agreements were for the manufacture of receivers to receive and decode satellite transmissions. As with the three-way battle between V.C.R., Betamax and Philips 2000, before it, and the two-way match between H.D. D.V.D. and Blu-ray since, there were two competing formats in the mid-1980s for satellite reception. One used the existing P.A.L. standard, like customers' television sets, and was inferior but inexpensive and the other used D-MAC, a high-definition service, better but relatively expensive. Sky used P.A.L., B.S.B. used D-MAC. In 1989 B.S.B. contracted with Philips for the latter to manufacture receivers in certain numbers for certain periods, and to maintain capacity until 31 December 1992. Between the two dates Sky acquired an untouchable market share in satellite broadcasting, B.S.B. could not operate economically with the number of subscribers it attracted, yielded to the inevitable and merged with Sky. There was a transition period of broadcasting in both P.A.L. and D-MAC, but it was a transition to P.A.L. alone at the end. There would be little call for D-MAC receivers. Philips sued the merged company for breach of contract alleging a variety of implied terms broadly to the effect that B.S.B. would not of its own motion (at any rate before 31 December 1992) reduce or eliminate the requirement for D-MAC receivers. The essential legal basis of the case is a familiar one, echoing *Stirling v. Maitland,*[82] *Whittle v. Frankland,*[83] *M'Intyre v. Belcher,*[84] *Hamlyn v. Wood*[85] and *Shirlaw v. Southern Foundries.*[86]

7.45 Both parties' counsel, and Tuckey J., who had held in favour of Philips and given summary judgment against the merged entity, British Sky Broadcasting, under R.S.C. Order 14A,[87] had accepted the formulation advanced by Lord Simon of Glaisdale on behalf of a majority of the Privy Council in *B.P.*

---

80 [1995] E.M.L.R. 472.

81 Which later merged with Sky to become British Sky Broadcasting.

82 Above, paragraph **7.17**.

83 Ibid.

84 Above, paragraph **7.19**.

85 Above, paragraphs **7.24–7.26**.

86 Above, paragraphs **7.39–7.43**.

87 A variant of the old RSC Order 14, under which the facts were accepted and the party bringing the application alleged that if one or more points of law were resolved in its favour, then judgment in its favour would necessarily follow. In other words, it was the same as the application for summary judgment under

Refinery (Westernport) Pty Ltd v. President, Councillors and Ratepayers of Shire of Hastings,[88] as 'an accurate and comprehensive statement of the law on implied terms'.[89] What Lord Simon had said was:

> Their Lordships do not think it necessary to review exhaustively the authorities on the implication of a term in a contract which the parties have not thought fit to express. In their view, for a term to be implied, the following conditions (which may overlap) must be satisfied: (1) it must be reasonable and equitable;
>
> (2) it must be necessary to give business efficacy to the contract, so that no term will be implied without it; (3) it must be so obvious that "it goes without saying"; (4) it must be capable of clear expression; (5) it must not contradict any express term of the contract.[90]

The Master of the Rolls, however, cautioned that this could be 'almost misleading' in its simplicity.[91] He went on to comment that:

> The courts' usual role in contractual interpretation is, by resolving ambiguities or reconciling apparent inconsistencies, to attribute the true meaning to the language in which the parties themselves have expressed their contract. The implication of contract terms involves a different and altogether more ambitious undertaking: the interpolation of terms to deal with matters for which, ex hypothesi, the parties themselves have made no provision. It is because the implication of terms is so potentially intrusive that the law imposes strict constraints on the exercise of this extraordinary power.[92]

After going on to discuss the paradigm cases for implication (for example, that **7.46** a surgeon employ due skill and care[93]), and noting the increasing difficulty encountered as a case moves further away from the paradigm,[94] the Master of the Rolls cited with approval the dictum of Scrutton L.J. in *Reigate*, already given above,[95] adding that '... it is not enough to show that had the parties foreseen the eventuality which in fact occurred they would have wished to make provision for it, unless it can also be shown either that there was only one contractual solution or that one of several possible contractual solutions would

---

Order 14, but permitted a significant dispute on the law, which Order 14, properly speaking did not (though in practice Order 14 applications and appeals often did involve extensive legal argument).
88   (1978) 52 A.L.J.R. 20, 26 (P.C.).
89   [1995] E.M.L.R. 472, 480.
90   (1978) 52 A.L.J.R. 20, 26.
91   [1995] E.M.L.R. 472, 481.
92   At 481.
93   See above, paragraph **4.47**.
94   [1995] E.M.L.R. 472, 481–482.
95   Above, paragraph **7.25**.

without doubt have been preferred',[96] citing as authority *Trollope & Colls Ltd v. North West Metropolitan Regional Hospital Board*.[97]

7.47   The Master of the Rolls then held,[98] allowing BSkyB's appeal, that he would not imply the term ('term 3', to wit that 'the defendant would not commit any act which would tend to impede or render impossible the marketing of the Receivers and/or to render the Receivers useless or unmarketable'[99]) which Tuckey J. had implied in giving judgment for Philips. He doubted whether the inclusion of the word 'impede' left it 'sufficiently clear to be reasonable',[100] but then dismissed the term on the 'more important' ground that 'we question whether, in this unusual factual situation, B.S.B. would have been willing to circumscribe its commercial freedom to this extent in advance' and that '[h]ad some protection been reasonable for Philips there is no knowing what form it would have taken, and no protection was necessary to enable Philips to perform the rather unusual obligations it undertook'.[101] He agreed with Tuckey J. in rejecting other terms, considering terms 4 and 5 as useless to Philips and term 6 (which would have inhibited BSkyB from warning the public that D-MAC would soon be useless) unreasonable.[102]

7.48   It is submitted, with respect, that the Master of the Rolls rather muddied the waters here. Having tentatively suggested that Lord Simon's formulation might be misleadingly simple (or, rather, might mislead people into thinking that it is simple), he then adopts some of its language. Or does he? He talks about the lack of clarity of 'impede', but apparently rejects term 3 on grounds that it was unlikely on commercial grounds that the parties would have agreed to it. Term 6, on the other hand, is dismissed because 'it could not be described as equitable or obvious; and it certainly was not necessary to give the contract business efficacy'.[103] But it is submitted that there is ample reason to suppose that 'obviousness' is a gloss on 'necessity', not a separate consideration, at least so far as previous authorities apart from the *Shire of Hastings* case are concerned. Moreover, the Master of the Rolls does not consistently apply a multi-staged test to each alleged implied term, or suggest that this should be done. *Philips Electronique* leaves us uncertain as to whether it was the intention of the Court of Appeal to adopt the Simon formulation or to disapprove it, or to warn against any such formulaic approaches.

---

96   [1995] E.M.L.R. 472, 482.
97   [1973] 1 W.L.R. 601 at 609–610 and 613–14. Also reported at [1973] 2 All E.R. 260.
98   [1995] E.M.L.R. 472, 483.
99   At 479.
100   At 483.
101   At 483.
102   At 484.
103   At 484.

Shire of Hastings, as a Privy Council case is only persuasive authority, and it is **7.49**
submitted that *Philips Electronique* is too equivocal in its treatment of the case
for us to accept that the Simon formulation has been brought into English law
as approved by the Court of Appeal. The single judgment, and lack of a clear
statement as to what the court thought the basis of implication of terms in fact
should be, make this case, the present author would argue, one of very doubtful
value as authority.

Given many strong statements, not least in *Reigate* in 1918 and in *Bunge* **7.50**
Corporation v. Tradax[104] in 1981, repeating the business efficacy approach and,
in the latter case, positively and expressly commending Bowen L.J.'s approach
in *The Moorcock*, and given the doubtful origins and significance of Mackinnon
L.J.'s approach in *Shirlaw*, we cannot with confidence say that the *Moorcock*
test suffered genuine competition, let alone replacement, in the century-and-
a-bit following its formulation.

4. Since *Philips Electronique*

Since *Philips Electronique, The Moorcock* has been cited in arguments or **7.51**
judgments in the courts of England and Wales, just in reported cases, over 90
times at the time of writing.[105] The most recent citation (at the time of
writing) in the House of Lords was by Lord Scott of Foscote, citing it with
approval as the test for implication of terms in *Concord Trust v. Law Debenture
Trust Corporation plc*, where he referred to it in dismissing the existence of an
implied term in a trust deed concerning Eurobonds:[106]

> [36] The act that would have to constitute the breach of contract is the giving of an
> invalid notice of acceleration, or, perhaps, having regard to the claims apparently made
> in the arbitration, the unjustified assertion of the occurrence of an event of default.
> There is nowhere in the trust deed any express undertaking by the trustee not to do
> either of those things. So a suitable implied term would have to be read into the trust
> deed.
>
> [37] Various tests for the implication of terms into a contract have been formulated in
> various well-known cases. In particular, a term will be implied if it is necessary to give
> business efficacy to the contract (see *The Moorcock* ...). The proposed implied term
> cannot satisfy this test. The trust deed works perfectly well without the implied term.

---

104   [1981] 2 All ER 513, [1981] 1 WLR 711, [1981] 2 Lloyd's Rep 1 (H.L.). Applied in *Locke v. Bellingdon*
      (2002) 65 W.I.R. 19 (Barb. C.A.).
105   March 2009.
106   [2005] U.K.H.L. 27; [2005] 1 All E.R. (Comm.) 699 at [36] and [37].

7.52 The following year, in the Court of Appeal, Buxton L.J. made reference to *The Moorcock* in refusing to imply a term into a franchise agreement in *Grow with US Ltd v. Green Thumb (UK) Ltd*.[107] He referred[108] to Bowen L.J.'s statement that 'the implication which the law draws from what must obviously have been the intention of the parties, the law draws with the object of giving efficacy to the transaction and preventing such a failure of consideration as cannot have been within the contemplation of either side',[109] before concluding that the instant case did not fulfil this criterion.[110]

7.53 More recently still, the *Moorcock* test was relied on by Sir Anthony Clarke M.R. in the Court of Appeal in *Legal & General Assurance Society Ltd v. Expeditors International (UK) Ltd*.[111] This concerned a lease agreement and the exercise of a break clause by the tenant. The question arose whether there was an implied term that the issue of certain notices would terminate the tenancy. The Master of the Rolls referred in passing to the officious bystander test, which the judge at first instance had referred to, and then cited the *Moorcock* test that the term must be necessary to give business efficacy to the contract,[112] concluding that in this case such a term was so necessary.[113]

5. *Belize Telecom* and *BNP Paribas v. Marks & Spencer*

7.54 Some attention might be expected to be paid at this juncture to the case of *A.-G. of Belize & Others v. Belize Telecom Ltd & Another*.[114] This case caused something of a flurry of academic comment as well as a flurry of references in the courts. The case concerned some of the sequellae to the privatization of the national telecommunications undertaking of Belize. It is not necessary to go into the details of the privatization, but they involved the establishment of a company called Belize Telecommunications Ltd in which the government initially retained a golden share (referred to in the case as 'the special share') and a holding of ordinary shares which would be gradually divested. A private company called Belize Telecom Ltd was set up for the purpose of acquiring a substantial part of the shareholding and control of the business. The immediate factual background of the dispute was set out in the following terms in the Privy Council by Lord Hoffmann, who gave the only judgment:

---

107   [2006] E.W.C.A. Civ. 1201, [2006] All E.R. (D) 435 (Jul).
108   At [24].
109   (1889) 14 P.D. 64, 68.
110   [2006] E.W.C.A. Civ. 1201 at [25].
111   [2007] E.W.C.A. Civ 7, [2007] All E.R. (D) 166.
112   At [64].
113   At [65].
114   [2009] U.K.P.C. 10; [2009] 2 All E.R. 1127.

[11] … In 2004 the first respondent, Belize Telecom Ltd (BT), acquired from the government the special share and a majority of the issued share capital, including majorities of both the B and C ordinary shares. It purported to appoint all eight directors: two as special shareholder tout court, two as majority B shareholder; two as special shareholder holding more than 37.5 per cent of the issue share capital and two as majority C shareholder. […]

[12] BT pledged the ordinary shares to the government to secure borrowings which had financed the purchase. Within less than a year, however, it defaulted on its obligations. On 9 February 2005, pursuant to the pledge agreement, the government took back a substantial number of the ordinary shares. The result was that BT was left with the special share and C shares amounting to less than 37.5 per cent of the issued share capital.

The holder of the special share had the right to appoint and remove two directors described as 'government appointments' and various other rights and vetoes, some of which depended on the level of holdings of ordinary shares, but most of which do not directly concern this discussion. What was directly in issue in the case was the fate of the two C shareholder directors not appointed by the majority of C shareholders but by right of holding the special share and holding 37.5 per cent of the paid-up capital of the company in C shares. BT had qualified to make these two appointments by dint of holding the special share and a majority of C shares. After the government took back ordinary shares under the pledge agreement, BT was left with the special share but without the qualifying number of C shares to appoint to, or remove from, these two seats on the board. The Articles of Association were silent as to what was to happen in this event. The appellants argued that there must be a term implied in them that in this event they automatically retire, as it would be absurd that they should remain indefinitely in office. The respondents argued contrariwise. At first instance in the Supreme Court of Belize, Conteh C.J. held in favour of the appellants. In the Belizean Court of Appeal this decision was reversed on the grounds that such a term could not be reconciled with the actual wording of the Articles. And so the case came to the Privy Council.

Lord Hoffmann's judgment is, with respect, apt to generate some confusion. **7.55** There is no rejection of the 'business efficacy test' or the 'officious bystander test'[115] nor of the dicta of Lord Simon of Glaisdale in the *Shire of Hastings* case.[116] Rather, there is an attempt to make sense of the process of implication in fact into a complex and detailed instrument, in this case Articles of

---

115 Indeed the headnote in the All England Reports states '[d]icta of Lord Bown in *The Moorcock* (1889) 14 PD 64 at 64 [sic. – presumably 'at 68' is meant] applied …'.
116 *B.P. Refinery (Westernport) Pty Ltd v. President, Councillors and Ratepayers of Shire of Hastings* (1978) 52 A.L.J.R. 20 (P.C.) and see above.

Association, as a method of construction of such an instrument. Repeated references are made to 'instrument' throughout the judgment, suggesting that this is not an approach which is necessarily applicable when considering contracts which are oral, partly oral and partly written, or oral but evidenced in writing.

7.56 This decision and the reasons for it were hailed by some commentators as a major change in the law, sweeping aside the *Moorcock* test of being necessary in a business sense to give efficacy to the contract and substituting a test, in effect, of whether the term would cause the contract to have the effect a reasonable business person would think it was meant to have.[117] Other commentators, however, have seen the case in subtler shades. John McCaughran argues that the test is ultimately not dissimilar to the *Moorcock* approach, making the implication of a term in fact depend upon the commercial aims of the parties and common sense,[118] while Hugh Collins, writing more broadly on implication, includes *Belize* in a useful discussion on the relationship between implication and interpretation.[119] It is probably fair to say, therefore, that commentators did not all see the decision in the same light. And despite a flurry of applications of the judgment in English cases there has not been unanimity in the courts. Notably, the Singapore Court of Appeal in *Foo Jong Peng & Ors v. Phua Kiah Mai & Ors*[120] not only stated baldly that the decision was not law in Singapore but also reiterated that implication and interpretation are two quite different things, with which the present author can only respectfully agree: see discussion in Chapter 2, above. The judgment of Andrew Phang J.A. in that case contains a fine discussion on the distinction and on the rules relating to implication, which rewards reading.

7.57 In the submission of the present author, the question seems to be formulated like this: 'We have an instrument before us, which is such as is meant to contain the whole agreement of the parties. It is not clear upon the face of that instrument what is to happen in such circumstances as have in fact eventuated. If a proper grammatical construction of the actual wording fails to reveal the answer then the court must construe the contract as a whole as meaning what a reasonable business person having possession of the relevant factual background (in the case of Articles of Association, which is published and available

---

117 See, e.g., C. Peters, 'Implication of Terms in Fact' (2009) 68 C.L.J. 513; K. Low and K. Loi, 'The Many Tests for Terms Implied in Fact' (2009) 125 L.Q.R. 561; B. Cain, 'The Implication of Contractual Terms in the New Millennium' (2011) 51 *Canadian Business Law Journal* 170; R. Hooley, 'Implied Terms After Belize Telecom' (2014) 73 C.L.J. 315.

118 J. McCaughran, 'Implied Terms: the Journey of the Man on the Clapham Omnibus' (2011) 70 C.L.J. 607.

119 H. Collins, 'Implied Terms: The Foundation in Good Faith and Fair Dealing' (2014) 67 *Current Legal Problems* 297.

120 [2012] S.G.C.A. 55, 149 Con.L.R. 117.

to anyone to read, this is only what is inherent in the document, excluding any extrinsic knowledge only available to some people) would think it meant. If it is *necessary* then to imply a term into the instrument to make it mean that, then it is legitimate to do so.' The fact that the actual words of the instrument cannot be made to state what it is thus concluded must have been intended is not a bar to the implication.[121] All this, however, assuming it is legitimate, does not appear to extend beyond implication into a written instrument as a method of giving effect to the outcome of a process of construction of that instrument.

The question of the true meaning and effect in English law of the judgment in **7.58** *Belize* has, it seems, been authoritatively settled by the United Kingdom Supreme Court (Lords Neuberger (P), Clarke, Sumption, Carnwath and Hodge) in the case of *Marks and Spencer plc v. B.N.P. Paribas Securities Services Trust Company (Jersey) Ltd & Anor.*[122] This case concerned the question of whether a term was to be implied into a lease of commercial premises that if the tenant exercised its break clause so as to terminate the lease after payment of a quarterly-in-advance rent instalment but before the next quarter began, the rent should be apportioned by the landlord and the appropriate portion repaid to the tenant. The Supreme Court were unanimous rejecting the implication of such a term. The leading judgment was given by Lord Neuberger, with whom Lords Sumption and Hodge agreed.

Lord Neuberger, after a survey of some of the leading cases and a discussion of **7.59** the general principle of implication as part of the process of construction or interpretation of the contract, as apparently suggested by Lord Hoffmann in *Belize*, drew the following conclusions:

[22] … Lord Hoffmann suggested that the process of implying terms into a contract was part of the exercise of the construction, or interpretation, of the contract. In summary, he said at para 21 that '[t]here is only one question: is that what the instrument, read as a whole against the relevant background, would reasonably be understood to mean?'. There are two points to be made about that observation.

[23] First, the notion that a term will be implied if a reasonable reader of the contract, knowing all its provisions and the surrounding circumstances, would understand it to be implied is quite acceptable, provided that (i) the reasonable reader is treated as reading the contract at the time it was made and (ii) he would consider the term to be so obvious as to go without saying or to be necessary for business efficacy …

Further:

121   See *Belize*, above, at [34].
122   [2015] U.K.S.C. 72.

[24] It is necessary to emphasise that there has been no dilution of the requirements which have to be satisfied before a term will be implied, because it is apparent that *Belize Telecom* has been interpreted by both academic lawyers and judges as having changed the law. [...] [In] *Foo Jong Peng v. Phua Kiah Mai* [2014] 4 S.L.R. 1267, paras 34–36, the Singapore Court of Appeal refused to follow the reasoning in *Belize* at least in so far as 'it suggest[ed] that the traditional "business efficacy" and "officious bystander" tests are not central to the implication of terms' ... The Singapore Court of Appeal were in my view right to hold that the law governing the circumstances in which a term will be implied into a contract remain unchanged following *Belize Telecom*.

Finally, Lord Neuberger observed that:

[31] ... Lord Hoffmann's observations in *Belize Telecom*, paras 17–27 are open to more than one interpretation [on the points as to the rule for implication of terms in fact and of implication being part of the exercise of construction] ... and ... some of those interpretations are wrong in law. In those circumstances, the right course for us to take is to say that those observations should henceforth be treated as a characteristically inspired discussion rather than authoritative guidance on the law of implied terms.

If an even more explicit statement were needed, attention might also be drawn to paragraph [26] in which Lord Neuberger states that: 'I accept that both (i) construing the words which the parties have used in their contract and (ii) implying terms into the contract, involve determining the scope and meaning of the contract. However, *Lord Hoffmann's analysis in Belize Telecom could obscure the fact that construing the words used and implying additional words are different processes governed by different rules*.' [Emphasis added.]

7.60   Lord Carnwath delivered a judgment assenting to the dismissal of the tenant's appeal but taking the view that the starting point from now on in cases of implication in fact should be *Belize* (a difficult proposition in those cases, like *The Moorcock* itself, where there is not a single instrument purporting to contain the whole of the contract). However, his Lordship states, in paragraphs [59] and [60], that the respondents in the instant case were correct in their argument that 'the judgment [in *Belize*] should not be read as involving any watering down of the traditional tests'.[123] If that is so, then it is hard to see how *Belize* takes us any further, or why Lord Carnwath '... would have been content to take [his] starting point not in the 19th century cases (such as *The Moorcock*), but in the most modern treatment at the highest level ... undoubtedly to be found in the judgment of the Privy Council in the *Belize* case'.[124] The *Belize* case does not involve an iteration of the requirement that the term

---

123   At [59].
124   At [58].

must be necessary for 'business efficacy' and be so obvious as to go without saying, and therefore in the submission of the present author is not of paramount assistance in deciding whether a term should be implied in fact, unlike *The Moorcock, Reigate v. Union Manufacturing* and *Shirlaw v. Southern Foundries*. Lord Carnwath's remarks are largely addressed, however, to the question of the relationship between interpretation and implication, leaning more towards the apparent gravamen of Lord Hoffmann's approach.

Lord Clarke, who had been on the panel in *Belize*, added some remarks of his **7.61** own, in agreeing with Lord Neuberger, both as to the outcome and the reasoning, explaining his own position as regards the relationship between interpretation or construction on the one hand and implication on the other, an explanation which his membership of the *Belize* panel makes particularly helpful. It is clear from his remarks that Lord Clarke does not share Lord Hoffmann's view that implication is merely a part of the process of implication, if that is what Lord Hoffmann meant:

> [76] As Lord Carnwath says at para 62, I did not doubt Lord Hoffmann's observation that 'the implication of a term is an exercise in the construction of the contract as a whole'. I recognise, however, in the light of Lord Neuberger's judgment, especially at paras 22 to 31, that Lord Hoffmann's view involves giving a wide meaning to 'construction' because, as Lord Neuberger says at para 27, when one is implying a word or phrase, one is not construing words in the contract because the words to be implied are *ex hypothesi* and not there to be construed. However, like Lord Neuberger (at para 26) I accept that both (i) construing the words which the parties have used in their contract (ii) implying terms into the contract, involve determining the scope and meaning of the contract. On that basis it can properly be said that both processes are part of construction of the contract *in a broad sense*. [Emphasis added.]

The present author respectfully agrees with Lord Clarke on this point.

It would be remiss not to touch on the question of comments made in both **7.62** cases about the dictum of Lord Simon in the *Shire of Hastings* case. In *Belize Telecom* Lord Hoffmann recited the conditions stated by Lord Simon[125] and said[126] that the Board:

> considers that this list is best regarded, not as a series of independent tests which must each be surmounted, but rather as a collection of different ways in which judges have tried to express the central idea that the proposed implied term must spell out what the contract actually means, or in which they have explained why they did not think that it did so.

---

125   See above, paragraph **7.45**.
126   *Belize* at [27].

Lord Neuberger says in *Marks & Spencer*:

> as Lord Hoffmann I think suggested in [*Belize*], although Lord Simon's requirements are otherwise cumulative, I would accept that business necessity and obviousness, his second and third requirements, can be alternatives in the sense that only one of them needs to be satisfied, although I suspect that in practice it would be a rare case where only one of those two requirements would be satisfied.[127]

It may be left to the judgment of the reader whether Lord Neuberger's interpretation of Lord Hoffmann's remarks accurately reflects the latter's meaning, which might be taken to be that satisfying any one of those conditions is sufficient alone to justify implication, or is intended as a corrective.

7.63   In his judgment, Lord Neuberger also made reference to dicta in two cases which had come before the Supreme Court since the decision in *Belize*. At paragraph [17] he said: 'More recently, the test of "necessary to give business efficacy"' to the contract in issue was mentioned by Lady Hale in *Geys* at para 55 and by Lord Carnwath in *Arnold v. Britton* ... para 112. The extent to which Lady Hale and Lord Carnwath understand the test in the same way or would apply it in the same way may best be gauged by reading the passages to which Lord Neuberger referred.

7.64   In *Geys v. Société Générale, London Branch*,[128] Lady Hale said this:

> [55] In this connection, it is important to distinguish between two different kinds of implied terms. First, there are those terms which are implied into a particular contract because, on its proper construction, the parties must have intended to include them: see *Attorney General of Belize v Belize Telecom Ltd*. Such terms are only implied where it is necessary to give business efficacy to the particular contract in question.

While in *Arnold v. Britton & Ors*,[129] Lord Carnwath said:

> [112] Another permissible route to the same end is by the implication of terms 'necessary to give business efficacy to the contract'. I refer again to Lord Hoffmann's words, this time in *Attorney General of Belize v Belize Telecom Ltd* [2009] 1 WLR 1988, para 22, explaining the 'two important points' underlined by that formulation:
>
> "The first, conveyed by the use of the word 'business', is that in considering what the instrument would have meant to a reasonable person who had knowledge of the

---

127   At [21].
128   [2012] U.K.S.C. 63; [2013] 1 A.C. 523; [2013] 1 All E.R. 1061; [2013] 2 W.L.R. 50.
129   [2015] U.K.S.C. 536; [2015] A.C. 1619; [2015] 1 All E.R. 1; [2015] 2 W.L.R. 1593.

relevant background, one assumes the notional reader will take into account the practical consequences of deciding that it means one thing or the other. In the case of an instrument such as a commercial contract, he will consider whether a different construction would frustrate the apparent business purpose of the parties ... The second, conveyed by the use of the word 'necessary', is that it is not enough for a court to consider that the implied term expresses what it would have been reasonable for the parties to agree to. It must be satisfied that it is what the contract actually means."

In the light of the above, the present author has no hesitation in stating that **7.65** *Belize Telecom* does not affect the law on implication of terms in fact, with the possible exception of being an instance of departure from the strict version of the rule that terms may not be implied into Articles of Association as to do so is a fraud on investors as seen, for example in *Bratton Seymour Service Co Ltd v. Oxborough*.[130] The comment of Lord Neuberger already set out above at paragraph **7.59**, namely that the judgment in *Belize* should and will be taken henceforth 'as a characteristically inspired discussion rather than authoritative guidance on the law of implied terms' seems apt.

Whatever some judges may have thought about it, *The Moorcock* has not gone **7.66** away. It is, as we have seen, still regularly cited and discussed in the courts, and it still provokes academic discussion, with lawyers and jurists trying in particular to establish the relationship between Bowen L.J.'s formulation and the 'officious bystander' test. As we have seen, Mackinnon L.J. clearly thought 'his' test was a clearer or more complete or just more accurate test, and quite distinct from Bowen L.J.'s formulation, while Lord Simon in the Privy Council in the *Shire of Hastings* case[131] saw the two tests as separate parts of a larger scheme for determining implication in fact. In turn, Sir Thomas Bingham M.R. cast doubt on the *Shire of Hastings* approach as being potentially 'misleading' by over-simplifying.[132]

Andrew Phang, then an academic, now a judge, in the article cited above, **7.67** seems to have concluded that the tests are essentially complementary.[133] Lord Steyn[134] and Lord Hoffmann[135] have each opined that the implication of

---

130   [1992] BCLC 693.

131   (1978) 52 A.L.J.R. 20.

132   Above, paragraph **7.45**.

133   A. Phang, 'Implied Terms, Business Efficacy and the Officious Bystander – A Modern History' [1998] J.B.L. 1. See also A. Phang, 'Implied Terms Revisited' [1990] J.B.L. 394, and 'Implied Terms in English Law' [1993] J.B.L. 242.

134   J. Steyn, 'The Intractable Problem of the Interpretation of Legal Texts' (2003) 25 *Sydney Law Review* 5, 11.

135   *South Australia Asset Management Corporation v. York Montague Ltd* [1997] A.C. 191, 212.

terms in fact is no more than an instance of the process of judicial interpretation and construction of contracts. Professor Sir John Smith clearly considered the *Moorcock* formulation to be at least as current as the 'officious bystander', and seems to consider both to be more or less equally stringent in their requirements.[136] Adam Kramer, after an excellent survey of the different opinions concluded that it is not necessary to take sides.[137] The present author believes he should take sides, nonetheless, and submits that the 'officious bystander' test, historically-speaking, at least, is simply a gloss on the Bowen L.J. formulation; a useful way of applying the *Moorcock* principle in practice.

7.68 In this chapter we have looked at the question of the essential permissiveness against the essential restrictiveness of the *Moorcock* test. The potential permissiveness no doubt accounts for counsel 'flushing' Bowen L.J.'s words at judges too readily, as Mackinnon L.J. saw it in *Shirlaw*. As has been pointed out, it is really neither purely or essentially permissive, nor purely or essentially restrictive, since whether one formulates the test in permissive language or in restrictive language, the resultant formulations are logically identical. Perhaps the reason is that both permission and restriction are bound up in the same passage: that is to say that it involves two statements, the first permissively-phrased and the second restrictively:

1.   It is permissible to imply a term in fact, where not to do so would lead to a failure of consideration (total or otherwise[138]) that the parties cannot have had in their contemplation at the time they made the contract; but
2.   In this case it is only permissible to imply such a term, and no more, as is necessary, in a business sense, to make the contract make sense.

7.69 These are not, however, entirely separate, still. Both relate to the presumed intentions of the parties. We presume that the parties would not intend a total failure of consideration, of course, otherwise there would be no point making a contract at all. Some failure of the consideration from one party's perspective, however, would need to be sufficient that, had the possibility been suggested at the time the contract was made, even the other party would have disowned such an intention. The court must then, in applying the second of the statements, consider what the minimum term would be that the two parties were at all likely to have arrived at, as practical businesspeople, as an acceptable solution. In this case we are clearly assuming that the party against whom the

---

136   J.C. Smith, 'Contracts – Mistake, Frustration and Implied Terms' (1994) 110 L.Q.R. 400.
137   A. Kramer, 'Implication in Fact as an Instance of Contractual Interpretation' (2004) 63 C.L.J. 384, 398.
138   There is, of course, no necessity for the consideration to have failed entirely. Clearly some benefit may have passed under the contract (for example, the cargo may have been unloaded under a contract such as that in *The Moorcock*).

term is alleged was the most effective of bargainers and kept the term to the least that could possibly be endured by the other party. Reasonableness is not, it is submitted, another limb to consider at all, as Lord Simon seemed to think in *Shire of Hastings*, but will necessarily be inherent in the process of arriving at the minimum term, since it is implicit in the notion that the alleging party will endure it, and is the best likely to have been got by the other party had the matter been negotiated over when the contract was originally made.

E. CONCLUSIONS

7.70 In this chapter, we have been concerned with the often vexed issues of what is the proper test for implication in fact and what is the relationship between the 'business efficacy test' and the 'officious bystander test'? Has the latter displaced the former? Is the latter supplementary in that, having established that a term is necessary to give business efficacy to the contract in question, one must then pose the officious bystander's question? Or even, as Lord Denning suggested in the Court of Appeal in *Liverpool C.C. v. Irwin*, are they alternatives: a term may be implied if either one of these tests is satisfied, implying that a term might fail one but not the other? Around these questions the fundamental problem of implication in fact revolves, at least so far as doctrinal law is concerned.

7.71 The earliest incidences of the application of the officious bystander test, *Reigate v. Union Manufacturing* (when the test was as yet unchristened) and *Shirlaw v. Southern Foundries* certainly do not support the hypothesis that they are alternatives. Nor do they support the hypothesis that both must be satisfied independently. It is equally clear that Scrutton L.J. in formulating the test in its original version had not intended it to supplant business efficacy: nor, indeed had Mackinnon J., as he then was, thought that business efficacy had been superannuated when he decided *Wallems Rederij A/S v. Wm H. Muller & Co, Batavia* in accordance with 'the principles laid down in *The Moorcock*'.[139]

7.72 It is submitted that the officious bystander test is indeed a descriptive gloss on the business efficacy test, which remains the fundamental basis for implication in fact. The test is flexible and compendious, rendering unnecessary such elaboration (which paradoxically results in over-simplification) as that in *B.P. Refinery (Westernport) Pty Ltd v. Shire of Hastings*.

---

139   [1927] 2 K.B. 99, 106.

7.73 To restate what has been suggested above, it is submitted that the rule governing implication in fact is best expressed in two limbs, namely that:

1. It is permissible to imply a term in fact, where not to do so would lead to a failure of consideration (total or otherwise) that the parties cannot have had in their contemplation at the time they made the contract; but
2. In this case it is only permissible to imply such a term, and no more, as is necessary, in a business sense, to make the contract make sense.

BIBLIOGRAPHY

Atiyah, P.S., J.N. Adams and H. MacQueen (2001), *The Sale of Goods*, 10th edn, London: Longman.

Austen-Baker, R. (2004), 'A Relational Law of Contract?' *Journal of Contract Law*, **20**, 125.

Austen-Baker, R. (2009), 'Comprehensive Contract Theory: A Four-Norm Model of Contract Relations', *Journal of Contract Law*, **25**, 216.

Beale, H. (ed.) (2009), *Chitty on Contracts*, 30th edn, London: Sweet and Maxwell.

Beale, H. and T. Dugdale (1975), 'Contracts Between Businessmen', *British Journal of Law and Society*, **2**, 45.

Cain, B. (2011), 'The Implication of Contractual Terms in the New Millennium', *Canadian Business Law Journal*, **51**, 170.

Carter, J. and E. Peden (2003), 'Good Faith in Australian Contract Law', *Journal of Contract Law*, **19**, 155.

Cohen, G.M. (2000), 'Implied Terms and Interpretation in Contract Law' in B. Bouckaert and G. deGeest (eds), *Encyclopedia of Law and Economics*, Cheltenham, UK and Northampton, MA: Edward Elgar Publishing.

Collins, H. (2014), 'Implied Terms: The Foundation in Good Faith and Fair Dealing', *Current Legal Problems*, **67**, 297.

Furmston, M. (2007), *Cheshire, Fifoot & Furmston's Law of Contract*, 15th edn, Oxford: Oxford University Press.

Goode, R. (2004), *Commercial Law*, 3rd edn, London: Butterworths.

Havighurst, H.C. (1961), *The Nature of Private Contract*, Evanston, Illinois: Northwestern, UP.

Hooley, R. (2014), 'Implied Terms After Belize Telecom', *Cambridge Law Journal*, **73**, 315.

Ivamy, E.R.H. (1976), *Chalmers' Marine Insurance Act 1906*, 8th edn, London: Butterworths.

Kitigawa, Z. (1997), 'Use and Non-Use of Contracts in Japanese Business Relations' in H. Baum (ed.), *Japan, Economic Success and Legal System*, Berlin and New York: de Gruyter.

Kramer, A. (2004), 'Implication in Fact as an Instance of Contractual Interpretation', *Cambridge Law Journal*, **63**, 384.

171

Lambeth, R.J. (1981), *Templeman on Marine Insurance*, 5th edn, Plymouth: Macdonald & Evans.

Low, K. and K. Loi (2009), 'The Many Tests for Terms Implied in Fact', *Law Quarterly Review*, **125**, 561.

McCaughran, J. (2011), 'Implied Terms: the Journey of the Man on the Clapham Omnibus', *Cambridge Law Journal*, **70**, 607.

McMeel, G. (2007), *The Construction of Contracts*, Oxford: Oxford University Press.

Macneil, I.R. (2000), 'Contracting Worlds and Essential Contract Theory', *Social & Legal Studies*, **9**, 431.

Peden, E. (2001), 'Policy Concerns Behind Implication of Terms in Law', *Law Quarterly Review*, **117**, 459.

Peel, E. (2015), *Treitel, The Law of Contract*, 14th edn, London: Sweet & Maxwell.

Peters, C. (2009), 'Implication of Terms in Fact', *Cambridge Law Journal*, **68**, 513.

Phang, A. (1998), 'Implied Terms, Business Efficacy and the Officious Bystander – A Modern History', *Journal of Business Law*, 1.

Phang, A. (1990), 'Implied Terms Revisited', *Journal of Business Law*, 394.

Phang, A. (1993), 'Implied Terms in English Law', *Journal of Business Law*, 242.

Rakoff, T.D. (1995), 'Implied Terms: Of "Default Rules" and "Situation Sense"' in J. Beatson and D. Friedmann (eds), *Good Faith and Fault in Contract Law*, Oxford: Oxford University Press.

Rideout, R.W. (1996), 'Implied Terms in the Employment Relationship' in D.R. Halson (ed.), *Exploring the Boundaries of Contract*, Dartmouth: Ashgate.

Scott, R.E. (2000), 'The Case for Formalism in Relational Contract', *Northwestern University Law Review*, **94**, 847.

Simpson, A.W.B. (1975), *A History of the Common Law of Contract*, Oxford: Oxford University Press.

Simpson, A.W.B. (2007), 'Historical Introduction' in M. Furmston, *Cheshire, Fifoot & Furmston's Law of Contract*, 15th edn, Oxford: Oxford University Press.

Smith, J.C. (1994), 'Contracts – Mistake, Frustration and Implied Terms', *Law Quarterly Review*, **110**, 400.

Staughton, C. (1999), 'How Do the Courts Interpret Commercial Contracts', *Cambridge Law Journal*, 303.

Steyn, J. (2003), 'The Intractable Problem of the Interpretation of Legal Texts', *Sydney Law Review*, **25**(5), 11.

Treitel, G.H. (2003), *The Law of Contract*, 11th edn, London: Sweet and Maxwell.

INDEX